"This is a magical book. You can read it as a story in its own right source book for ideas. The stories themselves will inspire though mind. It has a clear and concise explanation of the complex (and . behind Ken Wilber's work and Spiral Dynamics. The 15 rules for good writing alone make it worth buying. It is a book I have enjoyed reading, that I know will be a constant guide and source and one that has begun to inspire stories of my own. Thanks Nick."

Alex McKie, Futurist

"If you have your heart set on dynamic leadership in the classroom and school, then *More Magic of Metaphor* is an invaluable resource in any integral toolkit. It's a mind-stopper and a mind-blower, packed with stories that tell the importance of being the change you wish to see."

Nick Drummond and Mats Edin
Nordic Integral, www.nordicintegral.com

"Nick Owen has consistently led the way in applying the emergent field known as integral education. Here is his best work yet, where readers either new to his work or references can profit immediately by his personalized approach to leadership and education. His clear talent is immediately apparent as he explains in significant yet entertaining format the most compelling new approaches, while honouring the deep structures available to us all from archetypal storytellers. I could immediately see the relevance of Nick's approach to any leader. So sit back, and try to savour each story as it weaves its magic within."

Lynne D. Feldman MA JD
Founder, Integral Education Yahoo List
Chair, New Jersey Character Education Network Action Team
Founder, Teen Freedom Corps
Honored Social Studies Teacher, Northern Highlands RHS, NJ

"Stories are so important to individuals and organisations, yet we often take our stories for granted. Nick Owen weaves a spell with stories so elegantly that you have to think about them differently. You can read this book as a collection of fascinating stories, as an intriguing insight into possible interpretations and as a simple explanation of complex models. Understanding stories and how we use them, can enhance your effectiveness, whether you lead from the front or influence behind the scenes."

Dr Maire Shelly MB ChB FRCA
Consultant in Anaesthesia and Intensive Care, South Manchester University Hospital
Associate Postgradate Dean, Department of Postgraduate Medical and
Dental Education, NW Deanery

"Stories to change beliefs, stories to modify behaviours, stories to help people out of ruts, stories to open up new vistas … Nick Owen has provided us with a rich source of short tales we can readily use. Thank you Nick."

Mario Rinvolucri
Teacher, teacher trainer Pilgrims Limited and writer

"Be prepared to run a gamut of emotions as Nick walks you through a beautifully crafted collection of stories, woven together by a guiding narrative. Using two wonderful world theories as a foundation for understanding, Nick has created a magical source book for leaders, therapists, trainers and the curious."

Martin Woods
Head of Leadership Development, Norwich Union Insurance

"As the person who put Nick to sleep when introducing him to the ideas of Ken Wilber and Clare Graves, I have often felt responsible. This responsibility has now been alleviated by reading this book. Nick has integrated their ideas in a totally unique way. May this be the first of many to integrate the gifts of NLP, SD, and The Enneagram in a truly Integral way. And more great stories to steal!"

Peter McNab
INLPTA Master Trainer
Founder Member of Ken Wilber's Integral Institute
Author of the *Enriching Relationships* CD, the *NLP Practitioner Cards*
and *Integral Relationships*

"Nick has combined anecdotes, metaphors and stories from across the world into an exploration of the leader's toolkit. The book is of use both to those already in leadership positions and to those who seek to develop their leadership potential.
　"The book is a journey through time and space as Nick explores both eastern and western leadership heritage. *More Magic of Metaphor* is thought provoking and inspirational; it enables and supports learning, exploration and growth in both the reader and in the wider team."

Richard Coulthwaite
Director of Strategic Vision for Finance, Aviva Plc

"What a treat it was to receive this book. Having enjoyed and used *The Magic of Metaphor* extensively, I was expecting the delightful stories. I was also pleased to be reacquainted with the Apprentice Magician in the linking story, which brings a level of metaphorical explanation. This time he goes on a quest for stories about leadership, with a magic carpet as a companion and guide. What I hadn't expected was the bonus of Spiral Dynamics—the psychological model developed by Professor Clare Graves—and Ken Wilber's 'Theory of Everything'. The result is a rich exploration of leadership, influence and motivation—and a thoroughly enjoyable read."

Susan Norman
Co-Director of SEAL (Society for Effective Affective Learning)

"Nick weaves all of these threads into a beautiful story, a journey, full of adventure and discovery that follows the developing relationship between a wise elder and his young companion. Once I turned the first page, and took the first step, I was spellbound; you will be too."

Tim Watts
Tim Watts Associates

"I have found a magic well. The first time I drew water it was clean and pure. The next it was clean, pure and ice cold. The next time the pure, ice-cold water was drawn and poured for me by a beautiful, dark haired maiden with smooth olive skin. I spend many days travelling and talking to people from all corners of the world, but having found my magic well I know that my throat will never be dry again, and that each visit will be better than the last."

Jonathan Davies
Senior Vice-President, CNN International

"What is good leadership? Nick Owen's new collection of stories gives us a wealth of fresh insight into that question from the new and challenging perspective of metaphor. As well as presenting a fascinating new insight into what makes a good leader, the book is fun, original and inspiring—'Entertrainment' at its best."

Leslie Perrin
Senior Partner, Osborne Clarke, Solicitors

More Magic of Metaphor

Stories for Leaders, Influencers and Motivators

Nick Owen

Crown House Publishing Limited
www.crownhouse.co.uk

First published by

Crown House Publishing Ltd
Crown Buildings, Bancyfelin, Carmarthen, Wales, SA33 5ND, UK
www.crownhouse.co.uk

and

Crown House Publishing Company LLC
4 Berkeley Street, 1st Floor, Norwalk, CT 06850, USA
www.CHPUS.com

British Library Cataloguing-in-Publication Data
A catalogue entry for this book is available
from the British Library.

ISBN 1904424414

LCCN 2004110213

Printed and bound in the UK by
Gomer Press
Llandysul

We say more than we know that we say …
We know more than we can say that we know.

– Michael Polanyi

All truths are easy to understand once they are discovered; the point is to discover them.

– Galileo Galilei

Believe nothing, no matter where you read it, or who said it, no matter if I have said it, unless it agrees with your own reason and your own common sense.

– The Buddha

Fishing nets are for catching fish. But when the fish are caught, the nets are forgotten. Traps are for catching hares, but when the hares are caught, the traps are forgotten. Words are for putting across ideas, but when the ideas are understood, the words are forgotten. How I long to listen to a storyteller who has forgotten all the words.

– Chuang Tzu

To all dolphins …

In whatever waters they swim

About Nick Owen

Nick Owen has, at various stages of his life, developed successful and interconnected careers in education, the arts, journalism, overseas development and the world of corporate business. He has lived and worked in Africa, Asia, Latin America, and Europe.

He studied at Durham, Manchester and Oxford universities, is an NLP trainer and Master Practitioner, and holds qualifications in Spiral Dynamics having studied in the UK and the US with both its co-creators.

His clients range from FTSE 100 companies to small educational projects in remote regions of the planet.

His main areas of expertise are:

- enhancing professional performance
- enhancing life skills
- understanding how 'messages' are given, received, acted on or misunderstood
- resolving communication and relationship issues in order to create smoothly functioning organisations, and leadership that others actively want to follow.

In addition to being a partner at CMT, a successful London-based training provider, Nick operates his own independent programmes offering rigorous development opportunities in the following areas:

Business: communication, presentation, relationships, influence, creativity, cultural awareness, leadership, trainer development, unconditional responsibility, coaching and mentoring skills

Education: integral education, appropriate methodologies, leadership, classroom management, creativity, teacher development, coaching and mentoring skills

Professional development:	tailor-made courses for professionals
Personal development:	tailor-made programmes for individuals including personal life coaching
Executive coaching:	for senior managers
Certification courses:	NLP-based courses, including professionally geared NLP Diploma and Practitioner Programmes

For more information, e-mail Nick Owen on **NOwenOne@aol.com** or **nick@nickowen.net**

Contents

Acknowledgements iii
Foreword v
Introduction ix

Section 1: Preparations 1

Section 2: The Task...19

Section 3: Problem Solving 31

Section 4: The Stories...49
    Story 1 – Dances with Wolves 51
    Story 2 – The Premier League 56
    Story 3 – External Distractions 59
    Story 4 – Presence 62
    Story 5 – Holding the Space 66
    Story 6 – A Tibetan Meditation 71
    Story 7 – Silence is Golden 73
    Story 8 – Integrity: The Triple Distillation Test 76
    Story 9 – All at Sea 79
    Story 10 – The Fox and the Hedgehog 83
    Story 11 – A Close Shave 88
    Story 12 – This Strawberry is Delicious 91
    Story 13 – A Magic Carpet Ride 1 95
    Story 14 – Creating Dissonance 103
    Story 15 – Coping Strategies 105
    Story 16 – A Magic Carpet Ride 2...108
    Story 17 – The Lost Horse 113
    Story 18 – The Presence of Absence...115
    Story 19 – Personal Responsibility 118
    Story 20 – Collective Responsibility 121
    Story 21 – The Tale of the Rogue Monkeys 125
    Story 22 – Stuck in a Rut 128
    Story 23 – Gifted 132
    Story 24 – TRough Justice 137
    Story 25 – Taking Ownership 140
    Story 26 – The Heart of Darkness 145
    Story 27 – The Nature of Leadership 149
    Story 28 – Courage 154
    Story 29 – Rewarding Behaviour 157
    Story 30 – Hidden Resources 160
    Story 31 – Reflected Glory 163

Story 32 – Comfort Zones 166
Story 33 – First Fruits 170
Story 34 – Soil and Toil 174
Story 35 – MBA 177
Story 36 – Liquid Assets 181
Story 37 – Surface Tension 185
Story 38 – The Messiah 190
Story 39 – The Hat Trick 195
Story 40 – Illumination 199
Story 41 – It's About Time 202
Story 42 – Fate Non Accompli 206
Story 43 – The Counterintuitive Route 209
Story 44 – Go with the Flow 212
Story 45a – Good Enough 215
Story 45b – Not Good Enough 216
Story 46 – Resistance 219
Story 47 – Drying Out 223
Story 48 – Three Sheep 227
Story 49 – Peda-Stodgy 229
Story 50 – In Your Hands 233
Story 51 – The Difference that Makes the Difference 238
Story 52 – Random Acts of Kindness 243
Story 53 – The Cracked Pot 247
Story 54 – Wake Up! 251
Story 55 – The Prisoner 254
Story 56 – Wistful Thinking 259
Story 57 – Stuckness 263
Story 58 – The Sequence of Things 266
Story 59 – Out of Thin Air 269
Story 60 – Absence or Presence? 272

Section 5: Homecoming – Change, Learning and Transformation 275

Section 6: Attributes of Great Leaders, Influencers and Motivators 293

Section 7: Unravelling the Threads 301

Appendix A – A Short Introduction to Spiral Dynamics 307
Appendix B – Ken Wilber's 4 Quadrant 'A Theory
    of Everything' Model 325
Appendix C – Some Practical Benefits of Spiral Dynamics 329

Bibliography 331

Acknowledgements

For many years, the dolphin has been my guiding metaphor. I have never seen a "stuck" or bored dolphin. So, whenever I have felt stuck or blocked myself, I simply ask myself, "What would a dolphin do in this situation?"

From this perspective, especially when connecting to dolphin-like resources such as creativity, fun, grace, elegance and curiosity, my "stuckness" almost always seems to evaporate. And, when not, it is usually nothing more than my own stubbornness holding it in place. Just me, getting in my own way.

When I finally got round to swimming with dolphins – a curious, playful, energetic and welcoming pod of some seventy or so wild spinner dolphins in the Red Sea – I realised they were even more amazing than I had given them credit for. It would be hard to imagine many human beings so vital and adapted to their habitat as dolphins appear to be to theirs. And yet, deep down, hidden under so many layers, just as I can vaguely discern the dolphin potential in myself, I constantly meet its energy and effervescence surfacing in others too.

So I want to thank the many "dolphins" who have helped and supported me, in a variety of different ways, to spin and bottlenose this book into shape.

First, those who kindly looked at my manuscript and offered valuable feedback and suggestions: Binita and Rick Cooper, Alessandra Drago, Arielle Essex, Matthew Kalman, Alex McKie, Peter McNab, Maire Shelley, Carolyn Temple and Martin Woods. In particular, I must thank Christopher Cowan and Natasha Todorovic for their excellent and insightful comments, and for pointing out factual and interpretive errors in my understanding of Spiral Dynamics and its origins. Any remaining errors are my own. Also thanks to Don Beck and Chris Cowan for granting permission to use their story 'Interviews with Six People' printed in this book as Stories 13 and 16.

Second, the contributors who drew my attention to a wide range of stories in print, in movies, in the press, on the Internet and elsewhere: Arielle Essex, Eleonora Gilbert, Mark Hawkswell, Paul Holme, Alison Hood, Kathy Horton, Jacqueline Jager, David Jones, Carla da Silva, David Willis and Martin Woods.

Third, the storytellers from whom I have heard stories, or whose published stories have been sources for my own adaptations, and whose names are credited elsewhere in this book. And to all those who have created stories sometime, somewhere and whose work came to me via the Internet. Whoever you are, I thank you for your creativity and generosity.

Fourth, those who have given me support and strength at different times, especially when I most needed it: JB, Blackbird, AE, CF, EG, FCJ, SM, MP, SdiP, MS, CT.

Next, my publishers: David Bowman and the team who have given me so much support and encouragement.

And especially, to the teachers and mentors throughout my life from whom I have gained and learned so much: my father Evan Jones, and my uncle Colin Jones; my schoolteachers, Colin Turner and Ted Stead; my colleagues in education, Mario Rinvolucri, Sheelagh Deller, Seth Lindstromberg, Tony Wright and David Pammenter; my NLP trainers and colleagues too numerous to mention; my teachers of the Enneagram: Don Riso, Russ Hudson, and Sister Josephine Bugeja; finally, my Spiral Dynamics colleagues, and my SD teachers: Chris Cowan, Don Beck, Natasha Todorovic, and Christopher Cooke. Thanks to Christopher Cooke who first told me the story of 'The Fish and the Water'.

Water is an essential companion to my life and my writing. So thanks to three important aquatic locations: the River Thames, which continues to flow comfortingly and always entertainingly past my window, and to the islands of Hvar and Venice and the seas that surround them.

Finally, a future-thank you to all those of you who will select, use and spread your own interpretations of these stories to a waiting and expectant world. The world is looking forward to your wisdom.

Nick Owen
London, 2004

Foreword

I love stories, and always have. A long time ago, when my greatest goal was to have a train set on my sixth birthday, my father began to tell me stories set in an imaginary land peopled with kings and queens, mad inventors and carnivorous cheeses. (Carnivorous cheeses? Yes, truly, but that is another story). I loved those stories. Then the wheel turned its circle as the years passed and I found myself making up stories to my daughter at bedtime. These stories had princes and princesses, heroes and strange lands where normal rules were turned upside down and inside out. It was difficult but very rewarding to tell these stories every night, every story had to be new and interesting, and my daughter exercised strict quality control. I understood how good my father was at telling stories and how hard it can be to be creative every night to order. In the stories I told my daughter, I would sometimes have the hero's worries and fears reflect the worries and fears in her young life. While I never introduced carnivorous cheese, (surely the ultimate *'caseus ex machina'* for the storyteller), I usually managed to resolve my stories well and my daughter would go to sleep content that these problems did have an answer.

I would then go down and watch television or read the paper, to see and read the stories of the day that were important to me. These were the stories that I wanted to know about, ongoing stories of what was happening in the world, stories in which I participated.

Stories are important. We need stories; they are all around us, on television, in newspapers, magazines and books. Hundreds of thousands of people write new ones every year in the hope of getting them published. And that is just our conscious mind at work. Stories are so important that we tell ourselves several every night in the form of dreams. No one knows exactly how these nocturnal stories work, or what they do, but if we are deprived of them, we go crazy. So, too, daytime life without stories is intolerable. We want our minds and hearts stimulated by stories. We learn from experience and pictures and words evoke experiences. A good story gives you an experience you can learn from. When we are inspired by a story, it is because it speaks to us, it touches some nerve in us because the storyteller has made the theme a human experience and we connect with that experience, we identify with it and by understanding the characters more, we learn to understand ourselves.

Stories are the perfect teaching medium. What do we learn from stories? Everything. We learn how people are and how they act. We learn how the world is and how it could be. Everyone has goals, and goals are stories we want to happen and they have happy endings, (at least for us). Once we set our goals, we make action plans. Action plans are adventure stories with us as the hero accomplishing the tasks.

When we are young, we like to hear stories that end with 'and they lived happily ever after'. Even at a young age, I recognised that people do not live happily ever after. Bland stories of happy people with no challenges never interested me. The phrase 'living happily ever after', means that the story is over and the next story with its conflicts will soon follow. It is just another form of punctuation, like a full stop but longer.

There will be more conflict, because we make goals and very rarely does life grant us our goals without putting obstacles in the way. Once you have a goal and an obstacle, you have conflict and when you have conflict, there has to be a resolution and then you have a story. You have a life.

Nick Owen himself, as the storyteller is here throughout this story that you hold in your hands. The stories that Nick has woven into this book have everything that a good story should have. A cast of colourful characters, servants and masters, warriors and wizards, mothers and mystics that inhabit the stories that decorate the book. These stories are short, often funny and they show us something important, not by telling us, but pointing to it and letting us explore it for ourselves.

These short stories are bound together by another story of a young magician. And this story is in another story, a story of world famous psychologist Clare Graves, practical philosopher (not an oxymoron in this case) Ken Wilber, and authors Don Beck and Chris Cowan. They tell a story about evolution, of people moving through different values, struggling with obstacles and getting to new levels. This is a story about all of us and the world we live in. This story is about you and me, why we do what we do and all that remains is for you to take those ideas and apply them to your own personal story.

At every level, this book will stimulate you, and give you ways to make your own story more interesting, more exciting (if that is what you want) and happier.

These stories will give you inspiration to answer the questions you have, and to help you find your own answer, as every hero must. May your story be a good one, one worth telling. My congratulations to Nick Owen for telling such a good story and telling it well. Read on ...

> Joseph O'Connor
> São Paulo, Brazil
> August 2004

Welcome to a book for people who want to make a difference – in their own lives and in the world around them. It's not a pretentious instruction manual or a know-it-all quick-fix with five simple steps to solving all humanity's problems overnight. Instead, it represents a toolkit for thinking better, understanding more, and conveying increasingly conscious awareness powerfully to others.

Herein are three sub-books woven together. One thread is a careful selection of useful and illuminating stories and allegories which can be retold with great impact. Another is a metaphorical journey of exploration and personal development to more effective leadership, more positive influence, and enhanced motivation winding among the stories. And a third thread is an introduction to some new ways of thinking about human nature, change, and meaning making – essentials for positive growth. It's a powerful, multilayered tapestry which can be used and appreciated in chunks or as an integrated whole.

A challenge we've faced for nearly 30 years in applying Spiral Dynamics, my business and one of the models Nick Owen will introduce in this book, is how to teach the principles of a powerful model without either going overboard in theoretical detail or skimming through it so lightly that the outcome belies the intention of the theory – to recognize the elegant complexity of the process of human emergence. Nick avoids the traps of both over-complication and typology while leading his reader gracefully through these systems as parts of an interwoven, connected field – the nature of the human being in operation in this world.

One reason I'm very pleased to introduce this book is that it gives us all a resource for presenting the work in ways more people can grasp and use. It's not full of jargon or arcane references. Instead, it's packed with meaning and metaphor – ideas that can resonate with the reader and those who will then hear the stories retold. How much better to offer a great story with a lesson that's a fun read and even a great 'tell' so learning happens with a spontaneous 'ah, ha!' of discovery than to poured information from a pitcher of rote facts.

We humans are connection-seekers and meaning-makers, creatures anxious to draw parallels with our own being, patterns we see, and what we desire or reject. Nick's book is for people who want to understand and make a difference. If you are at all like me, you will thoroughly enjoy the tapestry Nick has woven and come away from this book enriched, entranced, and empowered.

Chris Cowan
NVC Consulting, Santa Barbara,
and the International Spiral Dynamics Organization
co-author, *Spiral Dynamics: Mastering Values, Leadership,
and Change*

Introduction

I've been fascinated by stories ever since I can remember. My parents used to tell me long stories at bedtime. I'd always fall asleep before I realised that their intention was to put me into a trance. It took me a long time to learn that stories were actually meant to have endings. They say boys are slow learners. And some say they never catch up.

By the time I was five, I was making my own stories. I never realised at the time, of course, that my own stories and fantasies were deep metaphors representing my core values. Looking back on one set of stories that I still recall vividly, I'm amazed to recognise how little these values have changed over decades.

These were tales I constructed in my mind's imagination about a tugboat skipper called Jim. I'd stand on the seat of a high-backed upholstered armchair, barely able to see over the top, one of my father's pipes clamped in my mouth, and test out my sea legs in this "wheelhouse" of my construction. From this vantage point I'd scan the horizon of my parents' living room for waves, whales and armadas.

Tugboat Jim lived in a cottage, by himself, and he'd go out to sea at all times of night and day when summoned to rescue stranded mariners and stricken ships.

Looking back now, I can see I'm less like Captain Jim and more like the tug. In my work as coach, facilitator, consultant, I'm constantly nudging, pushing, pulling and wheedling clients towards the changes they want to make. It may be supporting them to achieve safe havens in the future, or assisting them to move away from current problems. It may involve figurative firefighting or metaphorical whirlpools.

Like most tugs, I'm functional rather than elegant, present rather than charismatic, and very not there when I'm no longer needed.

As for my connection with Jim, I still endeavour to emulate his skills at scanning the horizon for future possibilities, reading the charts to seek out new depths and uncharted channels, scanning the almanacs for the most auspicious tides, streams and currents, and, whereas Jim used to rely on the stars and his sextant, I consult my metaphorical global satellite positioning system to find out where on earth I am.

Jim's values and the tug's values remain with me: be of service, get the job done with minimum fuss and attention, move on to the next challenge.

Water and solitude are both important themes running through my life. I live by water. I swim whenever I can. I get tremendous pleasure taking quiet walks along coastal paths. Water also gave me another, more recent, insight into the power of metaphor: the result of a discussion with friends about my long and sometimes fractious relationship with my father. As people with similar temperaments and attitudes often do, my father and I had fought for much of our lives, until we both mellowed and began to accept and respect our similarities as well as our differences.

The discussion centred on issues of space, challenge and identity. Where metaphorical images come from, I don't know. But I'm tempted to believe it's that part of our unconscious mind or higher mind that wants us to heal and be at peace with ourselves, if only we will be quiet enough to pay attention to it.

At any rate, an image materialised in my mind. My father and I were swimming in a pool, the same large, clean, blue pool, and had been all our lives. It was only then that I noticed we were swimming in the same direction, and we were swimming in different lanes. We could, if we chose, change lanes; one could join the other in his lane; or we could go our different ways, each with the acknowledgement and respect of the other. I can't begin to articulate with any precision what this metaphor meant to me. I can only report that it was incredibly liberating.

* * *

When my publishers asked me if I would write another book of stories as a sequel to *The Magic of Metaphor* (Crown House Publishing, 2001), I wanted to do something deeper and more challenging, something that would stretch me more, something that would make me think more deeply about things that mattered to me, and things I was curious about.

I recognise yet another pattern in my life here. A significant part of my work in personal and professional development revolves around communication and relationship skills. Why do I teach these areas? Because I myself have so much to learn about them. As one of the most influential teachers in my life once said to me, "We teach best what we most need to learn."

So I wanted this sequel to be a learning experience for me, and it took me two years to decide exactly what form this would take.

Personally, I like stories that stand alone and allow the readers or listeners to work out the meaning for themselves. But many people have asked me to apply stories to various contexts, and that's an interesting challenge, too. I have endeavoured to avoid making the stories specific to particular contexts, and have preferred to explore some possible interpretations. These interpretations are by no means exhaustive, and they only partly belong to me, as they come from the diaries of a seventeen-year-old apprentice magician who developed a personality of his own.

I wondered how to put together a book that would allow readers to access it at the level that was right for them. Some readers will just want to read the stories and make up their own minds about what to do with them and how to use them. Or they may just wish to read them for pleasure and nothing more.

Other readers may be interested in the possible interpretations that are suggested, which will no doubt be a springboard for their own stories and interpretations.

Others still may wish to read the book because they are interested in the topics of the subtitle of this book: *Stories for Leaders, Influencers and Motivators.*

My childhood reading influenced me greatly here. Every Christmas when I wasn't navigating my tugboat through the high seas of West London, I'd be avidly devouring Rupert Bear annuals.

These – for those who have never seen such a thing – provided one of the first mixed-ability texts. There were speech bubbles with simple dialogue for kids who preferred inference and brevity. But for those of a more literary bent there were rhyming couplets beneath each cartoon image, taking the narrative to a deeper level of exposition. And, for those six-year-olds who got a real buzz out of textual analysis and semiotics, there was a densely written paragraph of muscular prose that brought all the subtle nuances of characterisation and subtext into play.

This became the model for my book. You can read it at a variety of levels. You can dip into it, or read it sequentially. You can just read the stories, or you could read the general notes at the end. Or you can share the interpretations of the Young Magician as he attempts to make sense of what contributes to excellent leadership. You could also start with Appendix A if you're keen to explore some of the theoretical models used in the book before commencing on the narrative. It's up to you. There are merits in taking a sequential approach; there are merits in randomness and chaos.

* * *

The earlier book, *The Magic of Metaphor*, was subtitled *77 Stories for Teachers, Trainers & Thinkers*. Since that book was written I have become more and more fascinated by questions around leadership, influence and motivation. We stand at a crossroads in terms of the survival of this planet. And the crossroads is manmade. War, hatred, anger, genocide, pollution, deforestation and many other ecological and nonecological issues are omnipresent and almost universal.

What kind of leadership do we need to turn this around? How will such leaders identify the required and necessary changes, and influence and motivate others to make the required and necessary changes? What kind of leaders will these people be? How will they handle complexity? What maps and tools will they use to cut through the fog to bring light and clarity to factions bent on mutual destruction? How will they use these tools and models to influence the vast majority of ordinary people all around the world, who have no problem at all with peaceful coexistence on this paradise we share, to stand up and be counted?

And so the subtitle *Stories for Leaders, Influencers and Motivators* emerged. It may well be that the possibility of survival for the human race in the twenty-first century will depend upon the quality of these skills.

I don't mean by this that we should look to some distant leaders to save us. Change starts with ourselves and we are all leaders in some ways and at some times in our lives, whether as friends, lovers, teachers, parents, clinicians, coaches, managers or whatever.

This book is written with ordinary people in mind, as well as senior executives, politicians and other "important" people. It recognises that, while some lead from the front, many others can influence and motivate just as effectively from behind the scenes.

The stewardship of our planet is our shared responsibility. And this book is, in part, an attempt to make some of the most useful and effective tools for leadership and change available and accessible to everybody and anybody who cares. The future is in our hands and the future as ever starts now and continues always to do so. Now is a good time to start making changes.

* * *

Judith de Lozier is fond of saying, "There's no such thing as coincidence – it's just God's way of remaining anonymous." As chance or God would have it, the day I received my first five copies of *The Magic of Metaphor* from my publisher at the end of May 2001, I was booked to fly to California for a training programme that was to have a marked impact on my life and, as it turns out, on this book.

I spent a week studying with Chris Cowan and Natasha Todorovic in Santa Barbara, California. With Don Beck, Chris Cowan had taken a body of fascinating research into Levels of Existence theory, a theory that had originally been developed by Professor Clare Graves, and reworked it into a more simplified and accessible set of concepts and tools that they renamed Spiral Dynamics (SD). It is one of the most powerful change models I have come across. The title of their book, *Spiral Dynamics: Mastering Values, Leadership, and Change*, clearly sets out the scope of the model. But what is special about it is that it explains complexity with elegant simplicity. As Einstein would have said, they made it as simple as they could without making it any simpler.

As many great minds have done before them, they were able to use a model – which is to say a metaphor – to lay bare underlying patterns and structures that exist beneath, and make greater sense of apparent chaos. The great contribution of their work is to have identified eight distinct valuing and thinking systems at work in the world today. These distinct systems can be identified in individuals, groups, teams, organisations, institutions and geopolitical entities. And, while the systems can be separated out and identified, we can equally well recognise that each one of us carries inside him- or herself a range of several, or all, of these systems.

Don Beck and Chris Cowan would, I'm sure, be the first to acknowledge their enormous debt to Professor Clare Graves, whose research into Emergent Cyclical Levels of Existence theory began in the 1950s and continued till his death in 1986. Graves, a professor of psychology, working out of Union College, Schenectady, NY, was curious to answer the perennial question of most of his students: "Sir, which of the theories of psychology is the right one?" Graves recognised that he didn't know, either so he embarked on an exhaustive voyage of research. For eight years he systematically interviewed people who were unsophisticated in psychological theory and who would therefore give a more accurate reflection of their own views and values. He was curious to understand why they thought about things in certain ways. What did they value and why? Where did they put their attention and why? The core question he was driving at was, "What constitutes psychological health in a mature, adult human being?"

If you start to answer this question for yourself, and check out the responses of colleagues and friends, you'll begin to appreciate how revealing the answers are.

Graves collated the information and painstakingly developed his theories over many years. He was one of the first academics to begin to challenge the narrow specialisations of academia. He realised that understanding human beings requires more than a psychological perspective. Graves was a pioneer in the concept of a "unified field", engaging with the disciplines of biology, sociology, anthropology and neurology as well as psychology to take a multidisciplinary view of human development.

Don Beck and Chris Cowan, themselves highly qualified academics, were younger colleagues of and collaborators with Graves, and since the death of their mentor, have taken and developed the theories beyond the narrow confines of academia and out into the world of business, politics, governance, health, education and elsewhere. There are today practitioners of Spiral Dynamics in every corner of the globe, making useful differences, and applying effective change work in appropriate contexts.

During the last few years, I have been looking to find ways to integrate the ideas of Spiral Dynamics more and more into my practice, both at work and in my personal life. Above all, I have wanted to make Spiral Dynamics more available and accessible to a wider audience.

This collection of stories has offered me an opportunity to do this and, given the general readership at which it is aimed, it has been important to keep it as simple as possible without trivialising it in any way. The book offers a starting point for those who are new to the model, and a central outcome for me is that many who read this book may wish to find out more about this powerful and exciting model and tool for change.

Spiral Dynamics has far greater nuances and applications than are dealt with in this book, and I'm sure the curious reader will wish to go and find out more for him- or herself.

* * *

I first came across Spiral Dynamics and Ken Wilber's model of "a theory of everything" at the same time. It was 1999 and I was painfully working my way through my NLP Trainer Training certification. I have to confess that the models didn't do too much for me then. Perhaps my mind was on other things but I recall dozing off a couple of times during the presentation.

I have discovered quite often in my life that my brain has a tendency to switch off when presented with ideas that are of outstanding usefulness but require some rigorous and disciplined thought to initially get my head around. In fact, the better the idea the more likely I am to reject it. My reptilian brain simply does not like change. It's the younger, emotional and intellectual parts of the brain that have to persuade it to open up and learn because the chances of my personal survival will be increased. After all, survival is the only thing the reptilian brain cares about.

The ideas must have just sat there biding their time in my unconscious mind, which with the collective wisdom of centuries has learned to be patient with me. Occasionally, it would allow moments and memories, concepts and applications to surface into my consciousness. Mmm! That model could be useful here.

I came to the Spiral first, but when I finally got round to reading Ken Wilber's book *A Theory of Everything* in the summer of 2001, I was blown away. Here was a book that offered a single, powerful, integral model of reality, a model that made a great deal of sense to me, which, like SD, took complexity and made it accessible and metaphorical, just as Copernicus had done with the solar system, Einstein with $E = mc^2$ and Franklin, Crick and Watson with DNA.

In a four-quadrant model, Wilber divides the world into what is subjective and what is objective, what pertains to the individual and what pertains to the collective. Everything in the world, he argues, can fit into this model. One of the many really useful contributions this model makes is to create balance between aspects of external reality and inner perception that too often are kept apart and treated separately. The external, objective, right-hand-side quadrants are measurable. The interior, subjective, left-hand quadrants are not measurable.

One of the great imbalances in modern life is the yawning separation between what is measurable and what is not, what is pragmatic and what is ethical. This model elegantly integrates these aspects within a holistic perspective. It is not enough, for example, to run a business based solely on measurable aspects. In a modern economy of the twenty-first century, the organisational culture and the welfare and development of each and every employee make as much of a valid contribution to the health and progress of the organisation as does a healthy balance sheet, professional training and development and investment in state-of-the-art equipment.

And it doesn't take much to transfer these ideas from a business application and apply them to what might constitute an effective health service, or a well-run education system, or a happy family.

Wilber's model, in short, creates possibilities to look beyond short-term solutions and at new paradigms for saving not just our institutions but also the planet.

* * *

I have used the SD and Wilber models as the basis for analysing and exploring leadership, influence and motivation within the stories. Like all models, and all metaphors, they are not the truth, but a useful way to think about reality. Models are simply a way of testing a theory against our experience. And, as the Buddha himself, said, "Believe nothing, no matter where you read it, or who said it, no matter if I have said it, unless it agrees with your own reason and your own common sense."

So treat everything you come across in this book through the filter of your own knowledge and experience. Like everyone else on this planet, I am bounded by my own current limitations, and this book is a learning process for me. As you apply your own valuing and thinking processes to the stories and their possible interpretations, the book may well become a learning experience for you, too.

As to my interpretations of SD and Wilber, they are my own and I fully acknowledge that I may not yet have understood them in their full complexity. Although I have trained with Don Beck, Chris Cowan and Natasha Todorovic, as well as other excellent practitioners of SD, I still have much to learn. I have endeavoured to make these models as simple and accessible as possible without going too far. Only time and your feedback will let me know how far I have succeeded.

* * *

Finally, it is important to mention that very few of these stories are my own. They are stories I have found along the way as I have journeyed through my life by way of books, articles, the Internet, theatre, movies, television, radio, seminars, friends, colleagues and so on. Stories are part of our heritage. My life is a story, so is yours. The collective history of our species is a story, one that is as yet unfinished, and one to which we all can and do contribute.

The stories I have found, I have changed, adapted and embellished, some might say not always for the better. But I have done the best I could within my current allocation of time, energy, perception and awakening.

I have divided sources into three categories. Primary sources are the people from whom I first heard the story, the book where I first read it or the medium through which I was first introduced to it. Secondary sources are either the source that my primary source acknowledged, or a reference to books where you can find alternative versions of the story. General sources refer to stories that are widely known and exist in several variations. Stories that appear with the inscription "Original source unknown" beneath them are stories – usually sent to me by friends, colleagues or strangers as attachments to e-mails – where I have not been able to establish provenance or authorship. Where I have been unable to formally thank or credit the original copyright holders, please accept my apologies and contact the publisher, who will be happy to correct the text in future editions.

If you are interested in more information about the uses and applications of stories, the art of telling stories, framing and meaning, meaning and interpretation, stories as teaching and presentation aids, and multisensory communication, you may wish to refer to the introduction and final sections of *The Magic of Metaphor: 77 Stories for Teachers, Trainers & Thinkers*, where these topics are dealt with in depth.

May you enjoy the journey!

The Stories by Theme

Key attributes of leaders, influencers and motivators

The Integral Leader
Stories 2, 4, 5, 10, 11, 13, 16, 17, 23, 29, 33, 37, 38, 44, 46, 49, 50, 53, 58, 59, 60

The Pragmatic Leader
Stories 2, 5, 11, 17, 19, 21, 23, 25, 27, 29, 33, 34, 37, 38, 43, 45a, 46, 52, 56

The Present and Aware Leader
Stories 2, 4, 7, 10, 11, 12, 17, 18, 23, 26, 27, 29, 32, 33, 37, 38, 39, 41, 42, 43, 46, 47, 50, 56, 58, 60

The Leader who has Integrity
Stories 1, 2, 4, 8, 11, 23, 26, 27, 28, 33, 34, 38, 42, 46, 49, 50, 51, 53, 54, 55 58, 59, 60

The Leader who takes Personal Responsibility
Stories 1, 3, 11, 17, 19, 23, 28, 29, 32, 33, 34, 38, 39, 43, 54, 55, 56, 59

The Contributing Leader
Stories 1, 5, 11, 21, 23, 27, 28, 33, 34, 38, 39, 42, 46, 50, 51, 52, 53, 54, 59, 60

The Leader as Change Agent
Stories 5, 14, 15, 17, 23, 26, 27, 29, 32, 33, 34, 38, 39, 42, 46, 47, 50, 51, 52, 55, 56, 58, 59, 60

Other attributes of leaders, influencers and motivators

The Leader as:

Activist
The Leader who makes things happen: Stories 5, 27, 32, 34, 37, 55, 60

Boss
The Leader who leads assertively from the front: Stories 4, 20, 51, 58

Challenger
The Leader who challenges people, ideas and conventional wisdom: Stories 7, 8, 29, 38, 39, 47, 49, 50, 56, 57, 58, 60

Coach
The Leader who supports and consolidates change: Stories 6, 19, 23, 27, 46, 47, 50, 51, 58

Colleague
The Leader who walks step by step with you: Stories 23, 38, 51, 54, 55, 56

Compassionate
The Leader who demonstrates empathy: Stories 11, 15, 23, 26, 38, 42, 51, 52, 53, 54

Coordinator
The Leader who holds the space in which things can happen: Stories 5, 37

Courageous
The Leader who demonstrates selfless bravery: Stories 4, 11, 28, 29, 32, 37, 43, 49, 55, 58

Exemplar
The Leader who walks the talk and the walk: Stories 1, 11, 17, 23, 26, 28, 33, 37, 38, 49, 54, 55, 57

Expert
The Leader who demonstrates mastery and expertise: Stories 9, 10, 33, 34, 37, 47, 49, 59

Facilitator
The Leader who leads unobtrusively, as an equal: Stories 6, 11, 15, 23, 26, 27, 38, 39, 42, 50, 51, 56, 59

Father
The Leader as father figure: Stories 1, 28, 40, 50, 54

Tiger or Buffalo
Leaders displaying different temperaments: Story 27

Goal setter
The Leader as single-minded trailblazer: Stories 10, 33, 34, 40, 47

Fool
The Leader as "Trickster": Story 19

Good Wolf
The Leader who aggressively defends what is right: Story 1

Guardian
The Leader who is a protector and steward of people and values: Stories 28, 34, 40, 42, 50, 52, 54, 59

Hard worker
The Leader who rolls up his sleeves: Stories 33, 34

Humble
The Self-effacing Leader: Stories 2, 23, 26, 38, 51

Healer
The Leader who makes things whole again: Stories 11, 23, 46, 47

Helper
The Leader as assistant: Stories 15, 23, 42, 51

Inspirer
The Leader whose actions move others to act: Stories 6, 11, 23, 28, 38, 46, 47, 53, 54, 55, 58, 60

Listener
The Leader who speaks less, hears more: Stories 7, 21, 26, 27, 39, 51

Martial artist
The Leader who uses only as little energy as is necessary: Story 4

Mother
The Maternal Leader: Stories 11, 15, 51, 53

Motivator
The Leader who moves people to act: Stories 11, 27, 29, 38, 46, 47, 50, 55

Mystic
The Leader with the indefinable quality: Stories 40, 48, 57, 58

Questioner
The Socratic Leader: Stories 8, 49, 50, 58

Rapport builder
The Affiliative Leader: Stories 11, 17, 23, 29, 33, 39, 46, 47, 51, 53, 56

Role model
The Leader to be emulated: Stories 1, 2, 8, 10, 11, 17, 23, 26, 28, 32, 33, 38, 49, 58

Self-aligned
The Leader who appears all of one piece: Stories 2, 4, 8, 10, 12, 17, 18, 23, 38, 54, 55, 58

Self-effacing
The Leader who materialises when you need her: Stories 2, 7, 11, 26, 58

Sensitive
The Leader who is aware of others: Stories 11, 17, 20, 26, 27, 39, 42

Servant
The Leader who aims to serve the needs of those he leads: Stories 11, 50, 54, 59

Steward
The Leader responsible for overseeing, managing and preserving quality for future generations: Stories 27, 28, 33, 34, 50, 59

Storyteller
The Leader who works with story and metaphor: Stories 1, 13, 14, 16, 19, 22, 27, 28, 29, 37, 38, 46, 47, 49, 56, 58, 60

Strategist
The Leader as planner of action and decision-maker: Stories 10, 14, 17, 29, 37, 39, 40, 44, 47, 50, 52, 55, 56

Supporter
The Leader as enabler: Stories 17, 20, 51, 53, 54, 59

Taskmaster
The Assertive Leader: Stories 47, 58

Teacher
The Leader as educator: Stories 1, 3, 6, 11, 19, 27, 37, 49, 50, 51, 56, 57

Thinker
The Leader with provocative perspectives: Stories 3, 8, 23, 25, 27, 37, 49, 56, 58, 60

Visionary
The Far-seeing Leader: Stories 5, 27, 33, 37, 40, 47, 60

Warrior
The Leader who leads from the front: Stories 4, 28, 37, 55, 58

Zen Master
The Leader whose feet leave no footprints on the rice paper: Stories 3, 4, 7, 11, 38, 54, 57, 58

Wise
The Leader who possesses presence and awareness: Stories 1, 3, 5, 7, 8, 11, 17, 19, 23, 26, 27, 29, 37, 38, 39, 46, 47, 52, 57, 58, 60

Section 1
Preparations

It was 2.17 in the morning. A candle glimmered in a dimly lit study area. Not a sound could be heard except the occasional sighs of students sleeping in the dormitory. A Young Magician was putting the finishing touches to a paper he'd been writing on *The Uses of Story and Metaphor with Practical Applications*. It was the last written assignment of his apprenticeship at The Academy. He checked the clock on the wall, took another swig from his mug of cocoa and began a final read-through of what he had written.

Using story and metaphor with practical applications

If you could communicate "messages" with impact, wisdom and memorability, what difference would that make to your powers as a communicator? What difference would it make to other people's perception of you as leader, motivator, parent or teacher?

In business, if your team were to share the vision, direction and values that you do, how much easier would it be to drive your business forward, and create powerful and favourable impressions on your clients? You and your entire team would be operating as one, moving with confidence and commitment towards a set of common goals.

In education, how much more satisfying would your teaching be – both for you and your students – if you were able to:

- explain ideas more easily, more memorably, and more powerfully?
- create an environment to which all your students wanted to contribute and belong?
- motivate your students with a desire for lifelong learning?

So consider this question: What do the following teachers, artists and leaders have in common? Lao Tse, Jesus, the Buddha, Rumi, Chaucer, Shakespeare, Dickens, Tolkien, Gandhi, Winston Churchill, Einstein, Milton Erickson, John Harvey-Jones, Stephen Covey, Peter Senge and J. K. Rowling.

Answer: They all use varieties of anecdote, story, parable, case history and metaphor to put across their "message" in powerful and highly memorable ways.

Words by themselves are abstractions. A word is merely a representation of something, not the thing itself. Without a context or frame, words remain concepts, and concepts are open to a multiplicity of interpretations. Poor communication attracts poor results.

The meaning of your message is the response you get

In other words, the meaning of our communication is not what *we* think it means: it is what *our listeners or readers* think *we* mean. Poor communication, for example, is the reason many organisations and institutions fail to realise their full potential. Research suggests that 80 per cent of problems occurring within business contexts are communication issues. Mainly, this is the result of the vague interpretation of vague communication.

If we wish to ensure our words are understood in the way we want, we would do well to translate concepts and ideas into concrete, tangible, shared meanings. Anecdotes, stories and metaphors are very powerful ways to do this. They translate conceptual left-brain ideas into immediate and experiential right-brain recognitions. Stories connect ideas with people's lived experience. They make sense!

Three holy men from three religious communities were invited to give thanks following a fundraising dinner in New York. The Christian priest offered a prayer about tolerance. The Muslim imam offered a prayer about charity. The rabbi, however, told a story. And the story contained a "message" for the diners to reflect upon. A week after the dinner, nobody could remember the prayers. But everybody remembered the rabbi's story and the power of its message.

Stories can be used in many different contexts to get key messages across. They can be effectively used by coaches, mentors, teachers, trainers, therapists, parents, managers, team leaders, motivators and presenters, as well as in a raft of personal contexts. They work well in one-to-one situations, in small and large groups. Whatever the context, stories work brilliantly and are remembered.

In the rest of this assignment, I want to share some applications for storytelling, and show how stories can make a real difference to your impact and leverage, whether in business or education, in coaching or parenting, or simply when communicating and entertaining.

Contexts

You can use stories in every conceivable communication situation. They work particularly well when you "frame" them. Framing means that you give the listener a clue as to what the "message" is about. It is usually preferable not to explain a story. When the listener has to work to find a meaning it makes more sense and is installed much more deeply in their memory.

Here's an example of framing. Let's say the managing director of a company is holding a meeting with the intention of encouraging all employees to take more responsibility for the running of the business. The MD has in mind the development of a healthy organisational culture through the nurturing of a certain set of attitudes, but, rather than direct them, he would prefer his staff to work it out for themselves. So he talks generally about the kinds of people who work in successful organisations, and the kinds of attitudes they have. He goes on to use an anecdote to explain this:

> When JFK visited Cape Canaveral in the sixties, he'd met all the top people – the astronauts, the scientists, the technicians – and he was on his way out, walking down a long narrow corridor, when he came upon an old grey-haired man stooped over a mop and bucket. "What do you do here?" Kennedy asked. "Sir," said the old man, straightening up and looking the president right in the eye, "I'm doin' exactly what all the folks here is doin'. Workin' to put a man on the moon!" Kennedy, they say, was impressed.

In a different context – education, for example – you could use the same story to encourage students to take more responsibility for their learning and behaviour, whether in the classroom or the sports team. If Kennedy is not an appropriate model for your students, that's no problem. Simply translate the story into a more appropriate context, and instead of JFK use a person who will be a more appropriate role model for your students.

Applications

Anecdotes, stories and metaphors can be used to reinforce almost any message you want to get across. Here are some possible applications:

- motivating
- reframing an issue or problem
- giving feedback
- setting goals
- influencing others
- requiring responsibility
- teaching a point
- reflecting
- taking action
- modelling excellent behaviour

- demonstrating negative behaviour
- managing issues
- developing skills
- introducing new ideas
- challenging negative mindsets
- dealing with leadership issues
- enhancing creativity
- introducing a theme
- waking people up
- changing the mood
- realising potential
- getting attention
- making people laugh
- relaxing people
- easing tension or stress
- getting audience involvement
- shifting a paradigm
- simplifying a complex idea
- challenging complacency

Examples

Challenging complacency

Consider the parable of the boiled frog. If you put a frog in a bucket of very hot water you can be sure the frog will jump right out before he gets boiled. So would you! But put that frog in a bucket of water at room temperature and then ever so slowly turn up the heat, and you're going to have one very contented frog. And by the time that water gets to the temperature we were talking about earlier, he'll be far too groggy to do anything about climbing out.

Such complacency is classic in businesses and in individuals who have seen success as a reason not to change anything. When the market shifts it's already far too late to take effective action. Wake up!

For anyone, or any organisation, wishing to make the most of themselves it's useful to ask two questions: "Am I achieving more of my potential today than I was yesterday?" and "How can I achieve more of my potential tomorrow than I am today?" It is not enough to sit on past laurels or lily pads!

Skills development

Tiger Woods's ball was stuck in a sand trap. It was a very difficult shot. He took a long while weighing up how to deal with it. Finally, he addressed the ball, focused all his energy and played the shot. The crowd watched as the ball hung high in the air, dropped and then bounced twice and into the hole. "That was a real lucky shot, Tiger," a voice shouted from the crowd. "Yeah, it was," responded Tiger. "But you know what? The more I practise, the better I get, and the better I get, the luckier I get."

Effective behaviour isn't random: it's built upon an understanding of the structures and patterns that support excellent practice. Know-how is priceless and it can be learned. High-quality training and development are not expensive. Ignorance is expensive.

Taking responsibility

The baby mice were just a few days old. They were having fun when suddenly a large black shadow fell over them and they stopped playing. A huge tomcat was towering above them, licking his lips anticipating lunch. Quick as a flash, the mother mouse jumped over her babies, looked straight into the tomcat's eyes, and barked, "Woof! Woof!" The cat was so surprised it turned and ran. "Let that be a lesson to you," said the mother mouse. "Never underestimate the importance of learning a second language."

The key to success in life is learning skills that enable you to run your own life and achieve the goals you want. Without these skills you can be sure there are plenty of people willing to take control of you, and use you to serve their ends. What is the "second language" you need to learn?

Leadership 1: Walking your talk

A woman approached Gandhi and said, "Master, tell my boy to stop eating sugar." Gandhi looked at the chubby six-year-old and replied, "Bring him to me again in four weeks' time." The woman was surprised but did as she was told. Four weeks later, she brought the boy again. Gandhi looked at him forcefully and said, "Stop eating sugar." "Why didn't you tell him that a month ago?" the woman asked. "Because four weeks ago I myself was eating sugar."

Leadership is not taken but given. People choose to follow those whom they trust and whose behaviour and actions are totally congruent. If you do not walk your talk, people are unlikely to perceive you as a leader. This is as true for teachers and parents as it is for leaders and managers.

Leadership 2: Managing and leading

The two directors of Ecological Tours Ltd were guiding a party of tourists through a dense forest. While one director was showing the party the many fascinating aspects of the trees and the forest floor, the other wandered ahead along a path and into a clearing. The first director drew the attention of the tourists to a great number of extraordinary details. He showed them how to collect water, make a shelter and survive on forest fruits. The other director had meanwhile climbed to the top of the tallest tree from where he surveyed the surrounding landscape. A tourist shouted up to him, "Hey, this is amazing down here." "You're right," he called back, "but we're in the wrong forest."

Managing and leading are complementary activities but they have different functions. It is important to do both. Success requires attention to detail in the present *and* an ability to map directions for the future. In a world where the only constant is change, a leader must be like Mississippi steamboat captain: looking ahead for shifts in the current and obstacles in the stream, gauging the current depth, watching out for eddies and backwaters and taking stock of the journey so far.

The same is true in educational contexts where teachers will find it necessary to choose when to guide, when to coach and when to teach. It is important to generate greater choices in professional behaviour so that leadership styles can be matched appropriately to what is required in different contexts.

Realising your potential

Imagine a plank lying in front of you on the floor. It's 50 foot long, 1 foot wide and 4 inches thick. If I offered you £100 to walk along it, would you take it? Of course, you would.

Now if I tell you it's 100 feet up in the air, suspended between two buildings, with just 24 inches at each end resting on the buildings, would you take the money now?

Probably not.

But if I said that at the other end of the plank is your six-year-old daughter, and the building where she's standing is on fire, would you walk it now? I guess you would.

It is useful to embrace the attitude that the only thing that holds us back from achieving what we want in life is ourselves. Each one of us has to challenge the existing limiting paradigms – our habitual patterns of behaviour – that currently prevent us connecting with our true potential. We can always do more than we think we can. We all need to know what it is we want to achieve, take the necessary decisions and fully commit our resources to our outcomes.

So now you've got a taste for how easy and effective it is to use story and metaphor in your everyday communication in a wide variety of applications, why not start experimenting today? Who knows? The life you change may be your own.

* * *

The Young Magician put the paper down. That'll do for now, he thought. He took a last swig of cocoa and caught sight of the document that a friend had handed him earlier in the day. It was stuck on the pin board beside him. It made him smile.

Fifteen rules for good writing

1. Verbs has to agree with their subjects.
2. Avoid clichés like the plague.
3. Also, always avoid annoying alliteration.
4. Be more or less specific.
5. Parenthetical remarks (however relevant) are (usually) unnecessary.
6. One should never generalise.
7. As I've said a million times, never exaggerate.
8. Don't use no double negatives.
9. Never use a big word where a diminutive one will do.
10. Kill all exclamation marks!!!
11. Eliminate commas, that are not, necessary.
12. Use words correctly, irregardless of how others use them.
13. Use the apostrophe in it's proper place and omit it when its not needed.
14. Puns are for children, not for groan readers.
15. Proofread your work carefully to see if you any words out.
16. Check your speling throughly.

He yawned and stretched, then took a yellow Post-it. He quickly wrote a reminder to check his paper again in the morning for clarity and style. Then he stuck it on the frame of his computer screen, blew out the candle, and went to bed. It was 2.31 a.m.

* * *

The end of the school year, and consequently the end of his apprenticeship at The Academy, was fast approaching. The papers had all been written, the assignments were completed, the exams were over. All that remained was his final appearance before the panel of International Magicians and Wizards, who would decide if he was ready to graduate. Time dragged. The Young Magician passed his time playing football with his friends, swimming in the lake, reading and thinking about his future.

He wondered what he would be doing this time next year. If he passed his apprenticeship with high enough grades it would allow him to become a Travelling Magician. This would require him to leave The Academy, go out into the world and carry out some kind of task or ordeal that the High Master would require of him. He looked forward to that, and hoped he'd worked hard enough. He could only wait and hope.

* * *

It was the day before the International Panel of Magicians and Wizards convened. In fewer than 24 hours the results would be known. For some there would be joy, for others disappointment. The Young Magician could barely contain his impatience, anxiety and excitement.

And now, as he stood outside the simple residence of the High Master, he was aware of nothing else but the anticipation and curiosity he felt.

He entered the High Master's residence with a group of his fellow students. It was the traditional farewell meal for the departing apprentices. The High Master greeted them warmly. "Welcome, welcome," she said. "Make yourselves at home. Dinner will soon be served."

The Young Magician looked around. How was it possible for such a small residence to have so much space inside? Around a central fountain in the entrance hall were many rooms, each a different style, leading off in many directions. For a moment he was surprised. And then wondered why he was surprised. What should one expect of a Magician's house? The High Master was one of the most respected and innovative magicians of her day.

He wandered through some rooms taking note of the different features and themes of each. He looked through windows onto a variety of different landscapes. Finally, he entered an extensive and impressive library. There must have been thousands of books of all shapes, sizes and colours waiting patiently for attention on the many shelves.

He was curious to see how the High Master organised them. Did she organise books loosely and haphazardly under broad categories such as philosophy, science and literature, an arrangement in which a book was just as likely to choose the reader as the other way around? Or did she organise rigidly, alphabetically or even chronologically, so everything would be to hand and easily found?

It did not take the young man long to see that the High Master fell into the latter category. The library was organised with exceeding efficiency, each book assigned to its specific space, each book coded in its specific sequence.

Hmm, he thought, that's interesting information. A new insight into the High Master's character.

He took a book at random from the shelves. It was an old leather-bound edition covered in dust. He blew on it and a stream of fine particles made a small cloud in the room. Still some grime remained, so he moistened his thumb with a modest amount of spit and wiped it across the front cover. The embossed title emerged: *Fish Tales*.

Stories or recipes? Either way, he was hooked. As he carefully opened the covers, he happened to glance up and through the windows of the library and saw to his astonishment not gardens, or orchards, or allotments, but fish tanks – hundreds of huge fish tanks piled one upon another with a bewildering diversity of darting, gleaming fish, fish from every known and unknown ocean in the world.

The Young Magician sensed a presence behind him and turned around. It was the High Master. "I didn't know you kept fish," he said.

"No, my friend," she replied, "I don't keep fish. I keep water."

She smiled. The Young Magician had a sense he was missing something.

"What do you mean?"

"I think", replied the High Master, "some quiet reflection will allow you to work it out very well for yourself." Another smile. The eyes twinkled and she was gone.

The Young Magician was puzzled. He took a moment to think. He was still puzzled. What on earth did that mean? *I don't keep fish. I keep water.* What *could* that mean?

The more he thought about it, the more he felt confused by the simplicity of the riddle. It didn't seem to make any sense logically, yet he sensed from the High Master's tone and the expression in her eyes that something deeper lay under the surface of the words. Why would one want to keep water? he thought.

The Young Magician was curious now. He sensed there was something really worthwhile to be learned here if only he could tease it out. *I don't keep fish. I keep water.* The thought kept going around and around in his head. He sat down in a large leather-padded armchair, *Fish Tales* still in his hand, closed his eyes and began to think back over his long months of study. If he couldn't work it out with conscious thinking, perhaps his unconscious mind would offer some answers. His meditation teacher had never tired of telling him that.

He concentrated within himself. He focused his attention on the ticking of a distant clock, and the sound of muffled faraway voices. He felt his body settle into the soft inviting leather of the sofa, felt the warmth and texture of the material against his clothes and skin, sensed his breathing even and deep in his belly, and his eyelids becoming really heavy. A floorboard softly creaked. He noticed how calm and peaceful he was feeling. His head nodded slowly, then fell upon his chest …

The dream, when it came, was distant and fuzzy at first: pictures and voices began to form and swirl in his head. He noticed the book in his hands. It separated itself from the grasp of his fingers, opened at Page 73, and a line of red writing removed itself from the page and spoke to him:

"The last things to know about water are the fish." ~ Chinese Proverb.

The writing floated down into an ocean of fish with a soft splash, and the splash became a dot, which turned into a little yellow biplane flying low over the water. The biplane was pulling a streamer on which was written: METAPHOR … THE RIGHT BRAIN'S UNIQUE CONTRIBUTION TO THE LEFT BRAIN'S LANGUAGE CAPABILITY. It was a very long streamer.

Albert Einstein, dressed as a rainbow, jumped out of the little yellow biplane and parachuted gently down to the beach. He was shouting loudly in a strong German accent: "Make it as simple as you can but not any simpler." But nobody could hear him because they were in a different dream.

A huge cemetery stretched for miles beyond the beach. Hundreds of thousands of holidaymakers were sitting among the graves dressed in different colours as far as the eye could see. Rain started falling heavily, the graves opened, and the people cowered.

One particular Celtic cross rose high among the others and beckoned. On it were written the words: " 'There's no such thing as inclement weather, only inappropriate clothing.' ~ Celtic proverb." The cross spoke, the sodden people stepped out of their rain-soaked clothes, transformed into butterflies, and flew towards the sun. Some crashed to the ground, some flew straight, some flew up towards the sun.

The dream – or was it a nightmare? – was a roller coaster now. It seemed impossible to follow or make sense of its dips, and curves, and convolutions.

The Sun and the Rain were arguing. The Sun blamed the Rain for the floods, and the Rain blamed the Sun for the droughts. They couldn't see each other's point of view. Only the Rainbow, their lovechild, understood the depth of their attraction. She said, "You need at least three ways of experiencing the world before you can begin to understand what reality might be. All miracles require a shift in perspective."

"Creation is a miracle," said the little yellow biplane on its way back to the ocean. "That's right," said the Rainbow. "At its heart, creativity is simply the art of experiencing *what is* from new, unexpected or unusual perspectives. Creativity is how we learn to see in new ways."

"Yes, yes, yes," butted in another voice, full of impatience and frustration, which the Young Magician recognised instantly as his own, "that's all very well. But tell me, how does any of this explain just how and why the High Master keeps water, not fish?"

Silence.

"Aah," said the Rainbow, the Sun, the Rain, Einstein, the Little Yellow Plane, the Drop of Water and the Line of Red Writing from Page 73, "that's not just a good question: that's another story."

A distant gong reverberated deep inside the young man's mind. The voices mingled, swirled, danced together for some moments more and then began to fade. As they did so, he felt his sense of frustration and impatience fade with them. Is this a message, he thought to himself, some kind of cryptic set of clues?

He began to consciously relax and think. What do I have? A riddle, a Chinese proverb, Shlain's quotation on metaphor, Einstein's dictum on potent communication, a graveyard, an Inuit saying, a transformation, the multiperspective reality check and a definition of creativity.

What could it all mean? What did they all have in common? What did they all have to do with the High Master's comment that she didn't keep fish, but kept water? His head was starting to spin.

The gong exploded in his ears again. The Young Magician returned from his sleep with a start and opened his eyes. His head was resting on the arm of a padded leather armchair in a roomful of dusty books. *Fish Tales* was open on his lap. He was hot, there were beads of sweat on his forehead, and his fists were clenched.

The gong rang out again. It wasn't in his head at all but was coming from somewhere outside the library. He shook his head clear and realised it was a summons to dinner. Further reflection could wait. He was off to join the others. There is a time for contemplation, and a time for eating. Sometimes it was just better to be in the now.

* * *

It was the day of the initiation. The last test the Young Magician would have to undertake in order to be released from his apprenticeship. Once past this hurdle he could choose to become a Travelling Magician, journeying widely in the world, practising his art and making his contribution – whatever that might be.

"We are well pleased with you," said the High Master on behalf of the panel. "For in all respects you have done well. We simply ask you to remind us of the answer to the simple question: What is Magic?"

"It's the art of transformation and change," the young man replied.

"Good. And what is the role of a Magician?"

"To help people to make useful and beneficial changes in their lives."

"And how can this be achieved?"

The Young Magician took a moment or two to compose himself. He created a mental picture of the mind maps on which he made his notes, and which he'd used extensively for revision.

"In four ways:

- first, by knowing that everything has a structure;
- second, by believing that change is always possible;
- third, by accepting that there is always more than one way to look at things; and
- last, by understanding that the key to useful change lies in having both creativity and access to a greater number of choices."

"And what is the responsibility of the enlightened Magician?"

The Young Magician had no hesitation in replying. "The responsibility of the Magician is to use his or her power wisely, ethically and with humility."

This all sounded a bit formal and stilted to the Young Magician, but it was more or less what it had said in the notes taken from the textbook. And, since the High Master herself had written it, he reckoned it would serve him well.

"And what are the five key principles of Magic?"

The Young Magician took a moment to collect his thoughts again, and then replied, "The first principle is to look for the connections between things that are not always apparent on the surface and to see information in its wider context, for nothing exists or makes sense in a vacuum. You cannot understand a child's behaviour without understanding something of the family in which it lives.

"Second, to be aware that knowledge is always provisional, that there is always more to learn, and there's always more than one way to do things.

"Third, a Magician shares his knowledge for the benefit of others.

"Next, a Magician seeks to follow the rule of the four Rs: respect for self; respect for others; respect for ecological systems; and responsibility for all his actions.

"Finally, a true Magician believes that none of these things are true, but acts *as if* they are true. It is one's attitude and intention that truly matter. "

"You have learned well," said the High Master. "Now, we have all read with pleasure your final paper on *The Uses of Story and Metaphor*, so please answer this one question. Why would any self-respecting Wizard or Magician have an interest in communicating through the power of story and metaphor?"

The Young Magician felt his enthusiasm rising even before he began. "Because all stories are true and yet not true. Every story is complete in its own context, its own reality. Every story therefore reflects a system, a map of the world. Yet just as that map is complete in itself, it is also not complete because it represents only one among many perspectives.

"Stories offer us ways to see and understand our world in a new light, from a different angle. They allow us to challenge ourselves, and others, to recognise the limitations and shortcomings of our own maps of reality so that new insights become possible. Change becomes possible. Transformation becomes possible.

"A skilful storyteller can tell a metaphor or a story to someone in a way that creates a desire in them to change their behaviours, their skills or their thinking. It's quite possible for a story to create in a person a desire to change their life in a very deep way. I've seen it happen many times.

"In other words, stories are an important and powerful way to generate creativity and greater choice in people's lives. Stories are vehicles through which greater wisdom and compassion can be generated in the world.

"This is because storytelling is an art that is at the same time both simple and complex, both precise and vague, and one that speaks to both the conscious and unconscious minds.

"Actually, I can't think of any other art form that so effectively transmits both idea and action, structure and creativity, reason and emotion; which is so multisensory and speaks to so many types of intelligence; which can be short or long or something in between; and which is understood so easily by all ages and across all cultures.

"You know, it's really true what the sages of old have said: 'I am story.' For each one of us is no more nor less than our own story that we are still writing. And the history of the world, of both living and nonliving things, is the sum total of our collective story so far. Who knows what is possible or where it may end?"

The Young Magician looked around at the members of the Panel. They were smiling and nodding. He realised he hadn't taken a breath for quite a long time. He took a deep breath now, and then ventured a short, rather self-conscious laugh.

"Congratulations. You have spoken well," said the High Master. "You are now released from your apprenticeship and free to travel the world as a Travelling Magician to practise and develop your skills. We all salute you."

The Panel of Magicians and Wizards stood to honour the Young Magician's transition and, as he accepted his scroll of certification, a broad smile illuminated his whole being.

"The Panel has a task in mind for you," said the High Master. "We have noticed your progress with interest, your commitment and enthusiasm, your curiosity and willingness to learn and work. The journey is a long one and you have only just begun to embark upon it. Are you willing to accept the challenge?"

The young man looked around the room. He took in the many faces of wise and respected Magicians and Wizards who stood watching him and waiting for his response.

"It will be an honour," he said.

"Come see me tomorrow," said the High Master, "and we will discuss the journey we want you to take."

Section 2
The Task

The High Master looked at the newly qualified Traveller from across her desk.

"Congratulations, my young friend. The Panel has decided that you merit the status of Travelling High Flyer. This means you have been recognised as perhaps having the potential to one day become a member of the International Panel of Magicians and Wizards. You have a long way to go, of course, and many who set out upon the road do not have the stamina or desire to stay the course. And you have the right to refuse the challenge. Shall I continue, or not?"

"Yes, yes. Go on."

"Membership of the Panel is a great honour and carries many duties and obligations. Many challenges lie between you and your destiny and you will need to know how to deal with these challenges with creativity, firmness and integrity. And these, of course, are leadership issues.

"You will need to learn how to lead people, to influence them, and to motivate them. So the first challenge that the Panel has decided you must embark on is this: to seek out and explore key attributes of leadership. What inspires people to change, learn and transform, and – moreover – how can you influence and motivate them to *want* to do so?"

The Young Magician made to interrupt but the High Master continued.

"We have also noted your passion and enthusiasm for story and metaphor. So the Panel wishes you to discover and collect this information through the medium and experience of stories. Do you have any questions?"

The Travelling High Flyer shook his head, so the High Master continued.

"Now you have already learned, here at The Academy, much about leadership, and you also know there is much more to learn. My first question to you is: Where does leadership start?"

"Right here," said the Young Magician touching his breastbone with the four fingers of his right hand, "right here in me. It is my personal responsibility."

"Good," said the High Master. "We are talking of leadership, which begins and ends with you. You cannot lead others until you know how to lead yourself with integrity and alignment to your inner values. This is your starting point. You are to fulfil the challenge as it has been set down, and there is no reason why you cannot, at the same time, fulfil your own personal quest of solving the riddle and interpreting your dream. You'll find the two tasks have a comfortable fit."

The Young Magician was startled. "How did you know about that?"

"The High Master's eyes twinkled. "You enter a Magician's library at your own risk. I have to confess that the books in my library like to engage in a little gossip from time to time. So. Questions?"

"Is there any particular way the Panel wants this challenge done?"

"No, my friend. That is up to you. However, we will offer you some help and support. As you are now officially designated a High Flyer you qualify for transport befitting your status. Your transport will also act as your guide. The only drawback is that you will have to seek out and find this transport for yourself."

"How should I do that?"

"Just trust the universe. As we are fond of saying, 'When the Traveller is ready, the transport will arrive.'" She smiled again, and took a small leather-bound package from a secret drawer. "You'll need this," she said simply. "Good luck and have fun." She shook hands, turned on her heel, and was gone.

* * *

The Young Magician sat on the parapet of an ancient stone bridge. He looked down into the clear rushing water. Trout held their station in the current, moving lazily left and right as the water washed food towards them. He watched how effortless and elegant their movements were. They didn't strive for anything, they waited patiently and cunningly for whatever destiny brought them.

He felt the size and shape of the leather package in his jacket pocket. He'd held his curiosity back till now, but he'd been aware of its presence, bulky and demanding, ever since he'd left the High Master's office.

He took it out and laid it on the flat surface of the parapet. He carefully teased open the tight knots that bound its opening. Inside was – well, not very much really. A small scroll addressed to the Bursar of the school, an everlasting pencil in the spine of a never-ending notebook, a compass, a map of the universe, a folding pair of poly-tinted sunglasses, an apple and a plastic token.

Curious, he thought, as he made his way towards the bursary. I've no idea what the scroll's for. I wonder what the High Master wants me to understand by all this. Let's think. Clearly, the pencil and notebook are the tools of my trade, how and where I write down my experiences. The compass and map are probably for navigation …

He paused to reflect for a moment on the idea of covering the whole world with his one pair of good walking boots.

And the poly-tinted glasses? he thought. Mmm! That's more difficult. Could be that stories can be reframes, allowing us to see information, situations and relationships in different ways and in different shades from what's customary. That will do. And the apple of course must be the search for knowledge and wisdom. Or, knowing the High Master, it could all be completely different. As for the plastic token, I haven't got the faintest idea.

* * *

The door knocker at the Bursary was a large, black, iron ring set in the mouth of a huge-maned lion. A sanctuary knocker. Suddenly The Academy seemed a friendly and welcoming place; he had no real idea of the world outside or where he would be going.

He knocked three times. The door swung open smoothly on its hinges. The Bursar took the scroll, saying simply, "I've been expecting you. Take this gold coin, throw it as far as you can into the centre of the lake where the largest and sweetest trout swim, and wish."

"Wish for what?" said the Young Magician somewhat surprised.

"Wish for whatever it is you most need at this moment in your life. But take heed: you can wish for only one thing, nothing more. Now be gone. And good luck, young man."

* * *

Clutching the gold coin tightly in his left hand, the Young Magician once again passed the old stone parapet where not much earlier he'd watched the trout taking their favoured station. They were still there at that point where the current rushes fastest through the stanchions of the bridge. A wave of melancholy swept over him. He suddenly envied the simplicity of their lives. He himself had no plan, no itinerary – and no food, come to think of it, except the apple, stowed away with the plastic token in the bottom of his rucksack. He felt very alone. He stared hard into the riverbed to see if he could spot any carelessly abandoned gold coins that might come in handy, but all he saw were stones and pebbles of many shapes and colours.

He trudged on along the narrow road, following the river downstream, wondering where and how he'd find the transport he'd been promised. Already his boots were beginning to pinch his feet. Occasionally a car or bus passed him by, rushing onwards towards its distant destination, leaving him coughing on the exhaust fumes.

This is a great start to exploring the universe, he thought to himself. Welcome to adulthood!

The lake lay before him: calm, magnificent, reflecting in its surface the tall mountains and the thick forests. He walked out along an old and slightly worse-for-wear wooden jetty. When he reached the end, he looked at the coin gleaming dully in his warm hand, closed his eyes and wished with all his heart for … for what?

He opened his eyes again.

What was it he really wanted? What was it he really needed at this moment? He certainly felt lonely. Someone to travel with, to share his ideas and thoughts with, would be nice. A sympathetic and engaging critic would be ideal. But, on the other hand, they wouldn't be able to cover much of the universe if they had to go everywhere by foot. So some transport would be ideal, too. A bicycle didn't seem very ambitious; a spacecraft seemed pretentious. How to choose?

He closed his eyes, and breathed deeply to the very centre of his being. The High Master came to mind. "Trust the universe," her voice said. Two words came straight to the young man's consciousness. And he wished with all his heart. "I wish for nothing more than the bestest *travelling companion* in the whole wide universe." And, so saying, he hurled his gold coin far into the dark centre of the lake.

The coin sank slowly to the bottom, glinting as it fell, bounced off the fattest, sweetest, most enormous trout that fishermen dream of but seldom catch, and finally came to rest on the handcrafted blade of one of the finest, keenest scimitars ever made in the known and unknown worlds. Here the blade had lain for centuries, dropped from the dying hand of its last master, the last survivor of a band of noble brothers, who had served their Lord in the conquests of the North, but were destined never again to see the land of their birth.

Meanwhile, the Young Magician waited. He watched the ripples run in concentric circles far out across the lake from the spot where the coin had disappeared until they lost their shape and energy, and the lake's surface became calm and inscrutable again. He waited, scarcely daring to breathe.

A voice behind him said, "You called me, Young Master."

25

He turned around startled. There was nothing there. The old wooden jetty stretched away to the shoreline some twenty yards away. Beyond the road the forests climbed up steeply, and beyond them the cold grey cliffs of the mountains soared perpendicularly skywards. A single bird called forlornly, and the mountains just as forlornly sent the echo back.

"I am at your service, Young Master. What is it that you desire?" The voice was strong and firm. It was a dignified voice. It possessed both authority and confidence without the slightest trace of humility, even though – wherever it was coming from – it was offering service. And, underneath the cultured composure of the voice, the Young Magician sensed warmth, compassion and more than a hint of humour.

The young man looked down. At his feet lay a beautiful exotic carpet. It was not particularly large, measuring about six foot by three. It had a deceptively simple design. From the edge of the carpet, thirteen narrow bands of geometric shapes formed a border to an inner large panel. Along each long side of the panel ran a column supporting a lintel from which hung a large candelabrum. Below the candelabrum, at the foot of the panel was a decorative chalice resting upon a simple altar. Although the carpet was clearly old, and in some places a little threadbare, the colours remained rich and vibrant. Beneath the altar, at one edge was a small box containing Arabic script, which, the Young Magician guessed, was the name of the carpet's maker.

"Have you not before seen a prayer mat?" demanded the voice with the trace of a smile. "My design is Kula, a Turkish design, although I myself was created within the realm of the Persian kingdoms many centuries ago. My maker, whose name you see, was the greatest carpet maker of his time, perhaps of all time. Now, you summoned me, Young Master. What is it I can do for you?"

"Oh, I see. You are the travelling companion I prayed for. You're not what I expected."

"Of that I know nothing," answered the carpet, "and in my long life I have learned never to expect anything to turn out as you expect, unless you want to expect disappointment."

"Yes, that's probably true. Anyway, I'm very pleased to meet you. And, by the way, why do you keep calling me Young Master?"

"When your gold coin touched the blade of the scimitar of my long dead Master, by the law of contiguity, my allegiance was transferred to you. You are now my Master, Young Master."

"But you don't sound like a servant. You sound like, well ... a carpet with some experience. Some knowledge. You've been around, you've travelled, I can tell."

"Right now, Young Master, I am bound by the codes, obligations and duties of servitude. It is my honour and privilege to serve you. And I am proud to make the greatest contribution possible, whatever my current station in life. Do not make the mistake of disrespecting the vocation of service."

"But you ..." The Young Magician paused. "What do you mean, your current station in life? Have you ever been – um, how can I put this – anything other than a carpet?"

The carpet laughed. "No, I have always been what I am. But not always a servant. Once I was the pride of the Shah and his Queen. Weavers would travel the length of the known world to view my workmanship and marvel at the ingenuity of my maker. Once I was a king among carpets. But that was a long time ago and is, as they say, another story."

"Will you tell me?"

"Maybe one day."

"So what can I call you?"

"As you wish. Among men, I am known by the common name of Kula. Among carpets, I am called Al Sayyid, which means the Master, the Chief."

"Then I shall call you Al Sayyid." He bent down and began to roll up the prayer mat.

"What are you doing, Young Master?"

"I am rolling you up so I can carry you more easily."

It sounded to the Young Magician as if Al Sayyid was crying with laughter. Ripples ran the length and breadth of the carpet. The candelabrum shook. The young man let the mat unfurl itself. The laughter continued.

"Why are you laughing?" said the Young Magician when the carpet paused for breath.

"Because carrying me to reach wherever your destination is would be like leaving your own house, and walking right around the world from east to west, in order to visit your next-door neighbour."

The young man looked puzzled.

"You wished for a *travelling companion*. And, Young Master, you must have wished well. For now you have a companion, a companion who knows how to travel. A companion, moreover, who knows how to travel first class. I'm not just a rug that knows how to serve. I can fly you anywhere in the universe, anywhere you wish to go. Come on. Sit down. Take off your boots, put on your special poly-tinted sunglasses to protect your eyes, and let's get going."

No wonder the High Master was smiling to herself when I left, thought the Young Magician to himself. What could be more appropriate as a guide for a High Flyer than a magical flying Persian carpet? Perfect!

With a huge sense of excitement and anticipation, the Young Master took off his boots and carefully stowed them in his backpack. Then he seated himself gingerly between the chalice and the candelabrum, and asked, "How do I hang on?"

"Trust the universe. Where to?"

"Wherever we can learn. Wherever we can be of service. Wherever you think it's best to begin my quest. You're the expert traveller. You choose. You lead me."

The Young Magician closed his eyes. There was a sound like a long moaning sigh. He felt a slight kick in the pit of his stomach, the light caress of a gentle breeze in his hair, and then a deep and peaceful sleep took him.

Section 3
Problem Solving

He woke up in a meadow of buttercups. The sun shone on the snowy mountain peaks and a stream gurgled nearby. In the distance he could faintly discern the softly tinkling bells of grazing sheep. He rubbed sleep from his eyes. The view was magnificent, and the air smelled clean and fresh.

"Where are we?"

The carpet replied, "A good spot to weave together some thoughts and plans. If I am to serve you well, I need to know more about you, and what it is you are searching for."

The Young Magician told Al Sayyid about the task the Panel had set him, about the riddle of the fish and the water, and also about the dream. When he was done, Al Sayyid asked whether he had either a plan of action for his journey, or any idea about how he would organise his task.

"No, not yet on either count."

"Then I, as your Guide, will take responsibility for pulling the threads of our itinerary together if you take responsibility for working out how you're going to go about fulfilling the task."

The Young Magician swallowed. "That sounds like a lot of work. It's going to take me all morning. Let's have some breakfast first, and then we can think about it."

"As you say, Young Master. But we won't think about it: we'll do it. Now, what is it you desire?"

Even as he thought of piping-hot buttered croissants with black-cherry jam and a steaming mug of cocoa, Al Sayyid was already producing them from a hidden pocket just above the candelabrum.

"Magic," said the Young Magician and got stuck into his breakfast.

About leading

"I'm a bit stuck," said the Young Magician. "Leadership is a huge issue. Where do I start? I thought it would take all morning. Now I think it will take all month!"

"Well," Young Master, "we really don't want to spin this out, do we?" May a Guide be permitted to ask some simple questions?"

"Sure, go ahead!"

"What's your aim?"

"To find out about the nature and attributes of leadership."

"And who is this for, specifically? Leadership in what context?"

"Well, generally, really. Everybody is a leader at some times in his or her life. Not just in business and politics, but also teachers, doctors and nurses, police and fire officers, coaches, therapists, parents, friends, lovers. Even children, some very young, have responsibilities in their lives."

"And what's going to be different about what *you* want to say about leadership? What will distinguish your exploration from all the other books, seminars, courses, CD-ROMS and TV programmes?"

"That's hard. What I'm sure of is that there's no right way, no one best way to lead. It depends, I guess, on things like the different situations in which leading occurs and the nature of the relationships between people. Things like that."

"I hope you'll forgive me, Young Master, if – speaking as a carpet – I tell you that I find all this a little woolly. How exactly will you weave together your study of leadership that makes it different, unique? You need a design."

A sudden possibility occurred to the young man. "Well, I have to work through stories. And stories come from all over the world. They represent different cultures and ways of thinking, different styles and ways of doing. What if, as we bring together stories from East and West, we could bring together the best elements of leadership from different cultures as well?"

"And how do you propose to do that?"

The Young Traveller felt stuck again.

"Did you study Aristotle and Western philosophy at The Academy?" asked Al Sayyid silkily.

"Yes, I did."

"And, if you were to boil down all the great ideas that underpin Western thought and philosophy to two or three key concepts, what would they be?"

The young man racked his brains. "I guess a big one would be the division of things into different classes. This is this and that is that, and they are different."

"Ah, the concept of 'dichotomy', the division of things into two classes," said Al Sayyid. "Can you give me some examples?"

"Let me see. The Western world tends to distinguish between the spiritual and the material. So we often find a division between church and state. The mind and the body are considered different; most Western doctors treat them separately. Aristotle defined a world divided into subjects and objects, and the West continues to divide the world this way. This way of thinking means that I stop at my skin and then the rest of the world begins. So there is the one and the many – me and everybody else."

"And how does this differ from Eastern thinking, generally speaking?"

"Eastern thinking is more concerned with oneness, with indivisi-bility, with harmony and interconnectedness. Chinese doctors, for example, treat the whole person, mind *and* body."

"So, Young Master, what if you could interweave the wefts of Western tradition with the warps of Eastern tradition in a frame that combines them both, and into which everything fits?"

"But how?"

"By using what you already know, what you have already explained. You have said what exists in the Western tradition is the idea that there is the *individual* and that outside of this there is the *group*. Right?"

"Right."

"Good. Now watch my central panel."

Between the candelabrum and the chalice a simple grid appeared. On the left-hand side, the word "ME" was written alongside the upper box. And the word "OTHERS" was written alongside the lower box.

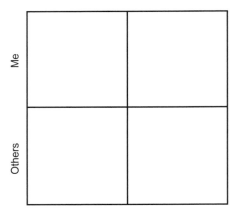

"And you also said that a key element of Western thinking is to divide the world into subjects and objects, what is inside you and what is outside you. Right?"

"Right."

The word "INSIDE" appeared above the left-hand boxes and the word "OUTSIDE" appeared above the right-hand boxes.

	Inside	Outside
Me		
Others		

"So, Young Master, we now have a division of the Western world into four separate and distinct parts or categories. Aristotle would be proud of us. Now, what elements of human life and activity do you think each box deals with?"

"Wow! That's cool. All life compressed into just four boxes! That's an interesting way to make complexity more manageable. So let me see ...

"The Upper Left box must be to do with all the things that happen inside a person, and that are individual to that person. These would be things that can't be 'seen' or measured, such as personality, temperament, attitude, awareness, personal values, wisdom and personal consciousness. So we could call this box 'Personal'.

"The Lower Left box is to do with all the things that happen inside groups of people. These would be things that identify groups of people as having something in common, such as shared 'language', shared values and shared culture. As we are talking about leadership issues we can call this box 'The team'.

"The Upper Right box is to do with what can be observed and measured on the outside of an individual. These would be things such as behaviours, skills, abilities, competencies, strengths, capacities and knowledge. We could call this box 'Professional'.

"Finally, the Lower Right box is to do with everything else that human cultures have developed. These are things that can be observed and measured on the outside. This box would include, for example, the different methods and styles that human beings use to organise politically, socially and economically. It would include things such as means of communication, means of transport, information systems and the ways in which these services are delivered. So we could call this box 'Infrastructure'."

Now the space on the carpet looked like this:

	Inside	Outside
Me	Personal	Professional
Others	The team	Infrastructure

"That's great," said the young man. "It really begins to organise and clarify what appeared so complicated a few moments ago."

"Remember," said Al Sayyid, "that the brain is a meaning-making organisation. It weaves together meaning by searching out and creating patterns. You always know more than you think you know. I simply asked questions that allowed you to frame and shape the knowledge you already had."

"What I can now see", said the Young Magician with excitement, "is that each of these boxes is an important area for a person who has to exercise leadership to think about and take into consideration. A good leader will want to consider each of these boxes, and also how they relate to each other."

"Precisely. Now what is there of human experience that is missing from our framework?"

The Young Magician thought hard and long. Finally he said, "Nothing. As far as I can see everything could find a place within one or more of these boxes."

"So we have four distinct categories, all of which have a relevance to leadership, and we have yet to thread in the weft of Eastern wisdom, which is what?"

"Harmony, wholeness, oneness, indivisibility."

"So how will you weave this in?"

The Young Magician reflected for a moment, and suddenly illumination hit him. "By recognising that these four boxes are not independent but interdependent. They have to work together, in balance, in harmony, as a unity. And how the balance is achieved will depend on the context and the environment in which leadership decisions have to be made.

"Now all I need to do is find stories from across the world that illustrate these elements, these arenas of inspiring leadership, and show how they work together. Result!"

"Congratulations, Young Master, you have begun to understand the key attributes of the effective leader, the one who can integrate and synthesise diverse strands of thought and action, culture and will, as surely as a master weaver integrates the yarns of the perfect carpet. You have begun to glimpse the notion of the Integral Leader.

About influencing

"So, Young Master, we have thought about leading. Now talk to me about influencing. And how do you distinguish it from manipulating? How do you keep these two yarns of such similar colour and texture apart?"

"Sometimes manipulation is necessary, for example in moments of crisis. If someone's about to get run over by a tram, give them a push. Or shout at people if the building's on fire. You don't need to observe the niceties in these situations.

"But, in normal leadership situations, manipulation – in my experience – is usually counterproductive. It makes me feel bad. And when I feel like that I'm probably not going to give of my best. On the other hand, when I feel that I've been influenced, I feel good and happy to give one hundred per cent to the task in hand.

"So the challenge for leaders is, therefore, how to make the team, or the individual, *feel good* about what they've been asked to do."

"So how does one do that, Young Master?"

"We studied this at The Academy. Manipulation is a strategy that goes something like this: 'I know what I want and I'm determined to get it. To hell with anyone who gets in my way, nothing's going to stop me. So do what I say, or else.'

"On the other hand, influence is a strategy that goes something like this: 'I know what I want and I'm determined to get it. But I know all of you probably want certain things, too. If I find out what your goals are and assist you in getting them, you'll probably help me in return.'

"While manipulators have to fight resistance and sabotage every time they want something, the influencers seek to build alliances for the long term, believing that people will be willing to work with someone who demonstrates they have their interests at heart, as well as their own.

"Manipulators operate out of a map of scarcity. They believe there is not enough to go around. If they don't take the prize, someone else will.

"Influencers, on the other hand, operate from a map of abundance. They believe there's plenty of what's truly important in life to go around. Whatever influencers give out, they believe they'll get back. Influencers dovetail their personal goals with the goals of others. They are aware of and pay attention to what's happening around them, and behave flexibly to accommodate whatever the situation requires. Above all, they work hard to build warm, long-term relationships with people because this is the secret of building trust and commitment.

"So, if I was also to consider the importance of thinking holistically as we did just now in the section on leadership, we could organise our thinking about influence in this way:

- a manipulator seeks a WIN for himself;
- an influencer seeks a WIN for himself and a WIN for the group;
- an influential leader seeks a WIN for himself, a WIN for the group and a WIN for the wider system.

"The influential or integral leader goes for the inclusive WIN–WIN–WIN."

About motivating

"A neat stitch," said Al Sayyid. "So what did you learn about the art of motivating yourself and others at The Academy? What is motivation and where does it come from?"

"I think I'll need some help with this."

"Young Master, what motivates you?"

"Doing things I like, the way I like doing them."

"And what does the word 'motivation' literally mean?"

"Movement."

"And what directions are possible?"

"Either towards something or away from something."

"Good, so would you agree that you are motivated to move towards the things that you find important in your life, the things you value, the things you want? And away from things that are not important, or not valued, or that you fear?"

"Yes, that's probably true."

"So you wouldn't attempt to motivate someone by offering them something they didn't like or didn't value, would you?"

"I guess not."

"Now, have your values, *the ways you respond to and think about things*, always been the same? Or have they changed over the last five, ten or fifteen years?"

"Mostly they've changed, although there are some values I know I've always had, and probably won't ever change."

"And does everyone have the same values as each other?"

"No. Of course they don't."

"So what have you learned so far about motivation?"

"That people get motivated by doing things they value and demotivated by doing things they don't value. But people don't all share the same values, or think about things in the same way. So what will motivate some will not motivate others, and vice versa."

"So ...?"

"So an effective leader will need to know how to motivate those he or she wishes to lead and influence through the ways that they differently and *naturally* get motivated."

"Precisely."

"Al Sayyid, there are an awful lot of people with different valuing and thinking systems out there."

"Individually, yes, but in terms of *types* of valuing and thinking, no. Young Master, do you recall the principles of Magic and how to achieve them? I believe you may have been talking about these very things with the Panel not long ago."

"Your emphasis on *types* is a clue, I guess. So that would be the notion that everything has an underlying structure and pattern, and that the observant magician looks to find what connects information below the surface of things."

"So ...?"

"So, perhaps just as we compressed the whole world and everything in it to four boxes, perhaps there may be patterns to be discerned generally in people's thinking and valuing systems. Is there evidence for this? Is there research?"

"Indeed there is. But perhaps you can work some of this out for yourself. Do you have younger brothers or sisters?"

The Young Magician was surprised at the question.

"I have a younger sister, yes."

"Tell me the main stages she went through in her development, starting at birth."

The Young Magician smiled at the memory of his little sister's early days. "When she was born she was completely dependent of course. She needed help and support and constant attention to get through the day. As she grew a little older she began to recognise us: Mother, Father and me. She developed a bond with us and we with her. We looked after her and made sure she had everything she wanted and needed.

"Later – she must have been around two and a half – there was a big change. She began to recognise herself as an individual human being. I think some people call these years the terrible twos. She could be a monster sometimes. Her motto seemed to be: I want it and I want it now. I think at times she ran the whole house and she was really creative in finding ways to do this.

"The next stage was that she began to pick up rules from our parents and her teachers at school. She started bossing her friends and schoolmates. She'd tell them what was right and wrong, what they 'should' or 'shouldn't' do. She'd even tell *me* how I 'ought to' do things. These rules ran her life, and our lives too for a while.

"The next stage was one where she began to experiment with the many things she was learning. She would apply her knowledge in a variety of ways. She'd take risks to get the results she wanted. She was keen on discovering how things worked and how to use them to her advantage.

"And finally, I suppose, there came a time when she broke away from her identification with our family and sought out her own circle of friends, her own small collective of companions, who did things together and invented their own ways of putting the world to rights."

"Now," said Al Sayyid, "gather up this tapestry of development that you have woven, these six stages you have teased out, and give them some simple labels. What is critical to the needs of each stage? What is it that each stage most values?"

The Young Magician thought hard for a while. And then with his finger wrote these bullet points in Al Sayyid's central panel.

- Stage 1: SURVIVAL
- Stage 2: SAFETY, SECURITY, BELONGING
- Stage 3: ASSERTIVENESS, EXPRESS SELF, CREATIVITY
- Stage 4: RULES, AUTHORITY, STABILITY, ORDER
- Stage 5: APPLY KNOWLEDGE, EXPERIMENT TO WIN
- Stage 6: COMMUNITY OF EQUALS, CONSENSUS, HARMONY

"And do you see any other patterns?" asked Al Sayyid.

"Yes, I do, and they were so clear as my sister grew up and developed. She went through some stages where her focus was completely on herself. These were the odd-number stages: one, three and five. And other times she was much more interested in fitting in with whichever group that she felt a part of: stages two, four and six."

"Now," said Al Sayyid, "these stages you have identified can also be observed in adult human development. We can see them in individuals, in groups, in organisations and even in nations. And this knowledge of patterns in *types* of thinking and valuing in people can be enormously valuable to the effective leader."

"Does this mean that each person operates in just one of these patterns?"

"Not at all," replied Al Sayyid. "People are complex and run many patterns. But it is often the case that a person, or group, or organisation may be *centred* mainly in one pattern – or perhaps two – and that will be very useful to know if, as a leader, you wish to influence or motivate them *naturally*."

* * *

The Young Magician was quiet for some time, reflecting on the ideas he had been sharing with Al Sayyid. Not long ago he had felt overwhelmed by the complexity of the information he was going to have to deal with. But now, with Al Sayyid's help, it seemed much more manageable.

He had a four-box model in which to analyse four aspects of leadership and into which, it seemed to him, everything in the world could be fitted. He had an understanding of the structure of influence and how it differed from manipulation. And now he was beginning to discern certain patterns or types of valuing and thinking in people that it would be useful to know about if he wished to motivate people successfully.

He thought of Einstein's dictum flapping on a streamer pulled by a little yellow biplane, and smiled: "Make it as simple as you can but not any simpler." I wonder, he thought, if I could make it simpler still.

He turned to Al Sayyid and said, "Perhaps we could code these six stages in some way. Just to make them simpler to remember."

"Good. How will we do that?"

"Let's give each stage a colour-coded flag where the colour symbolises the system. You choose." He passed his hand across Al Sayyid's central panel, erasing his previous work and, magically, these codes appeared:

Stage	Core value	Code	Reason
Stage 1	Survival	BEIGE	Like the savannah plain
Stage 2	Safety, belonging	PURPLE	Mystic, tribal
Stage 3	Assertiveness	RED	Expressive, hot emotions
Stage 4	Order, authority	BLUE	The blue sky above
Stage 5	Experiment to win	ORANGE	Molten steel
Stage 6	Consensus, harmony	GREEN	Liberal sensibilities

"Now," said Al Sayyid, "these are the colour codings used by a powerful model known as Spiral Dynamics, of which I shall say more soon. Each one of these stages in the development of people's thinking and valuing can be observed in the world today. And it will also be appropriate to add one more of these levels, a level that will represent the oneness, and indivisibility of the systemic, environmental thinking that we talked about earlier. The kind of thinking that embraces and supports all the previous ones."

And another level appeared in the list:

Stage 7:	Systemic, environmental	YELLOW	Sun that sees all things

And along the border of the panel, next to the appropriate descriptions appeared these coloured flags.

* * *

"So, Young Master, what has been the point of this whole exercise?"

"First, to give me a set of models, tools and structures around which I can organise my thinking about how leaders can influence and motivate people.

"Second, to give me some guidelines for organising and interpreting each of the stories I come across from East and West, and for considering what contribution they each might make to an understanding of what makes an inspiring leader."

"Congratulations, Young Master. Your goal is now as perfectly formed as a fine Persian carpet! This clarity will ensure you succeed in achieving the results you want. It is rather good, is it not, to have a rich, well-laid-out pattern to follow?"

The Young Magician paused and swallowed.

"Al Sayyid, I already have a lot to thank you for and we've hardly started our journey."

"Young Master, I am here to serve you. I simply gave you a frame through which to structure your thinking and knowledge for yourself. Remember, you already know much more than you think you do. And, if you want to know even more, there's plenty more to explore. Just slide your hand behind my left-hand pillar at the bottom near the chalice."

The Young Magician did so. He found a secret pocket and slid his hand inside. He felt papers and books.

"It's my secret library," said Al Sayyid, "my personal collection of books and papers. You asked about the research that supports the information you have been exploring.

"The four-box model is based on the work of the philosopher Ken Wilber. And the colour-coded stages of development in thinking and valuing systems, known as Spiral Dynamics, are based on the work of Professor Clare Graves as developed by his colleagues, Dr Don Beck and Dr Christopher Cowan. You can read their work as we travel, and deepen your understanding of their ideas, at your leisure."

The Young Magician shook his head. Al Sayyid was full of surprises. After a moment or two he asked, "So, I guess it's time to start out on our journey. Do you know where the Panel wishes us to begin?"

Al Sayyid replied, "Young Master, as you may imagine, I already have my instructions. Jump on, sit tight, put on your protective sunglasses. We're off to the plains of North America."

"What are we going to do there?"

"A good place to start, especially if you want to begin to address the issues and attributes of leadership, influence and motivation, is with a simple question: What is life all about?"

"A good question, which doesn't seem all that simple at all," replied the Young Magician.

Al Sayyid continued to follow his own thread. "I am reminded of an old Native American story about choice. Yes, this insight will be a good enough beginning to your quest."

"You know stories?" asked the Young Magician surprised.

"Young Master, it would be strange after five hundred years of flying over the universe with some of the wisest, most powerful and most knowledgeable of people if I did not have some wealth of stories woven into the richness of my design."

The Young Magician laughed at himself, once again appreciating how his new friend was already turning out to be one of his best resources. "You have my full attention."

"Are you sitting comfortably?" said Al Sayyid. "My story begins some years ago in North Carolina." The Young Magician closed his eyes and his pencil began writing magically in his notebook.

Section 4
The Stories

Story 1

Dances with Wolves

A white-haired Cherokee is teaching his grandchildren about life. He tells them, "A fight is going on inside me. A terrible fight, and it is a fight between two wolves.

"One wolf represents fear, greed, hatred, anger, envy, false pride, self-pity, resentment, guilt, inferiority, arrogance, deceitfulness, superiority and selfishness.

"The other wolf stands for peace, love, kindness, joy, truth, compassion, humility, transparency, authenticity, friendship, respect, integrity, benevolence, generosity, faith, sharing, serenity and empathy.

"The same fight is going on inside you, and in every other person too."

The children thought about this for a while. Then one little girl asked her grandfather, "Which wolf will win?"

The old Cherokee held a long silence. Then simply said, "Whichever one you feed."

Primary source: Eleonora Gilbert
General source: Native American tradition

* * *

After the story, the Young Magician sat quietly for a while and did some thinking. Then, he took out his never-ending notebook and his everlasting pencil and began to draw. First of all, he pencilled in a vertical and a horizontal line to make four quadrants.

In the upper left quadrant [UL], he quickly sketched out a picture of a person deep in thought. This icon in the PERSONAL box represented the *invisible interior* world of the *individual*: personal awareness and values, personal leadership style and attitudes.

 In the lower left quadrant [LL], he sketched a hand holding a group or family safely within its grasp. This icon in the TEAM box represented the *invisible interior* world of the *collective*: shared values, vision, and language; the webs of culture and worldview in which each individual operates.

 In the upper right quadrant [UR], he sketched a person working with a pair of compasses. This icon in the PROFESSIONAL box represented the *visible exterior* world of the *individual*: personal capabilities and competencies, professional behaviours, measurable performance.

 In the lower right quadrant [LR], he sketched a typical urban environment, although he could equally well have chosen any environment with visible social structures. This icon in the INFRASTRUCTURE box represented the *visible exterior* world of the *collective*: social systems, organisational systems, information systems, technical environments and so on in which people live and work.

When he had finished his work looked as shown on the top of the next page.

Then the Young Magician turned to a new page in his notebook, sketched in a small-scale version of the four quadrants on the left-hand side of the page, quickly drew in the icons for the UL and LL quadrants leaving the right hand boxes blank, and then began to write up his notes about the story: Dances with Wolves.

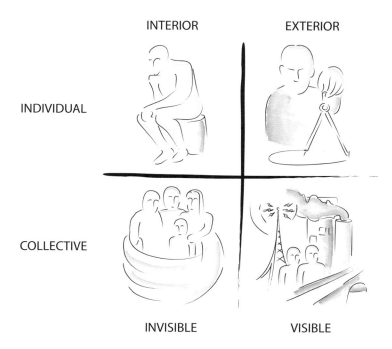

Leading

For the Cherokee leadership starts from within. It starts with a set of personal decisions about what is right and proper within his own individual worldview. So I'm putting an icon in the Upper Left (UL) *Personal* box. These decisions may be individual values and beliefs, or they may be rooted in the culture to which a person belongs. So I also score an icon in the Lower Left (LL) *Team* box. For me, the main message is that leadership starts with personal integrity.

Influencing

The old man uses a dramatic story as a way of capturing the attention of his grandchildren and teaching them about personal values. He also starts by telling them that the same battle is taking place inside him. He suggests that the battle for personal integrity goes on not just in ourselves but in everybody. Each one of us has a choice about how we will act. The story offers a WIN for the grandfather, a WIN for the grandchildren, and the possibility of a WIN for the world. The three wins we talked about earlier: a win for me, a win for you, a win for the system.

Motivating

This story connects with the listeners, and motivates them naturally, within the following valuing and thinking systems:

PURPLE:	**RED:**	**BLUE:**
tribal/family bonding; metaphors from the natural world.	heroism; survival depicted as a fight, a struggle.	order, structure, the way right-thinking people behave.

My insights

- The choices you make in your own mind determine the reality of your experience.
- Peace, love and kindness are not passive qualities. They have to be fought for and asserted. The good *wolf* wins, not the good *sheep*. Struggle is a natural and inevitable part of the human condition.

* * *

"Possibly," said Al Sayyid.

"What do you mean: 'possibly'?" asked the Young Magician somewhat taken aback.

"I mean, Young Master, that, while your interpretations are perfectly feasible, they are not the only possible interpretations. Always be aware that the way you interpret a story, or anything else for that matter, always says more about you, and your values and beliefs, than it says about whatever it is being interpreted. Each one of us is limited by our current knowledge and experience of the world."

But does that mean that I'm stuck in my views?"

"Not at all. And you'll learn a great deal more throughout your journey. But I shall always remind you, at the end of every story, to hold your current views and knowledge as nothing more than provisional. And, whatever *you* think, others may well think differently, including myself."

"And you, Al Sayyid, you've been around five hundred years or maybe more. Do you have more to learn?"

"Indeed I do. I may have kept young princes warm, and great sultans, kneeling respectfully on my soft pile, may have said their prayers on me, their heads bowed towards the east, but I have also been trodden on and walked all over. I know much and I know little. So tell me, what more do you have to say about this last story?"

"Well," said the Young Magician thinking hard, "one attribute of leadership that becomes clear to me from this story could be the importance of personal integrity."

"Indeed it could, among many other things besides, for as I have said all great stories are capable of holding many meanings. So, what is it that you would next like to explore?"

The Young Magician considered for a moment or two. "How does a leader get the best out of himself? Or herself?"

"A good question. Hold very tight, I know where we may find an answer to that. We are going to roll back the years to examine the very underlay of the modern fabric."

* * *

With Al Sayyid slung nonchalantly over his shoulder, the Young Magician was walking through a busy rural market. All the people wore the same blue clothes with red hand-stitched embroidery and silver buttons, men and women alike. Some wore leather slippers on their feet, most were barefoot. They were quite small and their eyes had only single lids.

"Where are we?" he whispered to the carpet.

"In Chao Li, on the Silk Road, in China."

"Why aren't these people paying any attention to us?"

"Because it's AD 717 and unlike us they can't shift through time, which is why we can see them, but they can't see us – unless we decide to make ourselves visible. Now these people are all going to an archery competition. Watch and learn."

Story 2

The Premier League

The new archery champion was very good indeed. He was also young, brash and rather full of himself. Arrogantly, he challenged a Zen master to a contest. The Zen master, who was highly skilled as an archer himself, was certainly impressed by the young man's technical ability. He watched as the boastful champion fired his arrow into the centre of the distant bull's-eye, and with his second arrow split the first.

"Beat that!" demanded the champion.

The older man smiled, said nothing, but merely beckoned the younger man to follow him. Curious as to the older man's intentions, the champion archer followed the Zen master through the twisting trails of the pine forests and into the high mountains.

They reached a deep chasm where far below mountain water roared and tumbled over rough-hewn rocks. Spanning the chasm was a rotten, moss-covered tree trunk. The Zen master calmly stepped onto the flimsy, slippery, unsteady log. He selected a distant boundary marker, drew his bow, and fired his arrow clean and true into the centre of the target.

Gracefully stepping off the log onto firm mountain rock, the Master invited the champion to take his turn on the treacherous trunk. But the young man was petrified by the prospect. He gazed in terror into the deep abyss. He could not even step onto the log, let alone fire an arrow towards the target.

"You have great skill with your bow," said the Master, "but little skill with the mind that lets the arrow loose."

**Primary source: *Zen Stories to Tell Your Neighbours* website
(John Suler PhD)
General source: Zen tradition**

* * *

Leading

 This story emphasises the personal characteristics of the great leader. The Zen master demonstrates command and control over the inner self (*UL Personal*). It also suggests that professional skills and behaviours, though important, are of little value without wise application (*UR Professional*). The story also reinforces acceptable cultural or team values – modesty and moderation (*LL Team*), and recognises that the effective leader operates across all elements of the infrastructure (*LR Infrastructure*). The chasm symbolises stress, crisis and danger as well as the separation in wisdom between to the two men.

Influencing

Metaphorically, the story reinforces the human desire for *balance* in each person's life. This balance requires both the development of appropriate professional skills and an inner composure that fosters personal stability and inner personal alignment. Again, the story stresses the benefits of a potential WIN–WIN–WIN.

Motivating

Stories that have icons in all the boxes suggest that they will appeal to all the valuing and thinking systems.

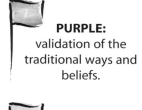
PURPLE: validation of the traditional ways and beliefs.

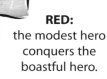
RED: the modest hero conquers the boastful hero.

BLUE: reaffirmation of order and stability: the right ways of behaving.

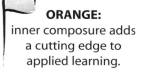
ORANGE: inner composure adds a cutting edge to applied learning.

GREEN: the humble, self-effacing leader

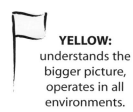
YELLOW: understands the bigger picture, operates in all environments.

My insights

- Leaders who have only technical competence remain technicians. Leaders who are authentic and modest, who lead by quiet example, and who are sensitive to the various demands of the *whole* environment, inspire others to pay attention.
- Stories are powerful ways to draw attention to the dangers of arrogance and boastfulness.
- Much wisdom resides in those who are older and more experienced.

* * *

"Possibly."

With Al Sayyid's words ringing in his ears, and before he realised they had even moved, the Young Magician found he was already in another part of China, even further back in time, listening to the wisdom of Confucius. It seemed the Panel had a point they wanted to impress upon the Young Magician.

Story 3

External Distractions

Confucius was saying, "Attaching too much importance to external concerns distracts you from internal ones. Consider an archer. If he is shooting for the prize of a mere certificate, he will be relaxed and focused and use all his skill and prowess. But, if the prize is a silver belt, he may become tense and hesitate. If the prize is a coveted golden trophy, he may shoot as if weighed down by troubles and cares.

"In all three cases the archer's skill remains the same, but in the second and third cases he magnifies the importance of material rewards and loses sight of his true nature. Whoever puts too much attention on what is on the outside gets clumsy on the inside."

General source: Taoist tradition

* * *

Leading

 Confucius is making the point that lack of inner psychological balance and composure leads to "clumsiness" on the inside (*UL Personal*). He is not denying the importance or existence of the professional and infrastructural (*UR and LR*) elements of archery but suggesting the wise archer should not be overconcerned with material issues or personal gain. As we are working with metaphor here, it is easy to substitute archer for leader, parent, teacher, coach and so on.

Influencing

The story influences because it describes something we all recognise from experience. Where does stress come from in situations like this? From being unable to control our negative inner self-talk. The story suggests the listener will gain more of what he desires when he develops his inner self and focuses on what is truly important in life. The story is primarily focused on a WIN for the self, although this is not in any way manipulative.

Motivating

My studies of Kung Fu-tse, Confucius's Chinese name, suggest that what most concerned him was the establishment of a system of morality and statecraft in order to bring about peace, stability and just governance in a time of warfare and tyranny. These are very much BLUE issues.

My insights

- Centre yourself totally before any high pressure event whether it is a sports event, performance, meeting, negotiation, or presentation.
- Know what is important in your life.
- Know what is not important in your life.

* * *

"Possibly. By the way, Young Master, "Have you ever heard of the great Chinese general Sun Tzu?"

"Yes, I have. We've studied him at The Academy. He was the one who said it was best – wherever possible – to win a war without having to fight any battles. His book, *The Art of War*, is as much about leadership as it is about warfare. In fact, I read in a newspaper that the coach of the Australian cricket team – the world champions – uses the principles of Sun Tzu to create the right psychological attitude in his players and their approach to the game."

"Young Master, dip into my secret library. See what comes to hand."

The Young Magician slipped is hand into the secret pocket and pulled out a slim volume.

"Read the introduction," said Al Sayyid. "What are the key points of Sun Tzu's philosophy?"

The young man scanned through the pages and read out the following:

- Avoid slaughter and destruction; win territory that is intact.
- Do not rely on numbers but on intellectual, moral and circum-stantial elements.
- Careful planning based on sound information is the basis of success and speedy outcome.
- The army completes what successful diplomacy has made possible.
- Make proper preparations *in the enemy's camp* so that the result is decided beforehand.

"These points strike me as influential leadership at its most supreme," said Al Sayyid, "and useful advice metaphorically in all manner of contexts where influence, leadership and success are critical."

"It's amazing, isn't it," said the Young Magician, "that a strategist who wrote in the fourth century BC remains able to lead and influence others at the beginning of the twenty-first century? Are we going to meet him?"

"Are you sitting comfortably, Young Master?"

Story 4

Presence

Sun Tzu was training a fighting cock for the Lord of Chu. After one week he was asked whether the bird was ready. Sun Tzu replied, "Not yet! He is too spirited, too quarrelsome and too eager to seek out a fight."

After two weeks Sun Tzu's answer was, "Not yet. He still bristles with aggression and pride when he sees another bird."

Another week passes and Sun Tzu's response is still, "Not yet. His fighting spirit is not yet diminished, and arrogance gleams in his eye."

At the end of the fourth week, Sun Tzu said, "Now he is ready. When he hears the crowing of another cock, he pays no attention at all. If you look at him, you would think he is a cock made of stone, so still is his demeanour, so centred his inner being. His inner quality radiates beyond him. He has no need to fight, because no other cock will dare face him."

**Primary source: Mark Forstater, *The Spiritual Teachings of the Tao*, Hodder & Stoughton
General source: Taoist tradition**

* * *

Leading

 To be able to lead oneself, to be influential, to achieve the maximum result with the minimum effort, requires training, patience and self-discipline. It is necessary to go beyond the ego. Inspiring leadership does not require macho displays of strength and power, unless there is a call for them as a last resort. Instead, the inner composure that comes from being the master of oneself impresses and influences others without fuss or ceremony.

Influencing

To serve a community well, the leader must be both strong and wise. The leader must be impartial yet ready to take action when necessary. Inner personal strength will therefore support appropriate professional behaviours and their application within the environment and infrastructure.

Motivating

Some of the great heroes in the movies, the ones who impress people with their strength of character and their moral values, are those whose behaviours are minimal and well controlled – as with the fighting cock in this story. I'm thinking of characters played by Humphrey Bogart and Clint Eastwood, for example. Their demeanour deters others from attacking them, but, if they *are* attacked, their response is ruthless. However, it is a ruthlessness that is necessary to uphold "right" values. So this story appeals to those whose values are formed through existing in both RED and BLUE environments.

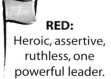

RED:
Heroic, assertive,
ruthless, one
powerful leader.

BLUE:
Order, control,
stability, authority,
one true way.

ORANGE:
Inner strength
will get the
results I seek.

YELLOW:
Personal alignment with self, others,
skills, and the environment; at one
with the habitat and the system.

My insights

- Stillness, inner strength and quietness can have much greater impact than posturing and displays of aggression or intellect.
- To play a powerful king on stage, do as little as possible. It is not what the powerful one does but how others respond to power that gives the king his authority.

* * *

"Possibly. And if I may weave in a few further observations on this topic," said Al Sayyid, "there is a book in my secret library on present day business organisations which reinforces your points.[1] It charts the progress of the most successful US companies over the last twenty five years, and makes the point that most people will probably not have heard of the CEOs who ran them. Their focus was on promotion of their organisation, not self-promotion."

The Young Magician made a note of this in his never-ending notebook, then said, "Al Sayyid, may I ask, how do you know where to take me?"

"I have a list from the Panel. You'll find another secret pocket cunningly hidden. Look at the chalice that stands on the altar in my central panel. In the mouth of the chalice you'll find the pocket."

The young man found the pocket, which was surprisingly large, fished around inside and pulled out an impressive parchment scroll covered in official seals.

"Is this it?"

"Open it up. What does it say now? Who's at the top of the list?"

"King Arthur."

"Then we have some flying to do. Halfway around the world, and some thousand years on in time. Sunglasses on? Let's go."

* * *

They were sitting in the corner of an austere banqueting hall within a great stone-built castle. At both ends of the room roaring fires blazed. And in between, long tables made of rough-hewn oak groaned under the weight of roast meats, turnips and pewter pitchers filled to the brim with beer, wine or mead. Men and women sat on long benches on each side of the tables, talking, shouting and singing. Streaming banners hung from the ceiling, and the armour and weapons of fighting men lay strewn on the floor, glinting in the flickering light of the fires.

"Where are we?" whispered the Young Magician.

"At the court of King Arthur. This is Britain in the sixth century. For many years, the land of the Britons has been ruled by chaos. Many have sought to seize the crown; but none until Arthur have succeeded. He has unified the kingdom once again, and repulsed the Saxon invaders, and now is the time to celebrate the peace. Order and harmony are once again restored in the land."

"Who are all these people?"

"Military commanders, knights, administrators, landowners, soldiers, poets and minstrels, mostly. And that man over there" – Al Sayyid flapped an edge loosely in a certain direction – "is Merlin the Wizard, who protected and mentored Arthur as a youth. From Merlin Arthur learned many gifts and much wisdom."

The Young Magician watched in amazement as another story magically wrote itself into his notebook.

Notes
1. Jim Collins (2001), *Good to Great* (Random House).

Story 5

Holding the Space

At the top table, Arthur sat. Behind him, on the wall and above the fire, hung the three great symbols of his power: the sword Caliburn, the shield Pridwen and the lance Ron. To his left sat his wife Gwenhwyfar, and to his right sat his three most trusted commanders: Cei, Bedwyr and Gawain.

Cei was the greatest and most feared of warriors and the brains behind Arthur's military campaigns. Bedwyr was responsible for the administration of the king's realm and the unification of the country. Gawain, whose charm and integrity were legendary, was responsible for all diplomatic and political dealings with allies and enemies alike

At another table Merlin sat with two of his most promising apprentices. While the knights and their ladies indulged in the food, entertainment and pageantry, Merlin's apprentices observed the events with curiosity and a certain amount of puzzlement. It wasn't till the festivities were almost over that they attempted to articulate their questions to their master.

"Merlin, Slayer of Dragons, it is indeed a pleasure and a privilege for us to be here with you at this great feast, and it ill suits us to be in any way critical or ungrateful, but there is something that we cannot help but notice. Can you help us solve what is troubling us?"

"What is your question? Let's see how you may unthread the puzzle for yourself."

"If we take each of King Arthur's great commanders one by one, we are humbled by their great gifts, their knowledge, their skills and the quality with which they execute their duties.

"Cei, Slayer of Saxons, is twice the warrior and strategist than is the king. Granted, Arthur is a fierce and committed fighter but he has neither

the strength nor tactical brain of Cei. Cei is a master of warfare. He knows exactly how to make maximum gain for minimal loss.

"Again, Bedwyr the Brave knows exactly how to achieve compliance and how to create efficiency. His approach is resolute and determined. If anyone can create discipline and unity in this kingdom, and create an effective administration, it is Bedwyr. Under his stewardship our troops are fed and armed, and our people live in peace and plenty. In these skills, his ability far outshines the competence of the king.

"Finally, in terms of nobility of blood, of grace and integrity, Gawain has no peer. His skills in tact and diplomacy are known and admired throughout the civilised world. He knows with whom to build strategic relationships, with whom to forge alliances and whom to threaten with the unleashing of Cei or Bedwyr. Surely, this inner knowledge and strength sets Gawain apart. He is a man who appears to be created specifically for the purpose of majesty and rule.

"And yet, despite the skills and brilliance of each of these great men, it is Arthur – a man who cannot hold a candle to any of them in their areas of expertise – who wears the crown, and who sits beneath those three great symbols of power: Caliburn, Pridwen and Ron. How can this be?"

Merlin reflected for a moment or two on the comments and questions of his two apprentices. After a pause he said, "Consider the web of a spider. What is it that determines the strength of the web as it hangs suspended in thin air enduring the furious struggles of trapped insects?"

"Surely it is the thickness of the thread," replied one apprentice. The other said, "Or is it the strength of its main spokes?" The first added, "Or perhaps the number of smaller lines that hold the main ones together?" They looked stumped.

"Consider," said Merlin, "that the webs of bigger spiders, whose silks are thicker, are not necessarily stronger than the webs of smaller spiders. Consider that webs of equal intricacy, and having the same number of lines, may also differ in strength. Consider, too, that the webs produced by similar species of spiders may differ greatly in quality and resilience."

Merlin paused for a moment to create a sense of expectation. "Look beyond the apparent to that which cannot be seen. A web is not made of silken threads alone. Just as important is the space between the threads. The art of the spinner is to introduce harmony and balance to the architecture it constructs. Its skill is to realise the space that holds and balances the threads within the web. So tell me, who is the spinner here?"

A log disintegrated in the fireplace behind them, sending a shower of sparks onto the hearth. The apprentices were thoughtful. Finally, one asked, "But how does a skilful spinner know how to create this harmony? By what secret gifts or guile does it bind all these threads and space together?"

"Think of a great teacher," murmured Merlin. "He gives away his knowledge, he supports and nurtures the development of his students, he speaks in a language they can understand, using examples they can apply. He recognises and validates their efforts, and the contributions they make. In everything he does he nourishes those in his care by giving away his energy and power. And yet the more he does this, and the more he appears to lower his own status, the higher the esteem in which his students hold him."

"That is exactly so," said one of the apprentices. "It's like the ancient riddle: What gains power the more it gives away?" "The sun," replied the second apprentice, "for the more it gives away its energy and strength that sustains all life, the more each flower and tree and natural thing grows towards it in praise and reverence."

"And so it is," said Merlin, "with a master spinner like King Arthur. He is so secure in his inner wisdom, his sense of harmony and balance, that he has no problem in putting talented people where they can shine and bring balance to his administration. And he achieves harmony between them by demonstrating how much he values each one of them for their highly distinctive and gifted contributions. And so, as all natural things incline towards the sun, just so does every individual in the kingdom incline towards Arthur with gratitude and respect."

Primary source: Martin Woods
Secondary source: There is a version of this story in
W. Chan Kim and Renee Mauborgne,
"Parables of Leadership"
General source: Adapted from Asian tradition

* * *

Leading

King Arthur's personal attributes and professional behaviours represented by the two upper boxes (*UL & UR*), allow the team culture to flourish (*LL*), and the nation to be well governed by efficient and pragmatic infrastructural systems (*LR*). The fact that all four boxes are fully represented suggests a great leader indeed, one who allows the whole "habitat" to flourish, so everyone and everything can give of its best. Thus the circle around the boxes.

Influencing

In this story we find the notion of the great leader as a coordinator. King Arthur's skill in bringing the best out of the great talent available to him and putting it to the service of the collective, the state, the common good is impressive while understated. In the same way great orchestral conductors, while not necessarily being the best musicians, know how to get the best out of the ensemble. They influence those they lead by wanting the best for the individuals and the best for the collective. This is a WIN–WIN–WIN story.

Motivating

This is a story that appeals to all the valuing and thinking systems. It gets six flags.

PURPLE:
King Arthur creates a sense of belonging, a unification of the people, the "tribe", the nation.

RED:
King Arthur is a hero, a conqueror, an undisputed leader who rules through chosen subordinates.

BLUE:
King Arthur has brought order and stability to the kingdom; he rules through rightful authority.

ORANGE:
King Arthur knows how to delegate; he rewards those who get results no matter their age, class or status.

GREEN:
King Arthur has restored harmony and leads with the consensus and counsel of others; he does not appear authoritarian.

YELLOW:
King Arthur is the most competent, the one who understands how to bring the best out of others, and how to run the system.

My insights

- Influential leadership does not necessarily have to be coercive and exploitative.
- Leadership can be nurturing and generative.
- President Harry S. Truman had this take on excellent leadership: "You can accomplish anything in life, provided you don't mind who gets the credit." That's just what King Arthur does.

* * *

"Possibly," said Al Sayyid. "Now, if you just take a look at the dictionary just inside the entrance to my secret library, you'll find it's open on a certain page. Look up the etymology of the word 'conductor'. You have touched on a very interesting aspect of leadership."

"Wow," said the Young Magician. "The Latin verb *conducere* means 'to lead together', which is certainly what a conductor does. But in certain contexts *conducere* means 'to serve'. So, we can add to the notion of the leader who is excellent at coordination, the notion of the excellent leader who is willing to serve."

"Precisely," said Al Sayyid. "Not a leader who sits on high and expects to be served, but one who identifies and recruits the brightest talents, ensures they are supplied with whatever they need and supports the whole culture in achieving the shared vision to which they all, according to their areas of expertise, contribute.

"The story of King Arthur is like hearing the sound of a fine Persian carpet being woven."

* * *

The two travellers were headed southeast. "Where are we going now?" asked the Young Master.

"Tibet, at least in spirit. Your Panel have suggested that every sixth story should take the form of a meditation. It should be something relevant, but in a relaxed and sometimes light-hearted way; something to reflect quietly upon, to chew over, to weave into our consciousness. If you slip your hand into my library pocket, you'll find the parchment there."

Story 6

A Tibetan Meditation

1. *Take into account that great love and great achievements involve great risk.*
2. *When you lose, don't lose the lesson.*
3. *Follow the three Rs: Respect for self; Respect for others; Responsibility for all your actions.*
4. *Remember that not getting what you want is sometimes a wonderful stroke of luck.*
5. *Learn the rules so you know how to break them properly.*
6. *Don't let a little dispute ruin a great friendship.*
7. *When you realise you've made a mistake, take immediate steps to put it right.*
8. *Spend some time alone every day.*
9. *Open your arms to change, but don't let go of your values.*
10. *Remember that silence is sometimes the best answer.*
11. *Live a good, honourable life. When the time comes to reflect on this, you'll enjoy it a second time.*
12. *A loving atmosphere in your home is the foundation for your life.*
13. *In disagreements with loved ones, deal only with the current situation. Don't bring up the past.*
14. *Share your knowledge. It's a way to achieve immortality.*
15. *Be gentle with the earth, and respectful of the seas and rivers.*
16. *Once a year, go somewhere you've never been before.*
17. *The best relationship is one in which your love for each other exceeds your need for each other.*
18. *Judge your success by what you had to give up in order to get it.*
19. *Approach love and cooking with reckless abandon.*
20. *Love as if you've never been hurt.*

Original source unknown

* * *

The Young Magician decided it wasn't appropriate to use the usual categories. Technically, it wasn't a story but it did offer some food for thought.

"This does have relevance," said the Young Traveller. "It has a lot to say about work – life balance, especially how to restore and improve the *life* side of the balance. For that reason it may not have so much appeal for RED, who might consider these suggestions rather woolly or flaky for their dog-eat-dog world. And ORANGE might wonder how these precepts will give them a cutting edge in achieving the success they strive for. There's plenty for the rest though."

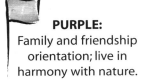 **PURPLE:**
Family and friendship
orientation; live in
harmony with nature.

 **BLUE:**
Rules; correct ways
for living.

 **GREEN:**
Harmony, consensus,
peace, sharing
and caring.

YELLOW:
Integration of left and right brain
thinking; preserve the whole planet
for the good of all its inhabitants.

* * *

"Possibly. Now, following on from these threads and knots of wisdom, let us travel across the great Himalayan mountain range to the nation of India," said Al Sayyid. "In the sixth century BC the Buddha, Siddhartha Gautama, set down the doctrines of one of the world's great religions. We shall profit by sitting at the feet of the Master."

* * *

Story 7

Silence is Golden

A young man joined a group of Buddhist monks after listening to their message and their prayers. The father went to the Buddha and in his anger and hurt accused him of many things: of corrupting youth, of stealing his son, of distorting the truth, of infamy, blasphemy and many other terrible things besides.

In response to all these harsh words the Buddha said nothing.

When the father had finally exhausted himself and his stock of words, and was quiet, he said to the Buddha, "Why do you remain silent? Why do you not defend yourself?"

The Buddha said, "If a man brought me a tray of sweet golden mangoes and I refused them, what would happen to the mangoes?"

The father said, "Well, they would remain with the giver."

"And it is just so with your words," said the Buddha. "They remain with you."

Primary source: Pete Nguyen
General source: Zen tradition

* * *

Leading

First, the Buddha appears to exercise strong personal composure and self-control (UL). The Buddha is true to himself. Second, this story makes a point of effective professional behaviour (UR). The Buddha acts appropriately. Third, there is the issue of conflicting values (LL). The Buddha does not attack the values of the father. He simply does not accept them, but he does so in a respectful way that opens the possibility of dialogue.

73

Influencing

The Buddha chooses not to match the emotional energy of the father. He waits until the father's negative emotion is exhausted and he is ready to put aside his anger and listen. The Buddha holds the space for the father to have his say, without disrespecting his values even though they are different. When calm is established, listening is possible, and understanding can take place.

The metaphor of the mangoes is simple and sweet. The mangoes represent the world of words and ideas and emotions. It is a metaphor of powerful simplicity that reframes our understanding in a very concrete and tangible way.

Motivating

Siddhartha Gautama, the Buddha, established a religion, a set of rules and precepts. He set out the Eightfold Noble Path consisting of right views, right resolve, right speech, right action, right livelihood, right effort, right mindfulness and right concentration. Rules and established pathways appeal to BLUE thinking. But RED and ORANGE may wake up to a negotiating strategy – silence – which they may find challenging to deal with. ORANGE may want to add it to their range of useful choices.

My insights

- This story can be interpreted in many different ways.
- Is it about nonacceptance? Or nonreaction? Or innocence? Or defencelessness? Or that the truth requires no defence?
- Anger (and other negative emotions) can overwhelm reason.
- Silence is a valuable discipline to develop.
- Emotion needs expression.

* * *

"Possibly."

"So where are we going next?" the Young Magician said, shrugging.

"The Buddha used silence and nonacceptance to handle certain situations. Let us experience a different way of filtering information. Not all information is equally valid. Sweet words on the surface may mask poison below, just as a rug with appealing designs may disguise the shoddiness of its backing.

"The technique of questioning to seek what lies below the surface is an art. In leadership it is a necessity. We are headed for France in the twenty-first century to meet a philosopher famous for both his ability to ask incisive questions, and also for his integrity."

Story 8

Integrity: The Triple Distillation Test

The Philosopher had just spent another hard day at the university asking lots of pertinent and challenging questions. On the way to his favourite brasserie for dinner, he was greeted by an acquaintance. "Do you know what I just heard about your friend Jean-Luc?"

"Just a moment," said the Philosopher. "Before listening to this I'd like to ask you a few questions."

"Huh?" said the acquaintance, who was eager to pass on this interesting piece of hot news.

"That's right. Before you talk about my friend Jean-Luc, it might be a good idea to just pause and consider what you are about to say. I call it the triple distillation test. The first distillation is through the filter of truth. *Have you made absolutely certain that what you are about to tell me is the truth?"*

"Well … no, actually, you see I just heard about it, and thought, well, you know …"

"All right," said the Philosopher. "So you have no idea whether the information is true or not. So let's try the second distillation through the filter of goodness. *Is what you are about to tell me about my friend something good?"*

"No, not at all, in fact—"

"So," interrupted the Philosopher, "you wish to tell me something bad about my friend Jean-Luc, but you're not at all sure that it's true. However, you may still pass this test, because there's one more distillation process remaining, the filter of usefulness. *Is what you are about to tell me about my friend in any way useful to me?"*

76

"Um. No. In fact, not in the slightest."

"Fine," said the Philosopher. "If what you want to tell me is not true, good or useful, why do you wish to tell me at all?"

Primary source: Mark Hawkswell
Original source unknown

* * *

Leading

 Personal integrity is a key issue here (*UL*). The philosopher also demonstrates the behavioural skill of asking excellent questions (*UR*). The acquaintance also demonstrates examples of unacceptable behaviour. Finally, the philosopher, through his actions and integrity, role-models values that – although shared by a community – are often conspicuous by their absence (*LL*).

Influencing

The story appeals to the reader, not to the acquaintance. The Philosopher seeks to influence the readers or listeners by referring to values that are generally shared by all communities: goodness, truth and usefulness. By demonstrating integrity and a passionate commitment to these values, by walking his talk, he is likely to influence people to wish to follow his lead. Were we all to follow the Philosopher's example, there would be a WIN for ourselves, a WIN for each other, and a WIN for the whole community.

Motivating

This story will appeal to several different valuing and thinking systems:

 RED:
will respond well to the strength of character, and the respect shown for the friend, Jean-Luc.

 BLUE:
will appreciate the championing of values that support social cohesion – in particular truth and goodness.

ORANGE:
will admire the Philosopher's ability to discover the facts and the way he doesn't suffer fools gladly.

GREEN:
will value the concepts of truth and goodness, and their role in creating a more equitable, caring and sharing world.

YELLOW:
will admire the Philosopher's fearless approach, and his inclusion of usefulness as an important criterion, in addition to truth and goodness.

My insights

• I'm beginning to realise how each different thinking system is likely to understand and interpret each story differently.

• Personal and professional integrity are essential if a leader wants others to follow him or her freely and with commitment.

• In contexts where gossip, rumour and innuendo are rife, this could be a good story to challenge the culture.

• The wise person pays attention to the wider consequences rather than immediate distractions.

* * *

"Possibly."

"I remember from my studies at The Academy," said the Young Magician, "that many philosophers throughout history have turned their attention to what the ideal leader might be."

"True," said Al Sayyid, "and we have already considered some of their insights in our previous stories. One pattern we have noticed repeated several times is that of the leader who understands, metaphorically, the harmony existing between all parts of the universe, and who is capable of ruling the just state. That is true of political leaders like King Arthur, but equally true of business leaders, parents and teachers in their different contexts.

"So let us remain with philosophers and thread our way back to Athens in the early fourth century BC," Al Sayyid continued. "Here is a story in which many different threads are woven into the complexity of the piece. I'm curious what you will make of it."

Story 9

All at Sea

A warship from the Athenian navy was lost at sea, far from land. And, given the fact this was at the peak of the Athenian democratic period, a mere 2,400 years ago, there was no reason at all why it should have been lost. People had been navigating by the sun and stars for centuries.

However, this was a ship that followed the rules of the current politics, not the custom of the sea. The captain had held a long meeting with his crew before leaving port, and after interminable discussions in which everybody was scrupulously listened to, whether they had anything worth saying or not, they had taken a majority vote to make all operating decisions collectively.

So now they were completely lost. However, there was on board a man who happened to be an excellent navigator. He knew exactly where the ship was, and how to reach the shelter of land where food and water could be found. But nobody wanted to listen to him. Individual excellence was frowned upon in this ship's prevailing culture.

Nevertheless, things were desperate. The captain convened a meeting to decide upon what action to take. Many sailors and soldiers spoke at the meeting. The navigator struggled to put his ideas across. Although brilliant with his charts and at reading the heavens, he was rather inarticulate – words didn't come easily to him – and he had few friends and allies among the crew. The argument was carried by a smooth-talking orator, the most charismatic and persuasive of speakers, who said exactly what the crew wanted to hear, but who knew nothing about navigation.

So they remained lost and ultimately starved to death. They valued collective ignorance over specialist knowledge. They valued sweet words that flattered over competence and integrity. They were influenced by the outer appearance rather than the inner wisdom.

Primary source: Plato, *The Politics*
Secondary source: There is a version of this story in
Annette Simmons, *The Story Factor*, Perseus Publishing

* * *

"Before you make your notes on this story, Young Master, may I suggest you read up a little on the work and ideas of Plato. You'll find the relevant reference materials in the usual place."

The Young Magician slid his hand into the secret pocket where the library was kept, extracted some books and began to read.

Sometime later his highlighted notes looked like this:

- This story is adapted from Plato's work *The Politics*.
- For Plato reason and logic were immortal and supreme.
- The ideal leader was both competent and knowledgeable.
- The ideal leader assured *ethical standards* and *objective scientific knowledge*.
- The relationship between a leader's inner harmony and the outer universe of Ideas brings order, intelligence and pattern to a world in a constant state of flux.
- Plato was generally distrustful of democracy, especially its more demagogic aspects.

Leading

 I interpret this as a story about what can go wrong when there is an absence of effective leadership. The elements of all four boxes are referred to but they are either absent or not integrated. Neither the captain nor the navigator demonstrates personal qualities of leadership. The navigator is strong on the professional skills and the infrastructural competencies that relate to his specialisation and the task at hand. But he is poor at the skill of presentation, and at communicating his ideas to people. There is a big values clash in the team box. The navigator values task, competency and functionality. The captain and crew value relationship and consensual decision making – *whether or not they are right*. The crew need the navigator's skills, and the navigator needs the skills of communication and rapport building. The captain needs to exercise responsibility, not court popularity.

The messages I take from Plato's story are that integration and synthesis of the qualities represented by the four boxes is essential if disasters are to be avoided. And, second, that it is important to distinguish between democratic participation and executive decision-making.

Influencing

Influence flows from the starkness of the message. I understand you want to live a life free from disasters. If so, heed the need for knowledge and competence, and do not be taken in by people who talk sweetly but know nothing. The story teaches through a LOSE–LOSE–LOSE scenario.

Motivating

This story will have resonance for the following valuing and thinking systems. And as we began to see in the previous story, resonance also means that some systems will react negatively towards a story instead of positively towards it. Each valuing and thinking system has *healthy* and *unhealthy* aspects, so stories can be just as effective in challenging values as connecting with them.

BLUE:
will lament the lack of authority exercised by the captain; he is the one who should create order through virtue of his appointed position; the boat/world needs underlying structure and order.

ORANGE:
will note the lack of efficiency; experts are present and challenges can be solved, but the prevailing culture is hostile to problem solving.

GREEN:
will be mortified by this attack on its prize values of consensual debate and respect for all views; however, healthy GREEN will recognise and note the inherent weakness within this system.

YELLOW:
will applaud the functional skills of the navigator and his understanding of wider systems (mathematics and astronomy); but will also recognise an inherent weakness in YELLOW thinking – inhibitions around connecting and networking widely.

My insights

- Values that are appropriate in some contexts may be inappropriate in others.
- The greater the complexity of a situation, the greater the need for recognition of knowledge and competence.
- The wise leader manages both task *and* relationship.
- Task and relationship are not either/or choices, but both/and requirements.
- The wise leader must sensitively acknowledge and manage different value systems.
- An ugly skin may hide a sweet and wholesome fruit beneath.
- Crises require flexibility of thinking and valuing.
- New ideas and systems, represented here as democracy, excellent as they may be in principle, can blind people to the merits of other ideas and systems. These other ideas are metaphorically expressed here as both knowledge of the science of navigation, and the responsibility of the leader (the captain) to govern *in the best interests of the whole system*.

* * *

"Possibly. And while we're in this geographical region," said Al Sayyid, "let's travel back a few centuries and visit another influential Greek thinker who's on the Panel's list, the storyteller Aesop."

"I've often wondered whether those simple fables have something to contribute to our discussion of the key attributes of leadership. Are you serious?"

"Especially if we weave a more modern spin into them. Sunglasses on, hold tight!"

Story 10

The Fox and the Hedgehog

The Fox knows many things, but the Hedgehog knows one big thing.

In a vote for the smartest animal on the planet, most people would probably put the Fox above the Hedgehog. The Fox is cunning, quick, sleek and creative. It is tenacious in finding ways to outwit its prey, and even in thinking of ways to get around the traps and barriers humans put in its way.

The Hedgehog on the other hand, though nimble on its feet, seems far less ambitious. A cross between a toothbrush and an anteater, it is mainly concerned with finding food and looking after its nest. Where the Fox is sensitive to whatever is happening within the wider environment, the Hedgehog seems preoccupied within its own small world, hardly aware of anything beyond the radius of a few metres.

So how is it, then, that the Hedgehog consistently outsmarts the Fox? The Fox lies patiently in wait at the crossroads for the unsuspecting Hedgehog. And when the Hedgehog arrives, with speed, stealth and guile, and from a cunning angle of attack, the Fox makes his move. But the Hedgehog senses the approach and, with a minimum amount of fuss, rolls himself up into a perfectly defended spiky ball, which denies the Fox any chance of success.

The Fox retreats, baffled, and slinks off into the forests to develop some newer, even more creative stratagems. But, despite his cunning, creativity, speed and slyness, the Fox hardly ever wins. Despite his many strategies, none of them can overcome the Hedgehog's one simple, unadorned, yet sufficient strategy. This battle, in some form or other, is played out every day. And almost every time the Hedgehog wins.

**Primary source: Adapted from Jim Collins, *Good to Great*,
Random House (adapted by kind permission of
Random House Publishing)
Secondary sources: *Aesop's Fables*; Isiah Berlin, *The Hedgehog
and the Fox*, Elephant Paperbacks**

* * *

The Young Magician was puzzled. "What has this story got to do with leadership? Surely you're not suggesting that a Hedgehog approach is more effective in leadership than the creativity and work rate of the Fox."

"Young Master, you should read more philosophy. Take a look in the library!"

The young man soon found a document written in 1939 by the philosopher Isaiah Berlin. In the essay, Berlin divided the world into Foxes and Hedgehogs. The Young Magician began feverishly scribbling some notes:

- Foxes are people who are curious and creative.
- Foxes pursue many goals and respond to the world in all its complexity.
- Foxes are "scattered and diffused, moving on many levels", unable to synthesise their thinking and behaviours into one overall concept or unifying vision.
- Hedgehogs have the ability to simplify a complex world into a single organising principle.
- Far from distorting reality, this organising principle unifies and guides everything the Hedgehog does so it can operate with effectiveness, appropriateness and complete functionality.
- For the Hedgehog, whatever does not relate to the Hedgehog principle is filtered out; it holds no relevance.
- Hedgehogs have the ability to see through complexity to perceive underlying patterns. They notice what is essential and pay attention to nothing else.

Leading

According to this story, and Berlin's essay, the key to success in leadership is to *know what business you are in*. And, once you know, you need to stick to it. The great leader seeks out underlying patterns in a complex world. This focuses attention on the infrastructure box. Within the chosen habitat, the leader can now focus on developing appropriate professional skills and behaviours. At the same time, the leader's clarity of vision and personal integrity allow the team to function effectively because they can share in the leader's strong sense of mission and purpose.

Influence

There are many examples of great thinkers who have cut through complexity to discover underlying patterns that simplify processes and understanding. The following come immediately to mind:

- Copernicus and Galileo with the solar system.
- Darwin and Russell Wallace with natural selection.
- Einstein with $E = mc^2$.
- Freud with the id, ego and superego.
- Jung with personal typologies.
- Myers and Briggs, following on from Jung, with their types inventory.
- Franklin, Crick and Watson with DNA.
- Bandler and Grinder with NLP.
- Clare Graves with his Emergent, Cyclical, Double Helix Model of Adult Bio-psychosocial Systems Development.
- Beck and Cowan with their simplified, more accessible version of Graves's work, known as 'Spiral Dynamics'.
- Ken Wilber with his 4 Quadrant 'A Theory of Everything' Model.

Motivating

This is a tricky one for me to assign valuing and thinking systems to. On balance, the big clue is that the Fox knows many things, but the Hedgehog knows *one big* thing.

ORANGE:
can be highly creative and strategic; it seeks out the best way among many ways; it desires results and rewards. This system has made many great contributions to the planet. But the downside of ORANGE is that it can, like the Fox, become too ambitious and overreach itself; it can become overcomplex and obsessed with sophisticated technology where simple functionality would do just as well.

YELLOW:
is functional: it prefers simple, elegant solutions that are planet-friendly and appropriate; YELLOW thinking seeks natural designs for complex problems; like the Hedgehog, YELLOW searches for organising principles that will preserve the habitat and everything in it.

My insights

- Know what business you are in, what your purpose is.
- Be focused, set clear goals.
- Know what is and isn't relevant; don't get distracted.
- Understand the role and purpose of creativity.
- Creativity has strengths and limitations.
- Recognise the dangers of too much complexity and overelaboration.
- Keep things as elegant and simple as you can – but not too simple!
- Seek out underlying, organising principles.
- Be aware of the whole habitat in which you operate.

* * *

"Possibly."

It was some time later that the Young Magician said, "I had no idea that there was so much to learn about leadership from fables and philosophy. And there's another thing I'm curious about. The Hedgehog seems to have one other additional advantage over the Fox. Perhaps because of its focus on the one big idea, it seems to be more present, less distracted than the Fox and so it seems more inwardly aware of what is really going on."

"You have touched, Young Master, on a very demanding discipline. Those who can develop the art of staying present to what is happening around them develop the aura that others call *presence*. They become more aware of themselves, their inner feelings and thoughts. They are also more able to pay attention to the many and varied things that are happening around them. They pick up clues from the environment; they read people's inner thoughts and feelings from their words and nonverbal communications.

"And so the quality of the interventions they make is wiser, deeper, more humane, more precise. In return, they are offered trust, loyalty, friendship, goodwill. These are things that no amount of money or power can buy or demand from people. Put on your special sunglasses. Sit tight. Let me take you to late-twentieth-century Argentina."

Story 11

A Close Shave

In the small town of San Martin de los Andes, in the heat of an Argentinian summer, Manolo, a seven-year-old boy, was recovering from an operation on a brain tumour. The treatment was working well but it had caused all of his hair to fall out. So, when he returned to school for the new term, Manolo wore a woollen ski hat to cover his embarrassment. Naturally, his classmates were curious about his unseasonal headgear and, after teasing him about it, pulled it off. When they saw what Manolo was attempting to hide, they became embarrassed themselves, and to hide their own embarrassment made fun of him instead.

Manolo was overcome with shame, and after the end of school pleaded with his parents not to send him back. They did their best to give him strength and encouragement. They reminded him that his grandfather had been a gaucho, *that he came from tough and hardy stock, and that it was a man's role to be a man, to take the rough with the smooth. They also reminded him of his duty to be a good and obedient son who had many things to learn at school. And they reminded him that the other students would soon get used to the situation, and that soon his hair would return, long, curling, black and glossy, as it used to be before.*

Next morning was another scorchingly hot day. When the teacher entered the classroom most of the students were already there, looking at Manolo and exchanging knowing glances and furtive smiles. Manolo was trying to make himself look as small as possible, wishing the floor would open up and swallow him. The teacher greeted the children, and then they noticed that she too was wearing a woolly winter hat. Then she removed it. Her head was as shaved and shining as the moon. She sat down at the desk next to Manolo and put her arm around him.

After school finished that day, many of the other children went straight home and told their parents they wanted their hair shaved off, too. The next morning half the class had shaved heads, and by the end of the week only two out of twenty still had their hair. The teacher had translated solidarity into a daring new game of self-expression and all the kids had joined in the fun. They had cut their hair together, and as it grew back their sense of comradeship grew with it.

Primary source: Claudia Moraes
Secondary source: Zander, R., and Zander, B.,
***The Art of Possibility*, Penguin**

* * *

Leadership

 The teacher in this story operates in all four boxes. At a personal level she demonstrates integrity and personal awareness. At a professional level she role-models desirable behaviours in such a way that everyone can take part, and no one needs to lose face or feel bad about their previous behaviour. This enables her at a team level to create a culture to which all want to belong, and in which all can thrive. She looks beyond diversity and difference to find what connects people. She notices what is happening within the classroom's social system represented by the infrastructure box and responds to it appropriately.

Influencing

Nothing separates people as much as perceived difference. Excellent leaders understand this and elegantly look beyond difference to find the commonality that unites us. The teacher finds a way of offering solidarity to Manolo in a way that neither patronises him nor confronts the rest of the class. Neither Manolo nor the other students have cause to be embarrassed by their actions.

The teacher *reframes* the meaning of baldness. She raises the question: What else could this mean? By the teacher's action, baldness no longer represents strangeness. Instead it becomes an act of personal expression, a gesture of solidarity, a fashion statement, a game to play. In so doing, she allows the class to explore issues such as compassion, curiosity and playfulness together.

Motivating

This story is likely to resonate with these valuing and thinking styles:

PURPLE:
creating a close bonding within the group, and a sense of safety and security.

BLUE:
the teacher asserts her natural authority and re-establishes order.

GREEN:
the teacher restores a sense of harmony and mutual respect to the group; inclusiveness is valued; no one is excluded, no one is shamed or humiliated.

YELLOW:
appreciates the commonality that exists beyond diversity; YELLOW also appreciates elegant, simple, functional solutions delivered without fuss, fear or fanfare.

My insights

- The importance of being present to what is happening around one, and responding to it in ways appropriate to those involved.
- The power of reframing: *What else could this mean?*
- Issues and conflict can be dealt with in nondirective, nonconfrontational ways.
- The power of story as one way to offer nondirective feedback.
- Giving feedback through action and modelling.
- Giving feedback through focusing on what is positive.
- Giving feedback at a behavioural, not an identity level.
- The power of just walking the walk.

* * *

"Possibly," Al Sayyid added. And then, "The lightness of this woman's leadership is like the elegance of the finest flying carpet, lifting effortlessly into the air."

* * *

"It's time for our sixth story. What do you have for me to meditate upon this time?"

"As we've started upon the theme of presence, let me offer you a timeless story from India," replied Al Sayyid. "It is a well-worn story though by no means threadbare. Take a moment to contemplate its design and simplicity, as well as its message."

Story 12

This Strawberry is Delicious

A monk was chased by a pack of hungry wolves until he came to the edge of a steep cliff. Having no other alternative, he jumped over the edge and clung tight to a small but sturdy branch that was growing out of the cliff face.

He looked down for a means of escape, and saw at the bottom of the cliff a hungry tiger. It was looking up at him with eyes full of anticipation, smiling a welcome, and licking its lips.

Just then the monk noticed a strawberry growing beside the branch. It was large, red, succulent and so very inviting. As he plucked the strawberry and popped it in his mouth, the branch gave way. And as he fell he thought to himself, "This strawberry is delicious."

General source: Zen tradition

* * *

Leadership

No story can be interpreted except as what it might mean for each reader or listener at a particular moment in a particular situation. This story, as do so many others, defies specific interpretation. I note extraordinary personal composure and presence. There is also the ability to focus absolute attention on what is happening in the present moment, in the *now*, which for me is an attribute of leadership in the professional behaviour and skills box. The monk's need to focus inwards is the result of his awareness of the crisis that is occurring in the infrastructure box.

Influencing

One way of reading this story is as a metaphor on the human condition.

We live in a precarious and fragile world, fraught with challenges and dangers. And yet life is also full of beauty and wonder. Where should we put our attention? How can we learn to appreciate what is? The only time in which we can do this is the present moment. There is no other time but now. The past is a coding of what we think happened. The future is an imaginary construct based on our past experiences.

In moments of crisis, it is necessary to put aside all other distractions and concentrate solely on the job in hand.

Motivating

The following valuing and thinking systems may respond to the messages they read in this story:

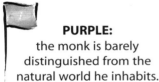
PURPLE:
the monk is barely distinguished from the natural world he inhabits.

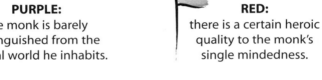
RED:
there is a certain heroic quality to the monk's single mindedness.

GREEN:
the monk appears to be at one with his universe.

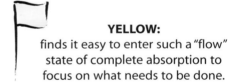
YELLOW:
finds it easy to enter such a "flow" state of complete absorption to focus on what needs to be done.

My insights

• What does the strawberry represent for me?
• What does the strawberry represent for you?

* * *

"No comment. You see, Young Master, there is learning to be found in the simplest of stories, just as the simplest designs of the most threadbare of carpets may sometimes illuminate the finest threads of its Maker's meaning."

"You may find that story simple," sniffed the Young Magician, "but for me that is the most complex of the stories so far. The more I think about it, the less sure I am of my own interpretations."

"And this is the way with skilfully woven carpets. Look on the surface, and the design may seem simple. But the art of the weaver draws the eye to the underlying complexity. Take a close look at the thirteen borders that are woven around my edges. Every single geometrical design has a meaning and a significance. What appears simple, may be complex. What appears complex, may reveal simple truths."

"This was the point we were making after the story of the Fox and the Hedgehog. There have been great thinkers, leaders in their field, who have cut through complexity to discover underlying patterns that simplify our understanding of natural processes.

"So while I've been assigning coloured flags in the Motivation section to represent different valuing and thinking systems, I've been taking advantage of your library, Al Sayyid, and reading up on the research behind it. It seems to me that the model of thinking and valuing systems known as Spiral Dynamics, on which my coloured flags are based, has made a huge contribution to my understanding of complexity."

"Indeed, Young Master, the ideas conveyed in this model will assist anybody in their quest to master leadership, values and change. So I think it's time you deepened your knowledge of the Spiral and of the valuing and thinking systems too. So slip on your sunglasses, hold tight: we're going to take a trip inside a book. We're going to meet six very different people, from different parts of the world, with very different thinking and valuing systems. Each one represents a thinking system from PURPLE through to YELLOW. All you have to do is ask them one simple question and take heed of how their answers differ."

"What question is that?"

"The one we started with in our very first story: 'What is life all about?' And as you listen to the answers of these six people you might ask yourself, 'How would I answer this question?', 'Which of these six people's views do I relate to and agree with?', 'Are you ready to explore a book of the world?'"

Story 13

A Magic Carpet Ride 1

Flying west from India, Al Sayyid and the Young Magician crossed the Indian Ocean, passed over Saudi Arabia and the Red Sea and turned south when they reached the Nile. They sailed high over Luxor and the Valley of the Kings, down the Rift Valley, until they dropped down fast, making their first landing in a rural valley in Bophuthatswana, South Africa.

Songoma *(PURPLE)*
The Young Magician sat in front of a middle-aged songoma, *a man who was sitting resplendent in animal skins and bead necklaces. The* songoma *was a man of importance in the village: a weaver and remover of spells, a man who could speak with the ancestors, and interpret the throw of cowrie shells and bones. He had a prodigious knowledge of ancient herbal remedies, which he would concoct from local shrubs and plants.*

"What is life all about?" the Young Magician asked him.

"To please and placate the spirits," the songoma *answered, a little uncertainly. He wasn't quite sure which tribe or clan the young man was from. "To honour our ancestors for they are still and always with us. We live for our own people, to support and give strength to each other. We know who we are, and who we are not."*

The Young Magician thanked him, and wished that good fortune would continue to smile on him and all his clan.

95

Al Sayyid wasted little time, flying high over the veldt, westwards over the Etosha Reserve in Namibia, and out across the Atlantic, then north from Recife on the Brazilian coast, skirting the Caribbean islands, along the eastern seaboard of the United States, until the towering skyline of New York came into view. Before he knew it, the Young Magician was sitting in a graffiti-covered subway car rattling along beneath the streets of the Big Apple.

Street kid (RED)
The Young Magician was sitting opposite a mean-looking street kid. Dressed in a beaten-up leather jacket and denim jeans, he looked at the Young Magician with cold, hard eyes. With some trepidation the Young Magician asked the question.

"It ain't none of your goddamn business," the street kid snapped back. He checked the Young Magician over to see whether he was carrying a weapon, or was perhaps a stooge for a rival gang. But, seeing he was pretty harmless, he finally replied, "OK, I'll tell you since you ask. But you better listen good, hear me? Life's a bitch. You gotta watch your ass 'cos there ain't no one else that gonna do that. Everybody's on the take, and everyone's got a price. And if you want something, you better go get it yourself. Do it, and do it now, 'cos tomorrow you could be dead. Anyone gets in my face, they gonna pay for it. That's how it is. Anyone who says different is crazy. All I want is you give me some respeck!"

The Young Magician kept his thanks short and was grateful that Al Sayyid made a quick smooth takeoff. The next leg of the journey was short, just a short hop west along the Hudson River. The Young Magician had now got a deeper understanding of two valuing systems under his belt. He thought about the street kid, and had to admit that, while he lived in a depressing world, he'd adapted pretty well to it.

In the distance, the Traveller could hear the strains of a military march as Al Sayyid landed smoothly on the marching square of the US Military

Academy at West Point. He found himself standing right below a statue of General Douglas McArthur. On the marble plinth were written the words DUTY, HONOUR, COUNTRY *in large bold letters.*

Military cadet (BLUE)

The Young Magician found himself standing in front of a young man about his own age, a fresh-faced seventeen-year-old cadet, and immediately asked him the question.

In a voice full of certainty and conviction the cadet replied, "Sir, it's about serving a higher calling that transcends all else. It's written on that marble, it's my religion. I learned it from my parents, I learned it at school. It's our nation's heritage. And, sir, I've taken an oath to defend it and sacrifice my life for it if necessary. It's God's will that we spread freedom and democracy around the world. God bless America!" The cadet snapped to attention and delivered a crisp salute.

As Al Sayyid soared high above the Great Lakes, the Young Magician reflected on his deeper understanding of another valuing and thinking system.

They took the polar route, across Canada and out over Alaska, over snow frozen Inuit villages. Looking down, the Young Traveller was reminded of similarities with the songoma, *but how different the lives of the Inuit with the worldviews of the street kid and the military cadet!*

Down the coast of Japan, past Hong Kong, and the Philippines, turn westwards to land with a bump on a busy but spotlessly clean pavement in Singapore outside Raffles Club. The contact arrived, an Asian yuppie. Elegant in an immaculate Armani suit, he stepped out of his Porsche Boxter, handed the keys to the valet and warmly shook the Young Magician's proffered hand. The Traveller was quick to notice the Rolex and the Cartier ring.

Entrepreneur (ORANGE)

The Young Magician sipped his tropical fruit juice while the entrepreneur savoured his Otard Cognac XO. Once again he asked his question and once again got a very different answer.

"Here's how it is. The world is my oyster. The challenge is to win the finest pearls, sell them at a profit, and then grow even bigger ones. You have to enjoy the best that life has to offer, and never forget that you can't take it with you. Trust in your reason, logical powers and judgement because that's what really counts. Work hard and play hard is my creed. There are risks, yes, of course there are, but that's what keeps us players at it. Now please excuse me, I've a teleconference to attend to with colleagues in Hong Kong, Mumbai and San Francisco."

Fruit juice drained, and another worldview glimpsed, the Young Magician slipped on his sunglasses again. While they passed high above the countries of the Middle East, he wondered what that New York street kid might have been like armed with massive oil money instead of a flick-knife, and also how similar in their mindset some of the Islamic mullahs were with the worldview of the military cadet. Both seemed to believe absolutely that they had the one and only true right way. And both appeared to think that God was undoubtedly on their side.

Social activist (GREEN)

The sight of Big Ben and the sound of its chimes confirmed it was midday in London. The Young Magician found himself sitting on some steps in Trafalgar Square right in the middle of a noisy human-rights demonstration. He was sitting next to an intense young woman. She was dressed in a duffel coat and knitted woollen hat. She had dozens of protest badges sewed onto her rucksack, inside of which were organic snacks and well-thumbed books on social injustice and international affairs.

The Young Traveller posed his question. She looked at him with deep meaningfulness. "What a deliciously interesting question. I'll tell you what I think, and then you must share your views with me. Life is all about people and belonging; about understanding the need for community and harmony. It all boils down – in the end – to love. We must move away from this dreadful materialism, greed and inequality that's destroying our planet. We must stop competition and capitalism if we are to preserve humanity. We must promote justice and peace everywhere. So ... now it's your turn ... "

But, before the Young Magician could even think of framing an appropriately sensitive response, finely attuned to the necessary amount of political correctness, Al Sayyid was impatiently dragging him off again, another values system in hand, towards the final destination on their global schedule.

Park ranger (YELLOW)

The Young Magician recognised the route. There was the Rift Valley again, and soon they were down with a bump in a game reserve in Tanzania. He was sitting on a log beside a park ranger who was brewing up some chai, the local tea, on a campfire. What was immediately noticeable was how functional and simple everything about the park ranger was. There was nothing fancy here. From the khaki kit he wore to the tough Land Rover he drove, there was an absence of frills and fuss. There were no designer labels, no consciousness of presenting the "right" image. The Young Magician immediately sensed an openness and candour about the man. So he went right ahead and asked his question.

The ranger pondered a while before answering. "Well, I've given that some thought and I've nothing spectacular to offer. But I can say that I *get a tremendous sense of satisfaction from working to reclaim and pre-serve our natural habitat. So I guess the kernel of my belief system is that we should celebrate and respect life as it is. Even more, it's about seeking to understand and discover how everything relates to everything else. How nature has its own flow and tempo of which we humans are only a very small part."*

Primary source: Don Beck and Chris Cowan, *Spiral Dynamics: Mastering Values, Leadership, and Change*, Blackwell

* * *

"So, Young Master, that's it. Possibly! What have you learned from our whirlwind tour of six very different worldviews. I wonder which mindset you most resonated with. One of them, or several of them? Which did you sense offered the right answers, the best responses? And why do you think so? Or did you find them all of equal value?"

"They certainly all have a contribution to make, and I have a number of questions I want to ask you in a while. But my greatest insight is this. That each valuing and thinking system is basically a set of particular coping strategies designed to deal with a specific set of external circumstances. Isn't that so?"

Al Sayyid replied by rolling himself up and then straightening himself out again.

The Young Magician opened his notebook and his pencil magically began to write:

Leading

My journey to the six locations, meeting six characters with very different worldviews, shows the relationship between how people use their inner attributes (*Personal*), their cultural norms (*Team*) and their behaviours and skills (*Professional*) as coping strategies to deal with the issues and challenges they face in their external environment (*Infrastructure*).

Influencing and motivating

To influence and motivate people it is necessary to meet them in their world-view. Do not impose your own, unless you are prepared to meet with resistance or hostility.

Spiral dynamics

Some notes I made from my reading:

- The thinking and valuing systems develop from less complex to more complex.
- Complexity of thinking is directly related to the complexity of the environment.
- Complexity is of value only when useful and appropriate.
- Each system includes and transcends all previous systems.
- Each system teaches the "codes" necessary for progress to the next system.
- No system is inherently "better" than any other system; a system's appropriateness to current external conditions is the most important factor.
- More complex thinking will generally be more effective than less complex thinking.
- The systems do not describe types of people, but *types of thinking in people*.
- Each system can display "healthy" and "unhealthy" characteristics.
- There are currently eight thinking and valuing systems; more will develop as our environment increases in complexity.

My insights

- The way we think about and value things derives from the way we cope with our external circumstances.
- Human nature has a capacity to develop from one valuing and thinking system to another.
- Systems are not "better" than others, just different and adapted to cope with different external conditions.
- Systems are interdependent and nested, in a *natural* progression. In nature there is a development in complexity from atom to molecule to cell to organism to ecosystem to biosphere to universe. It is the same with the valuing and thinking systems.

- If you destroy cells (less complex) you will destroy organisms (more complex). All systems rely on the health of all other systems.

- Understanding these systems is a *natural* way to lead, influence, and motivate people centred in these different systems.

* * *

"Possibly. Now, there is one thing I'd like you to explain to me, Young Master, based on your research. Why, if there are eight systems, have you assigned only six coloured flags so far?"

"According to the research, BEIGE is to be encountered mainly in situations of dependency such as when people are very ill, or seriously injured, or addicted, or homeless, or in deep grief. For this reason, BEIGE is a transitory state and few people are likely to be centred there. BEIGE is about survival at the most basic physiological level.

"The eighth system, TURQUOISE, is only just beginning to emerge in the world. Very, very few people on this planet have developed as far as this level of complexity yet, and so I'm considering it as beyond the scope of my work here."

"You said you had a question for me," said Al Sayyid picking up an earlier thread.

"Yes. I'd like to know more about how people change systems. And why it is that some people welcome change while others resist it."

"An important issue, indeed, for leaders to deal with. In my experience, most people change only when they need to, and see the purpose for it, within their own thinking systems. Those who wish to manage change will need to create dissonance in various forms so that individuals may want to seek change for their own reasons and in their own way."

"So how does one go about the business of creating dissonance, as you call it?"

"Metaphorically speaking, like this."

Story 14

Creating Dissonance

One evening an old farmer was walking along a country lane. He looked into a field and saw a group of young women bathing naked in a pond. The women noticed him at about the same time as he noticed them.

One woman shouted, "We're not coming out till you leave."

The farmer replied, "Oh, I'm not here to watch you ladies swimming naked, or running around in the meadow with nothing on.

"I'm just here to feed the alligator."

Primary source: Alain Haggar

* * *

The Young Magician hadn't expected this from Al Sayyid. He was a little taken aback. But he appreciated the point. He wrote in his notebook:

My insights

- Creating dissonance in people is the art of introducing a few "alligators" into their lives.
- Leaders need to introduce "alligators" to create the potential for change.
- The "alligators" need to be appropriate to the context, situation and valuing systems of those involved.
- Leaders need to think creatively, more outside the box.
- A simple, humorous story can carry as much weight and meaning, as much clarity and force, as a longer, more serious one.

* * *

"Possibly."

The Young Magician laughed, "And surely change can't always be that easy."

"True. It is a mistake, generally speaking, to think that change can be imposed without consequences. Especially when change programmes are not adapted appropriately to fit people's values or the prevailing conditions. It would be like using new nylon yarn to mend a hole in an old woollen carpet. In fact, badly thought-out change, or change that is applied ignorantly at best, and coercively at worst, can have serious consequences. "

Story 15

Coping Strategies

A woman was in the habit of taking her dog for a walk twice a day in her local park. She noticed a cocoon hanging from the branch of a bush. She wondered how long it would be before the butterfly would emerge.

One day she saw that a small opening had appeared, and she watched, fascinated, for several hours as the butterfly struggled to emerge. After a while the butterfly's progress seemed to slow down, and then movement stopped altogether. It seemed as if the butterfly had become worn out with the effort. So the woman decided to help.

She took a pair of nail scissors from her bag and snipped through the last part of the cocoon. The butterfly slid out easily, but she immediately saw that something was wrong. The butterfly was misshapen. The body was too large and the wings too small. The woman thought this would soon correct itself, but it didn't. All the butterfly could do was crawl around with its swollen body and shrivelled wings. It never flew, and soon died.

What this woman didn't understand was the bigger picture. She assumed kindness, compassion and speed would improve the butterfly's development. She didn't understand that the restriction of the cocoon and the effort required for the butterfly to emerge through the tiny aperture are nature's way of forcing fluid from the butterfly's body to its wings. Only when the butterfly has gone through this process in its own time will it be ready for flight.

Original source unknown

* * *

Leading

The infrastructural conditions in which we live (*LR*) require appropriate strategies for navigating safely through the challenges and conflicts that have to be faced. The quality of the coping strategies each one of us develops is directly related to the quality we generate in each of the remaining boxes (*UL, UR & LL*).

But in this story the person with most power is ignorant of what the other one needs in order to survive and succeed. Metaphorically speaking, her professional behaviours, based on her value system of "rescuing" the weak and struggling – though well intentioned – are ultimately disastrous. Such a clash of values in the Team box, expressed metaphorically here as between rescuing and struggling, will create ineffective leadership.

Influencing

The story demonstrates how not to be influential. Lack of knowledge, lack of awareness of another's real and underlying needs, no matter how well intentioned, can be fatal. There is no WIN for anybody in this situation.

Motivating

The butterfly could represent any of the thinking and valuing systems. In this respect, each of the systems will have its own way of going through processes of change. And often these processes will involve discomfort and struggle. Leaders need to be sensitive to the times when people going through change need to struggle, when they need support and when they need a combination of both. Change often takes time, and change often means a shift from one valuing system to another. The key question is how to motivate people to want to change *naturally* within their values, and from one system to another.

 PURPLE: responds well to rituals and making sacrifices for the group.

 RED: responds well to trials of strength and heroic challenges.

 BLUE: responds well to tests of loyalty and character.

ORANGE:
responds well to
tests of initiative
and achievement.

GREEN:
responds well to shared
and collective decision-
making processes; it is also
the system most prone to
wanting to "rescue" others.

YELLOW:
responds well to
ways of developing
knowledge and
competence.

My insights

- Change and struggle are natural and inevitable.
- When current coping strategies are no longer sufficient to deal with current conditions and increasing complexity, change becomes necessary.
- Change normally requires more complex ways of thinking in order to develop new learning, new strategies and a new awareness of how things are ... different.
- "Rescuing" others can prevent or inhibit the learning that only the struggle can teach them.

* * *

"Possibly."

"It was, I think," said the Young Magician, "Heraclitus who, two and a half thousand years ago said, 'You cannot step into the same river twice', meaning that change is constant and ever present. But does that mean change and complexity only flows one way?"

"Young Master, let's travel ten years on through time and go and visit those six people we met not so long ago. Let's see how time and experience have changed them, or – to put it another way – whether they have changed themselves."

Story 16

A Magic Carpet Ride 2

The Same Six People (Ten Years Later)

When they returned from the trip, the pencil wrote the following in the Young Magician's notebook:

Songoma (+ 10)
The songoma *has moved on. He has seized opportunities as they have arrived in the new rainbow nation of South Africa after the first democratic elections. He now owns a small chain of pharmacies selling both traditional and Western medicines. It appears he's left behind many of his former animistic and mystical beliefs and practices. On the other hand you're not sure what happens in the back room. There may well be a demand from many quarters for shamanistic services, which may well be met if the price is right.*

Street kid (+ 10)
A shift here too. The mean street kid has transformed into a militant urban evangelist. He has embraced Allah and now preaches a unique hell-fire-and-brimstone fundamentalist message. There is a puritanical strictness in his lifestyle and adherence to his unique style of Islam. Some of his

old buddies from the gang are now his bodyguards, and they ride around Manhattan in a white stretch limo with dark-tinted windows. He truly believes himself to have been called upon by a higher authority to promote the Truth, and he's prepared to take on any that oppose it.

BLUE

No change

Military cadet (+ 10)

The cadet graduated from the academy and served in various "peacekeeping" operations around the world. He has now left the army but remains true to his values. That said, they have mellowed somewhat, and he is now Academic Dean at a small military prep school in Virginia. He has become less rigid and more realistic, but continues to maintain his discipline and crusader spirit. His devotion to high principles is still intact.

ORANGE   GREEN

Upshift

Entrepreneur (+ 10)

The former Asian yuppie has left the high life and the fast lane far behind. No more Armani suits, no more flash cars, no more expensive liquor. He's been working for some time now as a volunteer in a poor sector of Negros, one of the many Philippine islands, on a major human-rights project. He's a lot more laid back and easygoing now. There's no longer any sense of self-promotion and fast-track ambition. He says, "I'm different now. I'm discovering what it means to be a human being. That triple heart bypass surgery really opened my eyes; there's no price you can put on the quality of that kind of peace of mind."

Social activist (+ 10)

How ironic. At that very same demonstration where we met the social activist, her beautifully hand-crafted posters were noticed by a passing art director at a trendy advertising company. She's now an account executive at a prosperous public relations company and thoroughly enjoys her BMW, designer clothes, fashionable Islington address and lavish lifestyle. Former activist friends don't speak to her any more. They say she sold out to the materialistic establishment. They feel betrayed. But she doesn't give a toss and has surrounded herself with more simpatico *friends who are much more in tune with "reality". The rucksack has been replaced with a Louis Vuitton briefcase.*

YELLOW

Park ranger (+ 10)

Sadly, the Park Ranger died a couple of years ago. He was buried in a simple ceremony, according to his wishes, in an unmarked grave in the heart of the reserve. He rests on a hillside beneath the sturdy shelter of a baobab tree. His colleagues say that he remained true to his principles throughout the last years of his life, completely committed to the idea of natural ecological systems while thriving on much simpler lifestyles. Less is more, as he often remarked. People from all walks of life – from different tribes, jobs and cultures – came to his farewell ceremony out of genuine respect for his contributions.

Primary source: Don Beck and Chris Cowan, *Spiral Dynamics: Mastering Values, Leadership, and Change*, Blackwell

* * *

Leading

The four boxes are represented in different ways in the cameo sketches. Changes in any one of the boxes may trigger changes in the other boxes. Change can be towards more complexity or less complexity, or there can be very little change. Some change can be quite startling, for example from sinner to saint, from entrepreneur to social worker, from do-gooder to go-getter.

Influencing

Look for the potentials in people. Each one of us is complex and most are capable of much metamorphosis in our lives.

Motivating

The following systems, according to my research, respond well to the following motivational and leadership styles:

PURPLE:
is nurtured by following rituals, finding reassurance, and working within close-knit groups.

RED:
gets energised by stories of heroism, by celebrating trials of strength and feats of conquest, and being given respect.

BLUE:
feels validated through appeals to tradition, just treatment for all, and by being honoured for loyalty and long service.

ORANGE:
needs recognition for its achievements, material symbols of success and challenges for improvement.

GREEN:
responds to the validation of people and relationships, the importance of feelings and a caring, socially responsible community.

YELLOW:
needs space to work functionally in their own way with free access to information and materials, doing things that fit who they are naturally.

My insights

- Changing life conditions activate valuing and thinking systems that can "emerge, surge, regress or fade".
- Human nature can develop new systems without eliminating previous systems.
- Changes in people can be surprising.
- No system is right or best.
- A question worth asking is: *What is appropriate?*

* * *

"Possibly.

"An influential leader," said Al Sayyid, "can be like the greatest of weavers. They have a light touch. They don't impose themselves on their material. Rather they let their material express itself, finding patterns and designs as they naturally emerge."

"I've heard", said the Young Magician, "that the great sculptor, Michelangelo, when asked by a young boy why he was hitting a large piece of rock with his hammer and chisel replied, 'Because there's an angel inside, and I'm helping him to escape.'"

"This is sometimes called taking the line of least resistance. Put on your glasses. We're going back to the early twentieth century to a small farm to meet a small boy growing up in the United States of America. His name is Milton Erickson, and he grew up to become one of the most successful and influential leaders in the field of communication and hypnotherapy."

Story 17

The Lost Horse

A horse with no identifying marks wandered into a farmyard. The farmer's young son said he'd take responsibility for returning the horse to its owner. The boy mounted the horse, urged it towards the road and let it choose its own direction.

The boy actively intervened only when the horse stopped to graze or wandered off the lanes and into a field. Otherwise, he just sat on the horse.

When the horse finally ambled into a farm several miles away, the farmer said, "How did you know to bring it here? Hey, how did you even know it was our horse?"

The boy said, "I didn't know. The horse knew. All I did was keep him on the road."

Primary source: Judith de Lozier
Secondary source: A version of this story can be found in
Sidney Rosen, *My Voice Will Go With You:*
***The Teaching Tales of Milton H. Erickson*, Norton**
(adapted by kind permission of Sidney Rosen)

* * *

Leading

This is a great example of leadership with a light touch. The boy is confident that the horse has its own resources for coping with the environment and will find its own way home. All he does is occasionally steer it back on track whenever it ambles off the desired path.

Influencing

The boy works within the horse's own frames of reference, not his own. He understands that each of us has our own natural ways of finding our own direction. And, if we try to force our preferred ways onto the preferred ways of others, it may take much longer to get the result we want. Result? A WIN–WIN–WIN situation.

Motivating

The applications of this metaphor offer something for all the valuing and thinking systems. What do you think?

My insights

- Each person is an expert in his or her own situation. They therefore already have the best access to solutions for their own problems.
- An important element of leadership may simply be to hold a space for others to work out their own solutions to their own perceived problems.
- Just sit on the horse, and the horse will find its own road.
- Adapt the job to what naturally motivates the worker.
- Do not expect to motivate workers who you force to adapt to the job.
- If the learner can't learn in the way the teacher teaches, the teacher needs to learn to teach in the way the learner learns.
- Do not give advice unless you are asked.

* * *

"Possibly."

"Time for our next meditation," said the Young Apprentice.

"I know exactly where to take you," replied Al Sayyid.

Story 18

The Presence of Absence

Emperor Hirohito of Japan was making a state visit to Thailand. Every day his itinerary was painstakingly planned to the last minute. It was a punishing and precise schedule. One particular Friday, the emperor and his entourage were booked to visit a small Buddhist temple for exactly ten and a half minutes to talk informally to some of the monks. The emperor and his party entered the temple precisely on time, but the monks were nowhere to be seen.

The aide responsible for the emperor's schedule was mortified. In panic, he first looked to find the monks, then made lame excuses for their absence. But the emperor was not perturbed. He stood silently in the centre of the room totally at peace with himself.

Precisely ten and a half minutes after they entered, the emperor signalled that it was time to move on. On his way out of the temple, Hirohito turned towards his aide and said, "Thank you. I enjoyed that appointment very much. Please schedule me another one tomorrow."

Primary source: Arielle Essex

* * *

Leading

When the environment requires much attention and the culture demands a fast pace, it is even more important for the leader to find quiet time to think, reflect and recharge the batteries. This is the art of taking an inventory of oneself. Stop, breathe, enter the present moment fully and connect with your centre. As Gandhi once said, "I have so much to do today, I will have to meditate twice as long." This is the art of self-leadership.

Influencing

Influencing oneself is a prerequisite to influencing others.

Motivating

All systems can benefit from meditation, whether it is quiet and introspective as for the Emperor Hirohito, or rhythmic and breath-centred for a swimmer, or intellectually absorbing for someone reading a good book, or self-focusing for the competitive athlete. The ability to "go inside" and enter a flow state that re-energises the self and reconnects thought to experience, and the inner world to the outer world, is a skill worth developing. Meditation aids personal direction, and direction is essential to motivation.

My insights

- Make good use of "spare" time.
- Meditate more.
- Reconnect the inner and outer worlds.
- Practise the art of slowing time down.

* * *

"Possibly."

"Where to next?"

"Young Master, we are weaving a journey through the warp and weft of time and space. There is not always a set route. What is your desire?"

"How about somewhere closer to home?"

"Mine or yours?"

"Yours. And what about something on the theme of personal responsibility? We haven't touched much on that."

"Then I know just the place to go."

Story 19

Personal Responsibility

A sultan invited a mullah to go hunting with him and his entourage. But he gave the mullah a camel that was very slow indeed. The mullah said nothing about this. Soon the hunt had left the mullah far behind and after a short time was completely out of sight. Then it began to rain. It rained very hard indeed.

All the members of the hunt got completely soaked. The mullah, on the other hand, quickly dismounted, took off all his clothes, folded them into a neat pile and sat on them under the camel for the duration of the storm.

When the storm abated, he dressed himself and returned to the sultan's palace for lunch. The sultan and his entourage were amazed that the mullah was completely dry, for even with the speed of their camels they had been unable to find any shelter on the plain. They looked at the mullah with suspicion.

"It was because of the camel you gave me," he said.

The next day, the mullah was given the fastest camel, and the sultan took the slow one. Once again it rained. The sultan, stranded in the middle of the plain, on a camel that moved at the speed of a tortoise, got absolutely drenched. The mullah, on the other hand, repeated the same procedure as the day before. When he returned to the palace he was as dry as a bone.

"This is all your fault," sneezed the sultan, "for persuading me to ride this snail of a camel."

"Perhaps," replied the mullah, "you took no personal responsibility for the problem of staying dry."

General source: Sufi tradition

* * *

Leading

The mullah cannot take responsibility for what happens in the environment. He is not responsible for the rain or for the absence of shelters. But he can take responsibility for how he deals with the situation. He takes personal control of his situation and behaves accordingly. This is in marked contrast to the sultan and his entourage, who seek to apportion blame rather than enquiring about what can be done. It is the mullah who has the more useful attitude rather than his social superiors.

Influencing

As far I can see the mullah's behaviour is not particularly influential. In fact he is rather rude. Perhaps Al Sayyid will have something to say about this. After all, it's his culture. Right now, there's only a WIN for the mullah. But I guess if the others learn about taking more personal responsibility there could be two more WINS.

Motivating

The desirability of taking personal responsibility for ourselves, and whatever situation we find ourselves in, is relevant to all thinking and valuing systems. The taking of personal, and sometimes collective, responsibility, is a great anti-dote to the blame culture, which can be pervasive in many organisations and institutions.

PURPLE, BLUE and GREEN:
are "we the group first" systems; they will tend to respond to collective responsibility.

RED, ORANGE and YELLOW:
are "me the individual first" systems and will respond better to taking individual responsibility.

My insights

- The acceptance of personal responsibility is a measure of integrity, attitude and strength of character in the upper left PERSONAL box.
- When the situation or environment is against you, think creatively.
- Taking responsibility for dealing with a situation – even if it is not my fault – liberates me.
- Blaming others or circumstances makes me a victim.

Blaming wastes energy and changes nothing.

* * *

"Possibly."

"Al Sayyid, I'm really curious about two things. First, why does the Mullah appear to be so rude and how does he get away with it with the sultan of all people? Second, I'd be interested to hear about an example of collective responsibility in action – especially in a work-related context."

"Young Master, your wishes are my command. Are your sunglasses on? Let's deal with your second request first. We're going back to Japan at the end of the twentieth century. We're going to take a visit inside a Japanese factory, which is actually a subsidiary of a US multinational company. You may notice an interesting clash of values at work. "

Story 20

Collective Responsibility

The troubleshooter flown in from the US was wondering how to handle this case. It was pretty serious. One of the Japanese workers on the machine belt of the factory floor had inserted a component the wrong way round. As a result the whole batch was ruined. It was going to cost the company a great deal of money to put it all right.

The troubleshooter asked the Japanese manager whether the culprit had been identified, and what action was being taken against her. It came as a surprise to hear the manager claim that he didn't know. "The entire work team has accepted responsibility," he said. "They have not told me who it is, and neither did I ask. Even their supervisor does not know, and if he did he would not tell me."

"But," said the troubleshooter completely amazed by this, "if everyone is responsible, then in effect no one is. They are all covering up each other's poor work."

"That is not our view." The Japanese manager was polite but firm. "The woman in question was so ashamed she went home. She offered to resign. Some of her team had to go to her house and persuade her to return. The group know she was responsible and she feels she has let them down. The group also are aware that she is a new worker. They say they did not help her enough, or give her on-the-job support, or make sure she had enough training. This is why the whole group have said they are very sorry. This is their letter right here. They are also willing to make a pub-lic apology to you."

"No, that's not what I want. I just want to make sure it doesn't happen again." She wondered what to do. This was not the way it was done back home at the parent company in Seattle. She wondered whether she should pursue this in the American way, or would it be better to deal with it in the Japanese way?

**Primary source: Fons Trompenaars, *Riding The Waves of Culture*
(reproduced by kind permission of
Nicholas Brealey Publishing)**

* * *

Leading

The story highlights a clash between valuing systems. Here the issue is not so much between individuals as between the differences between US and Japanese valuing and thinking styles. The values have a marked influence on both professional behaviours, and the organisation of the working environment. Knowing what you know about valuing and thinking systems, what would you do as a leader in this situation?

Influencing

The question is: does the group support or oppose high quality and high productivity? If the group supports these objectives, those who, in a communitarian culture, let the side down will experience shame. The idea that the individual must be punished for any mistake in order to become a better team member is not appropriate in this culture, although it may be in other cultures.

The troubleshooter's dilemma is whether to manage the situation with foreign heaviness or indigenous lightness.

Motivation

While there are messages for all systems here, the story will particularly resonate with these systems:

PURPLE:
while Japanese culture is rich in complexity and operates across all the value systems, much of its social organisation is deeply rooted in PURPLE; as the story illustrates, the group comes before the individual; collective responsibility is expected.

BLUE:
is structured and hierarchical and tends to be sure of the one right way; both Japanese and US cultures exhibit aspects of this. A downside of BLUE is that it has a tendency to rigidity.

ORANGE:
much US business thinking is centred in this system; it expects individual responsibility and accountability.

My insights

- What works in Seattle doesn't necessarily work Sapporo.
- The harder you push against a system, the harder it is likely to push back.
- Cross-cultural intervention usually needs to be appropriate to the receiver, not the giver.

* * *

"Possibly." After a while he continued. "A great weaver knows how to make an invisible knot. Let us see if we can thread together this theme of responsibility with your questions about rudeness, cheek and plain talking. In your studies of literature at The Academy, did you ever come across the concept of the Trickster?"

"You mean like Brer Rabbit in the southern United States, or the Tortoise, the Hare and Ananse in African stories, or the Wise Fool in the European courts of the Middle Ages?"

"Precisely. The story of the mullah and the camel is a tale about my old friend, Mullah Nasrudin. Stories about him contain both wisdom and humour, a wisdom and humour that can sometimes be deep and oblique, like the yarn of naturally dyed silk.

"The Trickster skates on the thin surface of what is just permissible. He is the only one who can tell the emperor that he is wearing no clothes and live to tell the tale. The Trickster reminds me of a carpet I once knew. It always surprised people by slipping out

123

from under their feet, just when they thought they understood something.

There are plenty of modern applications and contexts in which tricksters can thrive, especially around modern-day kings who live in ivory towers, and whose busy schedules keep them too far away and too insulated from the real world.

Story 21

The Tale of the Rogue Monkeys

In an experiment in animal behaviour, half a dozen monkeys were put together in a large cage. In the centre of the cage, suspended from the roof, was a bunch of ripe bananas. Below the bananas was a set of steps from which the monkeys could pluck the fruit.

However, the steps were wired and connected to a powerful pressure hose. As soon as the steps were touched, jets of cold water sprayed the whole of the cage, drenching all the monkeys. With amazing speed, the monkeys learned that the steps and bananas were out of bounds, and acted collectively to prevent any individual monkey getting too close to them. Social rules were established, and enforced.

Once this pattern was established, a monkey was removed from the cage and replaced with a new one. Naturally, the new monkey made straight for the steps. Before he could get close, the rest of the group jumped on him, forcibly preventing him from achieving his intention. Very soon this monkey learned the "rules" despite having never got wet. And, in fact, when the next new monkey was introduced, it was one of the most ardent in policing the rules.

Over time all the original monkeys were removed and replaced with new ones. The group taught each new monkey that the steps were off limits. Eventually there were six monkeys in the cage who had never got wet but who conformed to the rules because "that's how we've always done it". The water jets had been long switched off.

Finally, the researchers placed in the cage a bigger, stronger monkey. A rule-breaking monkey. This monkey resists the efforts of the others, breaks with convention, leaps up the steps and gets to eat the bananas. The others watch fearfully, but after a while all of them start to test the steps, and soon they have all changed their old behavioural patterns. All have benefited from the unconventional actions of a single rogue monkey.

Primary source: Robert Dilts

* * *

125

Leading

Leadership requires a balance. On the one hand it is important to develop a culture that harnesses collective energy and like-minded thinking and purpose. But this can have counterproductive consequences if taken to extremes: habits and conventions can lead to a dramatic fall-off in productivity, and resistance to innovation. Rogue monkeys are necessary to generate creativity and innovation, to challenge the old wisdoms and make things happen.

Influencing

On the other hand, leadership that regularly walks the corridors and visits the far-flung locations gets to hear a lot more about what is going on, builds better relationships with staff and gets a more hands-on understanding of the reality of the business and the issues that matter. Such leaders encourage rogue monkeys to dwell at all locations within the business. And they are always welcome in the leader's office, and they get invited to tell the truth as they see it, without fear of repercussions.

Motivating

The story has relevance to all systems. All leaders can become isolated and insulated from real issues, and the pace of change. Leaders who continue to do what made them successful in the first place, may find their success short-lived.

Rogue monkeys can exist at all valuing and thinking systems, and on rungs of any hierarchy. Look out for people who are creative freethinkers, who are curious and committed. Seek them out and listen to what they have to say.

My insights

- Rules and practices should be frequently challenged.
- Recognising that change is ever present and that strategies need to be constantly updated.
- It is too easy to programme people into compliance.
- Compliance is usually counterproductive in the long term.
- Rogue monkeys have great creative gifts to offer; equally they can be destructive if not recognised or given productive work.

* * *

"Possibly. And one of the problems with being an old carpet is that the traditional ways are ingrained like old desert dust. It's easy to become trapped in old procedures, tried and tested ways of doing things. But you know, Young Master, some tried and tested ways have been around for a very long time. And there's reason for this. Just bear in mind that there is frequently much to praise in traditional design."

"So what's our destination this time?"

"It's a long trip. All the way from the present moment to the first century BC."

Story 22

Stuck in a Rut

The US standard railway gauge – the distance between the rails – is four foot eight and a half inches. Or, to put it another way, 143.51 centimetres. Either way, these are not very elegant numbers. What could be the logical explanation? Why is this gauge used?

Well, it's because that's the gauge used on British railways, and it was British expatriates who built US railways.

So why did the British build them like this?

Because the first railway lines were built by the same people who constructed the pre-railway tramways, and this is the gauge they used.

So why was this gauge used for the tramways? Because the tramway builders used the same jigs and tools that had been used for building horse-drawn wagons, which used the same wheel spacing. Fine. So why did the wagon builders use this rather odd measurement?

Because, had they attempted any different measure, the wagon wheels would have broken on many of the old, long-distance roads in Britain. Why? Because that was the average spacing of the pre-established wheel ruts.

So how did those old rutted roads come into being?

Well, that's because Imperial Rome built the first long-distance roads in Europe and Britain so their legions could keep all those uncivilised people in check. The roads have been used ever since.

So what about the ruts in the roads?

Roman war chariots formed the original ruts. It was decreed that all roads built in the Empire had to match these so that their wagon wheels and axles wouldn't be destroyed. Now, because the chariots were made either by Imperial Rome, or for Imperial Rome, and Imperial Rome's bureaucracy set the standards, all chariots had the same wheel spacing.

The US standard railway gauge of four foot eight and half inches is derived from the original specification for an Imperial Roman war chariot. Specifications and bureaucracies tend to be self-perpetuating. So next time you are handed a specification, or told to do a certain job in a particular way, and wonder what ass came up with it, you may be exactly right.

The Imperial Roman war chariots were constructed exactly wide enough to accommodate the rear ends of two war horses.

But that's not the end of it.

Have you ever taken a close look at the Space Shuttle sitting on the launch pad at Houston? Attached to the sides of the main tank are two big booster rockets. These are known as Solid Booster Rockets, or SRBs. Thiokol manufactures these SRBs at its factory in Utah. The engineers who designed them might well have preferred to make them a bit fatter, but the SRBs had to be sent by train from Utah to the launch site in Florida.

The railway line between these two points has to run through a tunnel in the mountains, and the SRBs had to fit that tunnel. The tunnel is slightly wider than the railway track, and the railway track is about the same width as two horses' backsides.

So a major design feature of what is arguably the most advanced transport system in the world was determined over two thousand years ago by the width of a horse's backside.

Primary source: Paul Holme
Original source unknown

* * *

Leading

This story illustrates a leader's dilemma. The infrastructure is entrenched in history and is pervasive. In this case, it has been entrenched and deepened over a period of two thousand years. The infrastructure directly influences the behaviours and skills of designers, planners, engineers and many others. A culture of sameness and continuity has developed. The leader's problem is whether to accept things as they are, adapt what is as well as one can or do something completely different with the huge risks that entails.

Influencing

The story could be used to influence people who are reluctant to accept change to see the continuity that exists within a change programme. This and this and this are just like how it used to be in the past.

Equally, the story could be used to influence people to see the advisability of change, and how sticking to old ways limits our possibilities and potential.

The story could also be used to demonstrate how flexible the human race is at working within given parameters.

Or that truth is stranger than fiction.

Motivating

The thinking and valuing systems that resonate most in this anecdote are:

BLUE:
the true, tried and tested ways.

ORANGE:
pragmatic; keep costs low, make more profits, keep the trains as they are, just make them sexier.

YELLOW:
find simple, elegant, natural solutions to given problems; adapt design of SRBs to fit the tunnel.

My insights

- It can be difficult to transform material, methods, ideas, mindsets, cultures and values that may no longer be appropriate as the conditions in which we live change.
- Understanding why some people are reluctant to embrace change.
- The brain has an obsession with pattern and design.
- History is fascinating: far from being dead and buried, it covertly influences us in many profound ways.
- Progress creates new problems all of its own.
- The value of research.

* * *

"Possibly," said Al Sayyid. "You know, there is a wisdom in following traditional patterns and designs. They are like maps, navigational indicators that direct one along well-trodden paths. The weaver who made me followed a centuries-old tradition, just as the railway engineers followed a two-thousand-year-old tradition – whether they were aware of it or not.

"In the remote regions of the most barren deserts, pathways have been followed for centuries. Not just the pathways themselves, but the patterns of the terrain, and the mathematical movements of the stars and planets have been observed to guide travellers safely on their way.

"The desert is the most bleak and the most beautiful of places, and those who live in it, or travel through it, have developed their own kind of wisdom. Put on your sunglasses. We're travelling back to the desert where I spent my younger days."

Story 23

Gifted

A wise man was travelling by camel through the desert. His journey had been long, the day hot, and the wind searing. He arrived at a small village. He knocked at the door of a hut and asked for a cup of water. A young man brought him a goblet, filled to the brim with pure clean water, chilled in a clay pot.

The traveller brought it to his lips, paused for a moment to thank his god for the three great gifts of life, water and generosity, and drained the goblet in one long draught.

"I thank you," he said to the young man. "And for your hospitality, is there something I can offer you in return before I continue with my journey?"

"Yes, there is one thing," replied the young man. "There is discord in our family. Our father died some days ago, may God rest his soul, and in his will left his small herd of camels to me and my two older brothers."

"How can I be of help?"

"There are seventeen camels in the herd. My father's will says that half the herd must go to first brother, a third to second brother and one-ninth to me. But how can we divide a herd of seventeen camels? It doesn't go. And we don't want to kill any camels for they are worth more alive."

The traveller laughed. "The mathematics are confusing you. That is one problem. But let us see what can be done with a little ingenuity. Where are your family?"

The young man took the traveller through the house to a courtyard where the two other sons and the man's widow were talking heatedly. The youngest brother interrupted them and introduced the traveller.

"My friends, I believe you can sort this situation out for yourselves. Your brother has given me the gift of water. In return I give you my camel as a gift. Now you have eighteen camels. Does that help?"

"Let's see," says the young man, "one half goes to first brother, that's nine camels. One-third, to second brother, that's six. And one-ninth goes to me. That's two ...

"But ... but ... that only comes to seventeen altogether!"

"And by happy chance, the remaining camel happens to be the one I just gave to you. And, if you would be kind enough to return it to me, I shall continue my journey." And that's exactly what happened.

Primary source: Paola Menotti
Secondary source: There is a version of this story in
Joseph O'Connor, *The NLP Workbook*, Thorsons

* * *

Leading

The traveller is like a leader who can appreciate the complexity of a troubling situation and contribute elegantly to its solution. The story stresses politeness, openness, sharing and generosity – not just of material things, but more so generosity of spirit. The traveller works within the situation as it is, and behaves in a respectful and appropriate manner. He not only demonstrates a set of values that contribute to solving the problems that exist within a particular situation, but also creates a relationship in which reciprocity is likely to occur. His intentions and actions earn him trust, loyalty, respect, commitment, integrity and admiration – essential but intangible factors that no bottom line can show, and no amount of power or authority can demand.

Influencing

The problem for the family in this story is "stuckness". They can't figure a way through their problem. They have the resources, but they can't access them.

The traveller gives them an opportunity to do so. And he does it in a way that does not shame or embarrass them. In return for their gift, he offers a gift in return. The camel is a metaphor for whatever resources they need to solve their problem. The "camel" offers the family the possibility to see the problem from another perspective. It gives them the creativity to find a solution. The camel helps them to reframe their thinking.

And because the "camel" represents an idea, a notion, a set of solutions, the traveller can always have it back. This is WIN–WIN–WIN thinking.

Motivating

The story appeals to all the valuing and thinking systems:

PURPLE:
the traveller restores peace in the family, and respects the wishes of the ancestors, and the ancient ways.

RED:
the traveller treats the family with respect.

BLUE:
recognises goodness and decency.

ORANGE:
will admire the traveller's excellent leadership strategies, the efficiency of his solution and the minimal cost to the enterprise.

GREEN:
will respond to the traveller's relationship skills and his willingness to make a sacrifice for the common good.

YELLOW:
will recognise an elegant, simple solution that naturally combines task and relationship; the traveller has an ability to handle complexity and choose the appropriate solution for the circumstances.

My insights

- Don't make assumptions. A half, a third and one-ninth don't make one. They make seventeen-eighteenths.
- The young man offers water. Those who want help have to make an investment first.

- What you give freely usually comes back, and often with interest.
- Generosity creates reciprocity.
- You already have all the resources you need – you just need to find ways to access them.
- Resources can be internal and external.
- Take more than one perspective on things, especially when "stuck".
- To get the result you want, be flexible.
- An effective way to teach is to create a space in which others can do their own learning and access their inner resources for themselves.
- Think outside the box.
- Leadership is earned, not taken.
- The eighteenth camel is the contribution you make to the world.

* * *

The Young Magician opened his copy of *Spiral Dynamics* and got down to some more research. He was interested in the idea of the polite and respectful leader, as represented by the traveller in the story. His magic pencil wrote the following notes:

When a leader demonstrates politeness and respect:

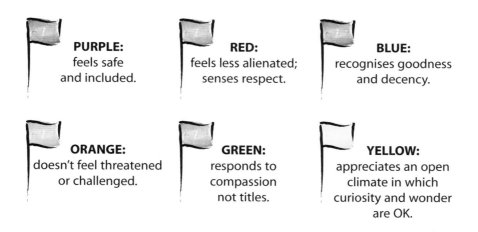

PURPLE:
feels safe
and included.

RED:
feels less alienated;
senses respect.

BLUE:
recognises goodness
and decency.

ORANGE:
doesn't feel threatened
or challenged.

GREEN:
responds to
compassion
not titles.

YELLOW:
appreciates an open
climate in which
curiosity and wonder
are OK.

* * *

"Possibly."

"Al Sayyid, the eighteenth camel I need right now is a light and amusing story. Do you have a route in mind to such a thing. I'm ready for some re-energising after so much writing."

"Then are you ready to take off for rural Spain? Naturally, I expect you will be looking forward to unravelling the threads and loosening the knots of the deeper meanings hidden beneath the light-hearted patterns of the surface."

"Lead on."

Story 24

TRough Justice

A pig farmer is working in his yard when one day a man appears and asks, "What do you give your pigs to eat?"

"Trash and leftovers from the farm mostly," replies the farmer.

"Well, that's a disgrace. I'm from the Animal Welfare Society and I hereby fine you a thousand dollars. It's outrageous giving your animals trash!"

A couple of months later two different men come to the farm and ask the farmer the same question. The farmer hesitates and then replies, "Well, generally speaking, it's high-protein, low-cholesterol. A typical lunch would start with lobster and smoked salmon, followed by a fillet steak and lightly tossed green salad, and a low-fat raspberry yoghurt cake as dessert."

The two men become very angry. "How dare you. This is criminal. People are starving all over the world and you are feeding such food to pigs. We represent a charity called Global Food Redistribution and we're fining you ten thousand dollars."

A month or two later a woman shows up at the farm with a clipboard and asks the farmer, "What do you feed to your pigs?"

The farmer gives her a long look and replies, "I give them a dollar each and they can buy what they want."

Primary source: Marta Genis Pedra
Secondary source: *English Teaching Professional* magazine
(adapted by kind permission of Modern English Publishing)

* * *

The Young Magician smiled and took out his notebook. His magic pencil began writing:

Leading

The story illustrates a number of different value systems at work, the various infrastructural considerations a farmer may have to deal with such as animal welfare and nutrition, and the range of behaviours the farmer uses in dealing with these challenges.

Influencing

At influencing, the farmer is a great example of what not to do. He has no strategies to find out the value systems of those who visit him; he fails to learn from his mistakes; and, above all, he appears to have no idea at all of what he thinks is right. His behaviour – amusing as it is – is reactive. He has not thought through the issues.

BLUE: compliance, rules and regulations, bureaucratic implementation.

ORANGE: this system can feel very challenged by BLUE rules and compliance: it has to make profits and survive – often by being "creative" within the rules.

GREEN: champions liberal values and causes, such as the redistribution of resources, cruelty to animals and so on. Political correctness is a GREEN issue: all should be treated equally and with respect.

Motivating

The story itself is fairly light, trivial and nonspecific, but with a bit of imagination the following could be argued:

Two important points:

• GREEN can be so sure it is right that it asserts BLUE rules to achieve conformity; political correctness can be an example of this.

- A valuing system is a way of *thinking about* things; so although the first two charities in the story may well represent GREEN values, they don't believe in the same things. The *container* is the same but the *contents* are different.

To give another example from a different system, BLUE thinking values authority, "the one true path". Both fundamental Christianity and fundamental Islam are BLUE – the container is the same. But the contents are different and can be quite hostile to each other.

My insights

- Who is right and by what criteria can things be judged?
- Any "-ism" when overzealously applied can seem ridiculous and counter-productive.
- What are the benefits of rules and regulations?
- What are the uses and abuses of compliance?
- People, including businesspeople, need to know what they think is right for themselves and for those they have a responsibility towards.
- It is useful to be able to read the motivational and valuing systems of others.
- It is hard to satisfy the demands, desires, and aspirations of everybody in an organisation, institution, group, team or family.
- Humour can raise many serious issues.

* * *

"Possibly."

"Al Sayyid, not far south of here, across a small stretch of ocean, lies the great continent of Africa. We've not yet travelled much to the southern hemisphere. I'm curious what wisdom, and insights into leadership, we can learn from these ancient traditions and cultures. Perhaps – and I'm thinking about the farmer in the previous story – there may be something to be discovered about the art of knowing what it is you want, and what it is you believe in."

"Let's find out, Young Master. Hold very tight, my coordinates are set for southern Nigeria, the land of the Yoruba, an ancient nation, rich in culture and complexity like a well-woven rug."

Story 25

Taking Ownership

Some problems are simple; others require some thought; and some seem beyond the knowledge of any to resolve.

Bakari owned many cattle and several wives. He was respected and admired far and wide in the land. He was considered to be a "big man". His senior wife had produced three sons and heirs, although the other wives were childless. But, as life is filled with pleasure, so is it filled with grief. If there are seasons of plenty, so there are seasons of drought. Life can change in the blink of an eye.

Bakari's eyes began to lose the light. He sold many cows to pay for healers, for the eyes are the guardians of light and life, but nothing could be done and soon he lived in endless darkness.

We can say that nothing is certain in this life. The gods send trials to test our strength. We live in hope that we will endure and pray our problems will be small. But, as Bakari's joys had been great, so were his woes, for soon he also lost his sweetest pleasure, the delight of sleeping with his wives.

To Bakari this loss seemed even greater than the first, and he spent huge sums on healers the length of the land searching for a cure. Soon Bakari's wealth was exhausted. Just a few cows and his compound remained. Even his wives deserted him just as the proverb has it: when the grasses burn, the jackals flee.

Only his senior and junior wives remained loyal. The senior wife took quiet delight in her husband's loss of desire. In her belly she felt the joy of knowing that the children of her womb would inherit when Bakari's time came to join the ancestors.

But the junior wife weighed matters differently. Bakari was the stem of her life, and to die without giving birth to his child was unthinkable. Her loins longed for nothing else. Neither did she give up hope. For, as the ancestors say, no snake is easy to kill.

One fine day, Bakari was resting on a log in front of his compound when a small bird landed lightly on his shoulder. It was breathing heavily and its heart was pounding. It whispered in Bakari's ear, "Blind Bakari, master of my fate, please help me. Do not let me die a cruel and unjust death. An eagle is close behind me. Save my life and I will return the power of light to your eyes." With hope in his heart, Bakari quickly took the bird and swiftly hid it in the folds of his agbada.

At that moment a great eagle landed elegantly in the dust. It cocked his head to one side and looked at Bakari. "May the great god, Olodumare, Owner of the Everlasting Now, protect you from the pangs of hunger because, My Lord, this my hunger is killing me today. Wherever you are hiding this small bird, I beg you give it me. Let me eat and I will restore to you that which you most long for, and you will desire your wives again. This I promise you."

Bakari was caught between two diverging roads to paradise. Which was more desirable? To have sight or to father more children? To feast his eyes upon his young wife's beauty without being able to touch and taste her, or to have many children but not be able to look upon them? It was a cruel dilemma.

Bakari sent for his senior wife and asked her advice. She was surprised, and asked him what lay behind his request. So he told her about the eagle and the small bird.

"There is nothing to discuss. Save the bird from a cruel and unjust death so that light will return to your eyes. If Olodumare, Creator of All Things, wishes that you hear the sound of young children, then wait until your sons have children. Besides, even if the power of your wood should return, your age will soon decrease it again. Your sight, you can enjoy for your whole life. The bird asks for life. Let the eagle hunt for itself."

Bakari considered the power of her argument. All the same he sent for his junior wife too. And when he explained the situation her response was quite different. "My Lord, I beg you with all my head, my heart, my body, my life on which you paid my dowry. Choose the power to sleep again with women. I dream to have a child for you. Oh God, bless me with the children of Bakari even if it is only one. Do not curse me as a childless woman. What do you want, My Lord, with eyes? How can you think of sight? How can looking at things that die compare with that great thing which truly makes you a man?"

Bakari's dilemma pressed upon him. Whichever advice he took, he could never be truly at peace. And, while he turned these things over in his mind, the eagle continued to make demands, and the small bird to tremble inside his gown. And then the realisation came to him. "Bakari, it is you who must solve your own problem."

Now that he trusted the power of his own mind once again, his brain began to work. He sent his young wife to the market to buy another bird which, while the eagle was distracted, he hid in his gown. Then he turned to the eagle, "If I end your hunger will you honour your promise?" When the eagle agreed, Bakari quickly slipped the second bird out of his agbada, and the starving eagle struck so quickly it never noticed the difference. Almost immediately Bakari felt the snake's head stir and begin to rise again. And, once the eagle had gone, the dove brought light back to Bakari's eyes.

As the presence of fish requires the presence of rivers, Bakari's life began to change for the better. His many wives returned; his compound filled with the sounds of joyful children; and money and riches once again made a nest in his house.

And so it is that the man upon whom the gods smile is the one who does not pay too much attention to the advice of others, but knows how to deal with whatever problems arise in his own way. For who else will ever have your particular interests hidden in the well of their heart? Consider well the example of Bakari. For even your own wife may not care whether you can see or whether you can seed!

Primary sources: I have heard versions of this story from both Femi Osofisan and Juma Bakari Secondary source: There is a version of this story in Gbadamosi and Beier, *Not Even God is Ripe Enough*, Heinemann African Writers Series General source: Yoruba tradition (Western Nigeria)

* * *

Leading

 The wise leader knows how to lead himself. He listens to the views, opinions and advice of others, but always bears in mind that their agendas – no matter how noble and compassionate – remain their agendas. The wise one makes personal decisions knowing that whatever risks are taken are based on knowledge of all relevant facts and what is right for his or her own personal *chi* (one's own personal spirit). The wise leader is also attuned to the whole habitat and everything within it. Above all, he takes responsibility for himself and for his situation.

Influencing

Bakari dovetails what he wants with what others want. By ensuring everybody achieves their outcome, and by being flexible and creative, he achieves the result he wants while keeping everybody else happy too. A WIN–WIN result.

Motivating

The story primarily concerns the following valuing and thinking system:

PURPLE:
Bakari is firmly centred in the traditional ways, beliefs, customs and values of his people. He hardly distinguishes between the world of humans and the world of nature; fear and fatalism play a significant part in his life; yet he still possesses enormous responsibility, creativity and dignity.

My insights

- Sleight of hand is a useful skill.
- Proverbial wisdom carries truth, dignity and beauty.
- Knowing what you want helps you get it.
- Pay attention to your inner voices and your gut feelings (the dove and the hawk).
- An effective leader knows how to discover and satisfy other people's needs as well as his own.

* * *

"Possibly."

"This is a great example of a teaching story," said the Young Magician. "And the African continent must be full of such stories. I'm curious, Al Sayyid, to hear other stories about leadership from other parts of Africa. Is there anything on the list."

"If you wish it enough, I am sure it will be there. Let us follow the old trade routes that crossed the whole of Africa, and see where we end up. Are your ready?"

Story 26

The Heart of Darkness

Hapo zamani palikuwa mtu mpofu. *Once upon a time there was a man who was blind. And yet this young man, Mapofu, had uncommonly good hunting skills. He could smell water at a hundred paces, sense the presence of a deer and hear danger before it came too close.*

After his sister got married, the blind man and his brother-in-law took a hunting trip together. In the forest they set their traps. The blind man covered his traps with grass and twigs with amazing skill and cunning. But, when the brother-in-law thought his blind companion wasn't looking, he kicked away the skilful camouflage. "How will he know when he can't see a thing?" he thought to himself.

The next day, they returned to the forest to check their traps. A scrawny dik-dik with short, spindly legs and a scraggy coat was caught in the brother-in-law's trap. But in the blind man's trap was a young kudu, the most magnificent of antelopes, with beautiful horns and a hide whose quality would shame a leopard. The brother-in-law knew how much that skin would be worth at the market, so, when he removed the animals from their traps, he cunningly exchanged them, giving the scrawny dik-dik to his fellow hunter. Mapofu took the dwarf antelope, gently passed his hand over it, and put it in his gunny bag.

As they walked home, they discussed many things, including a recent quarrel between neighbours about a boundary dispute. The brother-in-law was impressed with the blind man's thoughtful insights and asked him, "Why is it that people fight? Why do they dispute?"

"Kwa nini? Kwa sababu wanafanya sawa sawa umefanya. *Why? Because they do exactly what you have just done to me."*

The brother-in-law felt deep shame. He stopped and took the blind man's gunny bag. He removed the kudu from across his own back and put it around Mapofu's shoulders. "I am deeply shamed. My heart has become like stone. Forgive me."

They walked on in silence for some time. "Please tell me," asked the brother-in-law, softly, "how do people end a quarrel? How can friendship become possible again?"

Mapofu smiled so his eyes sparkled like the glaciers on Kilimanjaro, and he replied, "Rafiki yangu, wanafanya sawa sawa umefanya. My friend, they do exactly what you have just done to me."

Primary source: Ghonche Materego
Secondary source: There is a version of this story in
Annette Simmons, *The Story Factor*, Perseus Publishing
General source: East African tradition, Tanzania,
Zambia, Zimbabwe

* * *

Leading

When dealing with people who are cynical or self-interested, a direct assault on their attitude is unlikely to reap desired results. It may be much more elegant and respectful to use a story like this one. This story embraces both negative and positive aspects of human behaviour. The negative element allows those who have become cynical or disillusioned to acknowledge their attitude and behaviours for themselves. The positive behaviours, by contrast, model what is desirable. Such a story demonstrates that it is always possible to know how to change things, and ultimately heal negativity. This is the way of the aware or sensitive leader.

Influencing

The blind hunter waits for an opportunity to arise where he can naturally lead his brother-in-law to reflect on his behaviours. Because he doesn't blame or attack, he leaves space for the brother-in-law to apologise and *choose* to behave differently. The idea is rather similar to the way a martial artist redirects the force of an opponent's attack against the attacker himself. It is economical and elegant, and achieves fast results.

Motivating

The *politeness* with which the blind hunter responds to the situation and offers feedback to his brother-in-law will resonate with all the valuing and thinking systems:

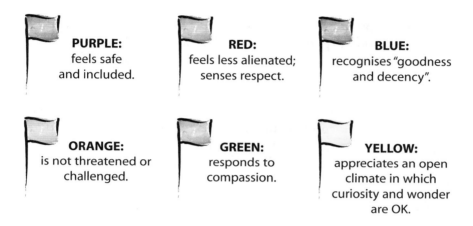

PURPLE:
feels safe
and included.

RED:
feels less alienated;
senses respect.

BLUE:
recognises "goodness
and decency".

ORANGE:
is not threatened or
challenged.

GREEN:
responds to
compassion.

YELLOW:
appreciates an open
climate in which
curiosity and wonder
are OK.

My insights

- Even if others can't see you, you can't hide from yourself.
- Even if others can't see you, it doesn't mean they don't know what is going on.
- Most people – given the chance – would rather make a contribution to the world than be mean to others.
- Being mean to others is an outer expression of how you are being mean to yourself.
- Sensitive leaders create opportunities for change in others through a variety of means.

* * *

"Possibly," said Al Sayyid. "And I have known many leaders whose style of leadership is exactly the opposite of the blind hunter's. Whereas he uses gentleness, they use force. Where he uses politeness, they use brusqueness. Where he is respectful, they are disrespectful. Where he works within the thinking of the other person, they impose their own thinking. Where he is placid, they are tempestuous. This is not to say one style is right and the other wrong, but to say that leadership is a question of choosing the strategy that is appropriate to the situation and to the relationship."

"I guess it's like a carpenter who has only one saw," the Young Traveller chipped in. "He'll do some jobs very well, and bodge the others. A good carpenter probably has lots of different kinds of saw and chooses the one that is most appropriate for the job in hand."

"Precisely. More choice is almost always better than less choice. Your carpenter is another thread you have woven into our ongoing narrative. But now we are going to travel to northern India to weave in a yarn of different hue. Pay close attention to a story that develops the theme of our blind hunter."

The Young Traveller felt that familiar lift in the pit of his stomach and they were airborne once again.

Story 27

The Nature of Leadership

When the Rajah of Sherpur died, his son succeeded him as the new ruler. Under the father's rule, the territory had prospered, conquering enemies, expanding into new territories and developing new trade links. But since the son's accession, events had taken a turn for the worse. Hard as he tried to assert his authority, the new lands fell into disuse, trade diminished, foes pressed upon him and the people began to mutter against him. And so he resolved to seek advice from the great seer and teacher, Guru Siddhartaji.

The Maharajah found Guruji gathering barks and medicinal herbs in the garden of his ashram. He explained his predicament and waited with expectation for a reply. But the sage said nothing, he merely signalled the young man to follow him.

They walked briskly until they reached the edge of the city, and at a bazaar beyond the city walls they engaged the services of a mahout, an elephant driver.

The three men and the elephant made their way into the jungle and it was not long before they picked up the spoor of a tiger. For three days, they tracked the beast, observing its habits, its rituals, its kills, its banquets, its liaisons. For each man, it was a lesson in power, guile, stealth and imperiousness.

On the fourth morning, they returned to the city. As soon as they had dismounted, Siddhartaji led the rajah along a path into the rice fields. "Pay close attention," he instructed the young man, "to the water buffalo."

Through the length of the day the two men sat under a banyan tree and watched the water buffalo plodding through the paddy fields. They observed the ease with which the huge beasts pulled their plough, turned over the soil and released the fecundity of the land. They noticed how willingly each buffalo submitted to its yoke, and put its strength at the disposal of those it served.

In the evening, as the sun was setting, Guruji turned to the young rajah and said, "Consider the tiger and the water buffalo. What have you learned about leadership? Why is it that you cannot do as your father did? Why is it that you find it so hard to influence your people and exercise authority over your territories?"

But the young man was lost as to the significance of the sadhu's wisdom. He gazed at the ground, and said, "Master, pity me. Speak to me in a language I may understand for I have no means to make sense of your message. What is it you want me to learn?"

"Consider," replied Guru Siddhartaji evenly, "the qualities of the tiger. It is dynamic and vital, arrogant and fierce, powerful and demanding. Like a true predator, it spares nothing; it destroys and consumes whatever gets in its way. It considers only itself and its own needs. It is completely focused on satisfying its personal desires. What can possibly withstand its limitless hunger and appetite?

"On the other hand, think of the water buffalo. It is patient and trusting. It puts its great strength and energy at the service of the community. It is satisfied with little and does not seek to live off the impoverishment or capitulation of others. It is slow and unhurried, and yet the job always gets done.

"My son, consider the qualities of these two great animals. The fierce tiger, that walks by itself, and goes its own way without regard to the needs of others, serves only itself. When its energy is spent, and its ambition and desire satisfied, what has been achieved? Nothing, save for its personal pride and sense of satisfaction. What is its contribution to the jungle except for death, destruction, and the marking out of territory?

"Now think of the water buffalo. What gifts does it offer? It carries great burdens, it tills the soil, it nurtures the land, it serves the community. It never thinks of promoting itself, and yet in its own humble way it promotes the wellbeing of all. Through its contribution it supports and succours all living things. It leads through service, and its power is subjugated to the wider needs of the community as a whole."

Siddhartaji paused so that the young rajah could reflect on his words. And then he added, "Learn from the rhythms and lessons of the natural world. For as it is in nature, so should it be in all things, including politics and power. The true leader is not like the tiger but like the water buffalo. Just as the water buffalo redistributes soil and water, nurturing the land and the people alike, just so does the great leader serve, succour and develop his people and his lands.

"Those who win the affection of their people, and create prosperity in their state, are not assertive, self-seeking and all-consuming like the tiger, but benign, deep, humble and life-giving like the buffalo. These are the leaders who win the affection of the people and encourage them to create prosperity. Maharajahji, open your mind to your Oneness! What is your true inner nature? What kind of ruler do you aspire to be? Perhaps your meditation on the tiger and the buffalo will lead you to the answers you seek."

The rajah was quiet, absorbed in his thoughts. The burning desire for glory that he had long carried within him was extinguished. His former pride and arrogance ebbed, and now humility, inner strength and the desire to serve flooded and permeated the recesses of his heart and mind.

The excitement that the tiger had earlier generated within him diminished, while the rising moon, dancing in the waters of the paddy fields, illuminated everything that had been achieved – season after season – by the selfless, committed, noble service of the water buffalo.

Primary source: Nick Jones
General source: Asian tradition

* * *

Leading

The story suggests that, like the unassuming water buffalo, the complete leader nurtures the land, serves the people, protects the present, guards the future and gives a great deal more than he takes. Personal integrity demonstrates skills and behaviours that are nurturing and generative. These in turn support the people, their values and the culture so that there is harmony in the environment and the whole habitat can thrive.

Influencing

Guru Siddhartaji elegantly influences the rajah through a teaching story, a natural and powerful metaphor that compares the tiger and the water buffalo. The sadhu – the wise one – holds the space for the young man to think through the metaphor and work it out for himself. Although the rajah is unable to do so, his curiosity is opened and he connects with the vital attribute of humility. He admits his ignorance and asks for illumination. Now he is open to listen to and understand the message. At no time has he felt himself attacked or humiliated. The process of feedback is a gentle one. When and if effected, the result will be a WIN for the rajah and the guru, a WIN for the people and a WIN for the habitat as a whole.

Motivating

There is something in this story for all the systems:

PURPLE:
responds to references from the natural world.

RED:
may sit up and take notice of the danger of violent self-expression and self-consuming power.

BLUE:
will recognise the "authority" of Siddhartaji's wisdom and his championing of natural order.

ORANGE:
will take note of effective strategies and efficient governance.

GREEN:
will respond to a nurturing leader who rules the country for the common good, and who serves the people.

YELLOW:
will appreciate the guru's leadership style, which allows all the systems to respond and thrive in their own way; YELLOW also appreciates the use of natural design in problem solving.

My insights

- A nation state or an organisation can grow and develop as a natural, living organism.
- Inspiring leaders are more concerned about the success of the enterprise and the community than their own self-aggrandisement.
- Natural leadership regenerates itself through the development of new talent and resources.
- Leaders hold the space in which others can learn and change.
- A shooting star cannot be compared to the sun.
- A tiger and a water buffalo have different attributes. Both are mighty forces, and both in different ways may need to be contained.
- The style of the tiger is for the short term; that of the water buffalo is for the long term.
- Change takes courage.

* * *

"Possibly," said Al Sayyid. "And it takes courage in a man or woman to stand up to the Tiger and other popular conceptions of leadership. I'm going to fly you west, to the middle of the twentieth century, to a leader who had the courage to stand up to another kind of animal, the arrogance of a conquering army."

Story 28

Courage

Shortly after the fall of Copenhagen to German forces in April 1940, Christian the Tenth, the King of Denmark, looked out of his palace window and saw the swastika flag flying above the government buildings.

The king immediately requested a meeting with the German commander. He politely asked that the flag be taken down. His request was denied.

The king was thoughtful for a moment or two, and then turned again to the commanding officer.

"And what if I send a soldier to remove it? What will you do then?"

"There is a simple answer to that question. I will have him shot on the spot."

"I don't think so," replied the king, "not when you see the soldier I send."

"How so, Your Majesty? Please explain yourself."

The king looked squarely into the commandant's eyes and replied in a calm, even voice, "I will be that soldier."

It is said that the flag came down within the hour.

Primary source: Mette Theilgaard

* * *

Leading

 The king's personal determination and integrity, demonstrated in his behaviours, would surely serve as a powerful model around which his people are likely to unite. He is prepared to risk his life so that he and his people, though defeated, can maintain their dignity and self-respect. In another story about King Christian X, it is reported that, when told by German commanders that all Jews would be required to wear the infamous star on their clothing, he replied that all Danes would in that case do so since no distinction was made between races in that country.

Influencing

As the representative of the Danish people, the king displays courage and self-less behaviour that is certain to influence his subjects. He represents the whole cultural group and therefore each individual too.

How exactly he influences the German commandant is not so clear. There is no reason why a man with so much power should respond to the threat made by the king. Perhaps it is the manner in which he states his intention that impresses itself upon the German.

Motivating

All the valuing and thinking systems can respond to the king's refusal to accept national humiliation:

PURPLE:
will appreciate the gesture of sacrifice for the "tribe".

RED:
will respond to the heroism of the gesture.

BLUE:
will acknowledge rightful authority and self-sacrifice in a noble cause.

ORANGE:
will applaud a calculated risk that succeeds splendidly.

GREEN:
will appreciate the gesture of noble sacrifice for the sovereignty and dignity of the people.

YELLOW:
will salute the integrity of the man, and the simple elegance of the solution.

My insights

- When a person is fully committed to something, they are much more likely to get it.
- Adversity frequently brings out the best in people.

* * *

"Possibly. There are many kinds of courage," said Al Sayyid. "Exercising leadership when one is seen as an outsider, as different, as beyond the norm requires courage, dignity and creativity. These attitudes and their behaviours are more elegant and more likely to make subsequent integration possible than resorting to more confrontational methods such as force or the law. An old carpet may reject a new repair if it is done without skill and sensitivity. An excellent weaver finds ways to match the new threads to the old, and work within the existing framework. Hold tight, we're on our way to an unnamed country where many peoples of different race and culture are learning to cooperate and coexist."

Story 29

Rewarding Behaviour

A stranger from a distant country moved into a house on the edge of town. It was a town that wasn't much used to outsiders, and so it wasn't uncommon for the local kids to gather around his fence at various times of the day or night and hurl insults at him, and throw all sorts of litter into his garden.

One morning, the man surprised the kids by coming out to greet them. He said, "Where I come from people can shout much louder than you. And they're more creative, too. I'm getting bored hearing the same things from you every day. I'm sure you can do better. So I'll tell you what. I'll give you all a dollar if you come tomorrow with the loudest and most unpleasant insults you can think of."

The kids thought this was a great idea. They came back next day with some really choice insults that they'd got from their parents and elder brothers.

"Pretty good," said the stranger, handing out the cash, "but is that really the best you can do? Come back tomorrow and, if you can improve on today, I'll give you fifty cents each."

The children returned next day and hurled some very colourful abuse at the man. They chanted long and loud, and, when they were done, he gave them their promised reward. "Excellent," he said, "much better. Come again tomorrow, but I can only afford ten cents."

"Only ten cents?" responded the children, deeply affronted. "You're joking!"

So they stayed away. And they never came back. It wasn't worth it.

Primary source: Joseph O'Connor

* * *

Leading

The stranger demonstrates remarkable self-control and self-restraint in the face of considerable provocation. But through his behaviours he recognises, accepts and even validates the valuing system of his tormentors and, through subverting it, creates a change in the relationship and in the habitat.

Influencing

Where does motivation come from? Within. Where does financial reward come from? Without.

What is motivation? By definition it implies movement towards or away from something. In my experience, we tend to move towards things that we value, that give us pleasure, and away from things we don't value, that give us pain. Motivation, then, is based on people's valuing systems, and wise leaders recognise that different people are motivated by different things.

This story demonstrates how a reward system can actually demotivate people, rather than engage them. The rewards become expected and lose their pull. "It isn't worth it," say the kids. By contrast, the stranger uses excellent leadership skills to achieve the result he wants through working with, and through, the value systems of the children.

The children celebrate and recognise their own and their culture's identity by distinguishing what differentiates them from the outsider. This reflects their value system. The stranger accepts this and encourages it. By doing so he builds a relationship with them. By contrast, had he shown resistance to their behaviours and values he would merely have perpetuated the situation. Perhaps he would have exacerbated the situation.

So, first, he recognises and accepts their value pattern of identification without judgement. In fact, he lets them know that his culture is not so very different from theirs, and challenges the kids to raise their standards. It's a smart move because most kids can't resist a heroic challenge. Then he creates a dependency in them by rewarding them. This distracts them from their original expression of values.

The stranger then encourages the kids to "blow out" their aggression by taking the issue to extremes. The kids find that their behaviours are not getting the results they expected, the ones that made it fun in the first place, and then they find that their material rewards are diminishing, too. So what's the point in continuing?

Motivating

The story will resonate with the following systems:

PURPLE:
tends to define its
own group by
knowing what it is not;
can be suspicious of,
and antagonistic
towards strangers.

RED:
responds to
demonstrations of
power and heroic
action to overcome
challenges; RED also
appreciates instant
gratification.

YELLOW:
will appreciate the
stranger's elegant
and creative
solution, the natural
way he uses the
valuing systems of
the kids to create
desirable change.

My insights

• Excellent leaders take time to find out what each person values.
• The easiest and most elegant way to engineer change is to do it within people's natural valuing and thinking processes.
• Creativity can be more effective than confrontation.
• Monetary reward can demotivate people and create dependency thinking.

* * *

"Possibly."

"Another sixth story," said the Traveller. "What skein do you have for me to unravel this time?"

"As you have seen, Young Master, adversity can be the ideal provocation to explore hidden reserves of attitude and character that may lie unacknowledged and untapped below the surface of things. All leaders will face adversity from time to time. Then is the moment to dig deeper and reflect on the discoveries with patience and wisdom. If you want to know about the quality of an ancient and fine carpet, take a good look at the backing. Hold on, for this story we could be anywhere in the Jewish Diaspora, and many other diasporas beside.

Story 30

Hidden Resources

Three young men sit around the bed of their dying father. With the last of his energy, he tells them there is treasure buried under the family fields. "Where? Where is this treasure?" they ask. But it is too late. He has gone.

After the mourning and the funeral, the three men take picks, hoes and shovels, turning the soil, digging deep, leaving not one part of the family land untilled. They find nothing. Deeply disappointed, they give up their search and return to the city.

The next summer, the farm yields its best harvest ever.

General source: Jewish tradition

* * *

Leading

Action is required to unearth resources, whether these resources are available inside oneself or accessible in the external world. These men take action but fail to reflect upon it, or to connect the relationship between cause and effect. They are too impatient and look only for immediate rewards. Their concept of treasure is limited to matters of material gain. They appear to have little awareness of the contents of the interior left-hand boxes.

Influencing

The story speaks to the reader or listener rather than to the men. It raises the question: what is treasure? It is not only material things: money, gold, artefacts. This story suggests that all resources are treasure. In this case it is the land, the earth and the human effort needed to prepare it to bring forth its bounty.

The men influence the land by their action, but they are unaware of its response. The dance of relationship is incomplete; they are unaware that the earth moves at a different speed and so they ignore its gifts.

Motivating

The story may have particular resonance for these valuing and thinking systems:

PURPLE:

is only hinted at in the sense of a close-knit family; PURPLE values the ancient traditions and ways; its time frame looks back to the past to ask: what would the wise ancestors have done in this situation?

RED:

looks for instant gratification. It is not afraid of hard work and heroic struggle but wants instant rewards or may lose patience; RED's time frame is very much focused on the present moment.

BLUE:

BLUE's time frame is past through to future; BLUE is the first valuing and thinking system to value sacrifice today for rewards tomorrow. BLUE thinking created Paradise and pension funds; hard work and personal sacrifice for higher goals are prerequisites for future rewards and success.

My insights

- Look beyond the meaning of surface things.
- Learn to connect cause and effect over longer periods of time.
- Treasure means different things to different people.
- Do not put too much attention on material things.
- Disappointment in the present moment might be exactly what is required for success later in life.

* * *

"Possibly."

"That story reminded me of some of the previous stories, "said the Young Magician. "I'm thinking in particular of Confucius's comment: 'Whoever puts too much attention on what is on the outside gets clumsy on the inside.'"

"And this is also part of the message from our next story from India. Hold very tight."

Story 31

Reflected Glory

A tramp, shuffling along a dusty road, noticed a large shiny rock on the ground ahead of him. He picked it up and saw that inside was a beautiful stone. So he took it to a jeweller and had it valued. As luck would have it, it was an enormous example of a rare and precious gem, which he then sold for a huge amount of money.

Now prosperous beyond his dreams, he continued his habit of looking down at the ground. Maybe he would find another precious rock. Then he'd be even richer! In fact, he spent most of the rest of his life searching the ground for such another stone until one day he saw a shiny round object lying in the dust.

When he picked it up, he discovered it was just a broken mirror. Pondering this, he suddenly realised that it looked so shiny and sparkly only because it was reflecting the most beautiful blue sky inlaid with a few fluffy, high, white clouds. He looked up, and for the first time in years saw just how beautiful the sky was. In his endless searching for another precious rock, he had completely failed to notice and appreciate anything of the beauty and richness that was all around him.

Primary source: Arielle Essex
Secondary source: Swami Paramahamsa Prajnanananda

* * *

Leading

 The tramp's attention is focused on the external, material world. He has discovered a strategy that has brought him wealth, and he appears to believe that continuing the same strategy will increase his wealth. This limited behaviour, which is not dissimilar to the behaviours of the monkeys in Story 21, "The Tale of the Rogue Monkeys" (see page 125), prevents him from seeing or connecting with

163

any of the limitless resources that are available to him in the universe. This is a trap leadership can fall into when it remains stuck in behavioural patterns that were once successful and no longer are, or pays insufficient attention to the complexity of the environment, or the opportunities that are available.

Influencing

The story may influence the listener or reader to pay attention to the dangers of operating only in the right-hand exterior boxes without sufficient attention to the left-hand interior boxes. Perhaps quality requires the presence of individual or collective values. If quality is not present inside of ourselves, how can we expect to recognise it on the outside?

Motivating

The story may appeal to individuals in all the thinking and valuing systems who may have become distracted by living in the past or future, or who have become so focused on material things that they have lost sight of what is truly worthwhile. The tramp has acquired more than he needs; his behaviours and motivation strategies are obsessive.

My insights

- Beware of the seductive power of lust and greed.
- It is harder to change a successful strategy than an unsuccessful one.
- One of the best ways to become unsuccessful is to continue doing what made you successful in the first place.
- Live in the *now*: savour your strawberry.
- There are many ways to lose concentration and become distracted.

* * *

"Possibly. As I recall," said Al Sayyid, "it was Saint Augustine who drew attention to the three *presents*. That is the present of the past, the present of the future and the present of the present."

"Al Sayyid, you've lost me. What are you talking about?"

"There is no other time but the present moment. The past is merely a sensory coding of what we think happened. The future is merely a sensory coding of what we imagine will happen, and even that is based on our past experiences. The only real time is the present moment.

"Leaders who wish to develop the art of *presence* can achieve this only by being in the present moment. It is presence that allows people to become more aware of themselves, their inner feelings and thoughts. People who are present are also more able to pay attention to the many and varied things that are happening around them. They pick up clues from the environment; they read people's inner thoughts and feelings from their words, and tone, and nonverbal communication. And so the quality of the interventions they make is wiser, deeper, more humane, more precise. In return they are offered trust, loyalty, friendship, goodwill. These are things that no amount of money or power can buy or demand."

"Like the wise traveller on his camel, or the teacher in Japan," offered the Young Traveller, "in the earlier stories."

"Precisely. And now that we are considering the importance of how we pay attention to time in ourselves, we can also observe how the same patterns – metaphorically speaking – are woven into nature. If you are ready for a story from Russia you had better get a grip."

Story 32

Comfort Zones

Two seeds lay in a shallow depression in the field where the farmer had thrown them. As the autumn days passed, birds searching for worms, and the wintry wind, loosened the earth, which slowly began to cover them.

Patiently, they waited as the nights grew longer and the days grew colder. They huddled together for warmth. Even below the surface of the earth they noticed the changes going on above them. They felt the quality of the rain change as the warm squally autumn winds from the west gave way to the sleety slanting winter winds from the north.

They waited patiently as the hardness of winter set in. They felt the first sharp clasp of the frost upon the ground and then the weight of the winter snows piling high above them. And they huddled together even closer. And they waited.

Eventually, the pressure changed, the snow began to melt, and the soil once again became soft and moist. Warm spring winds gently began to caress the fields and both seeds began to feel strange and powerful urges within themselves.

The first little seed pondered, "I wonder what's up there," and he began to push curious little green shoots upwards in the direction of the earth's crust. "And I wonder what's down there," he said, and began to push enquiring little roots into the soil below.

But the second little seed said, "I've no idea what's up there. It could be scary. And I don't know what's down there. That's really frightening. So I think I'll just stay here a little longer."

Soon, the first seed had pushed through the earth and was enjoying the sensation of warm spring sunshine, the freshness of the air, and all the wonderful things that she now saw around her. Her roots too were pushing deep into the soil below, drawing energy, nourishment and strength from the richness of the environment.

But the second little seed continued with its inner monologue. "It could be dangerous up there. Who knows what's down there? I think I'll just stay here a little longer."

By the end of spring, the first little seed stood strong and tall, surveying the fields from some height and with considerable pleasure and sense of achievement. Her roots were deeply centred in the ground, providing a foundation from which she could blossom and grow even stronger.

Meanwhile, the second little seed was still continuing with its risk-free strategy.

Until a chicken came along, and ate it.

Primary source: Kathy Horton
General source: Russian tradition

* * *

Leading

The story compares two sets of personal attitude. The first seed demonstrates curiosity, wonder and a willingness to listen to, and take action upon, the deepest stirrings in its heart. The first seed is prepared to take risks. The second seed, on the other hand, suppresses these feelings. Anxiety prompts it to choose what it considers to be the safe option. One message of this story is that in times where growth and development are required pro-activity or reactivity are better choices that inactivity. If you don't act upon the world, the world will act upon you.

Influencing

Readers or listeners who may have excellent strategies for putting off decision making are invited to do a contrast analysis.

The habitats in which we live are not risk-free. We have to make choices, make decisions and sometimes push beyond our comfort zones if we are going to live a life that is useful, purposeful and fulfilling. If our DNA hadn't taken the risk to open itself to the acquisition of new intelligence on a regular basis, we'd still be amoebae.

Motivating

All thinking and valuing systems can demonstrate the healthy and unhealthy attitudes illustrated in the story. Perhaps the story would particularly resonate with these systems:

BLUE:
can sometimes have problems taking initiative; can wait to be told what to do by those who have "authority" – sometimes called "public-sector syndrome" by detractors.

ORANGE:
values risk taking and the application of knowledge and discovery to create possibility in the world; ORANGE loves to break free from constraints and rules and make the best of itself.

My insights

- Life requires risk.
- Sometimes it is safer to move towards danger than away from it.
- Without some risk there is unlikely to be some result.
- Lack of action may indicate an unwillingness to take personal responsibility.
- Excessive comfort can seriously diminish learning and development opportunities.
- Contexts: education, healing, therapy and coaching, business, investment.

* * *

"Possibly."

"Research exists," said Al Sayyid, "that shows how laboratory rats, released into the wild, develop twenty-five per cent bigger brains over a three-month period compared with captive rats. The real world is a great teacher.

"There are two ways through which you can make time your enemy," Al Sayyid continued. "One is, as demonstrated by the second seed in the previous story, by waiting too long to take action. The second is by taking action too quickly, without taking time to think and plan. Reach into my library pouch and see what you find inside."

The Young Magician gently inserted his hand into the concealed pouch by the chalice and withdrew a magazine with a shiny cover. It was a back number of the *Harvard Business Review*.

"Take a look at the article entitled, 'Beware the Busy Manager'. You may want to make some notes."

After he had read the article, the Young Magician's magic pencil wrote down the following points:

- A big problem in contemporary Western businesses and organisations is damage done by managers taking action without sufficiently thinking through consequences.
- This has a lot to do with cultural expectations especially the JFDI mentality.
- JFDI means "Just Flipping Do It!"
- JFDI may work well in crisis and firefighting situations.
- However, organisations stuck in such knee-jerk responses will do well to reassess the long-term effectiveness of this strategy.
- The wise leader strikes a balance between:
  - action and reflection;
  - achieving goals and avoiding problems; and
  - managing the present and thinking through future consequences.

"Let us continue on our journey of exploration," said Al Sayyid, "and let us deepen our study of time, risk and resources. You may also notice how other themes relevant to inspiring leadership are also woven into the rich fabric of the following Sufi teaching story. Let me take you back to the land where I was first created."

Story 33

First Fruits

A certain farmer planted an ancient type of raspberry of a kind that was known to have the sweetest and subtlest flavour but that took many years to mature.

The shah, himself a keen gardener, chanced to pass by one day and, noticing the young shoots climbing up the bamboo framework, asked the farmer if he had enough patience to wait for the first fruit since this type of ancient raspberry usually took twenty years or more to bear fruit.

The farmer replied that he was planting not for himself but for the future of his family and the enrichment of the earth. If he himself did not live long enough to see the fruit it was God's will. On the other hand, should he be fortunate enough to survive so long, he would personally bring the shah the first fruits, provided of course that the shah himself was still around.

Both men laughed heartily at this and the shah went on his way.

Many years later the raspberry canes bore fruit. The farmer took the first crop to the shah, who, delighted to see the farmer again after so many years, lavished him richly with gifts.

Word spread around the land that the shah was rewarding simple farmers who brought baskets of raspberries to the palace with gold equal to the weight of the produce.

So it was that a certain opportunist, anxious to make some easy money, bought some raspberries in the market and took them to the palace, demanding to be rewarded in similar fashion.

The shah personally threw the self-serving treasure seeker out of court, saying that he was rewarding craft, commitment and determination, not raspberries. He pointed out in no uncertain terms that shallow imitation was no substitute for skill, application and experience.

The second raspberry bringer was so angered by the slight he had received at the shah's court that he never bothered to discover the extraordinary circumstances that had led to the exchange of gifts in the first place.

Primary source: Nossrat Peseschkian,
***Oriental Stories as Tools for Psychotherapy*, Sterling**
Secondary source: Sufi tradition

* * *

Leading

The shah and the farmer, although widely separated in terms of social and political status, are completely at ease with each other because they are so at ease with themselves. They also have common values, and it is perhaps this more than anything else that allows them to go beyond the trappings of society and status to treat each other with respect and as equals. Just as the farmer is the guardian of his farm for future generations, the shah is the guardian of the state and its people. Their attitudes, their values, their behaviours all create a desirable impact on the habitat, not just for now but the future. Both men are models of desirable behaviour and action.

Influencing

Both men influence their environment through their actions. They live by certain codes that create a positive effect on the cultural and economic health of society. As with many great leaders, their main concern is with husbandry – the careful management of resources through time. Their goal is not for themselves, and there is no trace of ego. Their goal is that their land will continue to prosper for future generations. The opportunist is the perfect foil for these values. And he doesn't even bother to find out why his ruse failed to work.

Motivating

The story appeals to all valuing and thinking systems:

PURPLE:
the ways of tradition are observed and honoured; the group is preserved against threats.

RED:
a strong leader is to be respected; the leader respects those who deserve respect and is tough with those who don't.

BLUE:
hard work, good husbandry, delayed gratification, ethical behaviour and right-minded leadership confirm the existence of order in our lives.

ORANGE:
appreciates expertise, efficient leadership, the successful outcomes of projects and "shareholder" value.

GREEN:
may appreciate the easy relationship between the shah and his subject, but may also disapprove of the rough treatment of the opportunist; may consider that the "system" has failed the opportunist and that the shah would do well to divert resources into giving such people more equal opportunities.

YELLOW:
will salute the absence of barriers between the two men, knowing it is based on their mutual respect for the competence and knowledge within their own fields of expertise.

My insights

- Do not underestimate the importance of future planning, hard work, determination to succeed, craft and commitment.
- Great leaders are more concerned with their contribution to future generations and the sustainable development of their "habitat" than their own self-gratification.
- Success requires rigour and discipline, and the nurturing of talent and resources through time.
- When you see success, look beneath the surface for the planning, persistence, knowledge and skills that have supported it.
- Successful people take responsibility for their actions; unsuccessful people prefer to blame others rather than notice their own shortcomings.

- Blame perpetuates cycles of ignorance.
- The quick fix creates dependency cultures.

* * *

"Possibly. Young Master, many people look at a carpet like myself and, while appreciating the surface qualities of design, pattern, weave, colour and so forth, completely fail to realise what effort and energy has gone into the creative process. It took nine months for my Maker to create me. That is a labour of love as well as of expertise.

"The opportunist in the previous story looks for a quick fix, an easy way to make material gains, but, generally speaking, life is not like this. Dedication, determination and the awareness of possibilities are vitally important. The universe is certainly benevolent and surrounds us with riches of all kinds, but it is up to each one of us to recognise what these riches are, combine them in different ways and make the most of them for the good of the whole planet.

"My Maker found fabric, wool, silk, dyes, needles and a loom. But without his skill in weaving them together, without his commitment to the hard work and the time it would take him, nothing would have been created. There is no magic solution, as all Magicians know.

"Are your sunglasses to hand? We're off to the Midwest of the United States of America."

Story 34

Soil and Toil

A priest was driving his station wagon along a remote country road. As he reached the brow of a hill, he slowed down and whistled to himself. Stretched out below him, nestling in the valley, was one of the most beautiful farms he had ever seen. The fences were trim, the crops a lush green and a line of trees led up to the farmhouse, which though set back from the road was clearly kept in immaculate order. There were flowers and vegetables growing in the cottage garden, and white-painted stones demarcated all the borders. The scene was worthy of a travel agent's brochure.

On the other side of the road were more fields. The soil was rich and black, and clearly had just been ploughed into the straightest furrows the priest had ever seen. On the far side of the fields the priest was able to pick out the distant figure of the farmer sitting on his tractor, moving slowly back towards the road, finishing the last of the ploughing.

It was a beautiful sunny day, and, having not much to do, the priest coasted down the hill into the valley, parked his car and walked over to the paling fence. He stood there enjoying the sun on his back, the smell of the freshly turned earth and the satisfying sense of God's beneficence.

The farmer looked up from his work and saw the priest. He carefully continued with his last row, switched off the engine, slowly dismounted, and then – taking all the time in the world – ambled across to where the priest leaned against the fence.

As the farmer got closer, the priest smiled and greeted him, "Beautiful farm you have here. God has certainly blessed you with this land."

The farmer took a sweat-stained handkerchief from the pocket of his overalls and wiped some beads of perspiration from his forehead. Then he took a long moment to cast his eyes over the whole spread. He removed the piece of straw he'd been sucking from between his lips, and, still holding the silence, allowed his eyes to engage with the priest.

Finally, in a slow, deliberate voice, he replied, "Yes, Reverend, you're right. God has indeed blessed me with a beautiful farm. But, I just wish you could have seen it when He had it all to himself."

Primary source: Bob Proctor

* * *

Leading

We live in a world that is full of resources. Both the farmer and the priest appreciate this. But the priest has failed to consider a vital element that has produced the beauty and productivity of this particular piece of land. Prayer is not enough. Prayer and action are required. The farmer has appreciated the potential of the land and invested time, energy, skill, labour and risk in it. And the land has rewarded him in turn. The farmer, taciturn by nature, leads by example. His personal commitment and attitude, supported by a set of values that include a strong work ethic and sense of independence, plus his particular farming and building skills, have shaped the environment. And in its turn this environment reshapes the response of others.

Influencing

The story works on the reader or listener by contrasting two ways of seeing the world. The priest's way is to see things as they are rather than ask how they have become so. The priest's belief system influences him to scan mainly for God's contribution. The farmer, without denying the existence of any god, has a belief system that scans for the effects of hard work and vision upon the environment. It is not either/or but both/and. In this way the farmer includes the priest's views and then transcends them.

Motivating

The story will probably resonate best with these thinking and valuing systems:

BLUE:
the priest's view that "God's in his Heaven and all is right with the world" will resonate with BLUE thinking and so will the work ethic and future-planning mentality of the farmer.

ORANGE:
the farmer has ORANGE tendencies as well as BLUE: he has applied his skills to the environment, taken risks, invested for the future, created material comforts, and is now harvesting the rewards.

YELLOW:
will appreciate this story as a metaphor that might be useful in shifting BLUE thinking, where it is no longer appropriate for the conditions, gently towards more ORANGE ways of thinking and doing.

My insights

- We are surrounded by resources; it's up to each one of us what we do with them.
- Success may require:
  - a clear set of outcomes and a vision of the future;
  - being aware of the responses to our actions;
  - having the discipline to work hard and handle adversity; and
  - being flexible and having the courage to take risks.
- Success often takes time to create: rigour, discipline and tenacity can be valuable attributes.
- Developing a farm is no different from developing our personal and professional skills, or learning to play a musical instrument, or training for sports.
- We each have a responsibility to use the resources available to us to make a contribution to the planet.

* * *

"Possibly.

"Hard work can be a good thing," said Al Sayyid, "but not if it isn't productive or useful. Just like a motif that doesn't contribute to the overall integrity of a carpet's design and purpose, too much of anything can detract from, and even cheapen, the value of the original idea. Do you like guacamole?"

The Young Magician nodded.

"Excellent. We're going to Mexico."

Story 35

MBA

An expensive yacht docked in a tiny Mexican port. The owner, a successful business consultant from the north, complimented the local Mexican fisherman on the quality of his fish and asked how long it took to catch them.

"Not so long. A couple of hours only."

"So why didn't you stay out longer and catch more?" enquired the consultant.

The Mexican explained that his catch was more than sufficient to meet his own and his family's needs.

"So what do you do with the rest of your time?"

"I sleep late, play with my children, take a siesta with my wife. When it gets dark I go to the village to see my amigos, have a few drinks, play some cards, sing a few songs. I have a good life, my friend."

"Hang on a moment, fella," the consultant butted in, "I have an economics degree from Harvard and an MBA from Tufts, and I can sure give you some help. Look, here's what to do. Fish a bit longer, and fish every day. Then you sell the extra fish for a profit. With the extra revenue, you can buy a bigger boat. With the extra money you earn from that, you can buy a second boat, and a third one, until you have a fleet of trawlers.

"Instead of selling your fish to a middleman, you will now have power and authority to negotiate directly with the canneries and processing plants. You could even open your own plant.

"Then you could leave this ramshackle old port of yours, and move to Cancún, or Mexico City, or even LA or New York. From the centre of the universe you can direct your whole operation."

"How long is that gonna take?" asked the Mexican wide-eyed.

"Hard to be exact. Twenty, maybe twenty-five years."

"And then?"

"Well, then it gets to be real interesting," said the consultant, eyes glittering with calculations. "When the whole enterprise gets really big, you can start selling stocks and make millions!"

"Wow, millions. Talaga? And after that?"

"After that you'll be able to retire, live in a small village near the sea, sleep late, play with your children and grandchildren, catch a few fish, take a siesta with the one you love, and spend your evenings drinking and enjoying yourself with friends."

"Thank you, señor. But I think I'll just stick to this, my simple life."

Original source unknown

* * *

Leading

This story challenges the assumptions that hard work, investment and the markets are always good things. The story raises the question: What is appropriate? We do not live in a one-size-fits-all world. For the fisherman, his way of life suits him: it is appropriate to his lifestyle and the social and economic conditions with which he appears very content. The other way may be appropriate to different cultures except that – as the MBA suggests – the hardworking go-getting achiever of the northern hemisphere actually really aspires to what the fisherman already has.

Influencing

The story influences through gentle humour and a circular logic that allows us to make up our own minds about what we really want, what makes sense, and what is appropriate to us. It raises the question: am I really sure that I am using my energies and resources in ways that get me what I really want and desire?

Motivating

The story will probably resonate with the following systems:

PURPLE:
will respond to the natural rhythms of life of the fisherman, and to his close bonding with family and friends.

ORANGE:
may be shocked and surprised at the idea that the capitalist dream may not be a universal shared goal or the panacea for all economic "deficiencies".

GREEN:
may be delighted at the gentle puncturing of the MBA's economic vision; GREEN favours redistribution of wealth rather than its accumulation.

YELLOW:
will see this story as ammunition in explaining why undiluted ORANGE and GREEN solutions will never be appropriate in developing countries that have not yet progressed beyond PURPLE and RED thinking and valuing systems; only solutions appropriate to the political, economic, social and cultural conditions in these countries are likely to succeed.

My insights

- Leadership must be applied within the particular thinking and value systems of the individual or the group for it to:
  - make sense;
  - be understood;
  - be appropriate; and
  - be motivating.
- Science has its limitations, especially when applied through a particular lens.
- Hi-tech creates its own complexities.
- A nut is best opened with a nutcracker, not a sledgehammer.
- A solution should be appropriate to the problem and to the need.
- A simple software upgrade may be much more sensible than the latest, most powerful computer.

* * *

"Possibly.

"The difference between science and religion", said Al Sayyid, "is that religious truth is permanent and scientific truth is provisional. What is true in science today may be challenged and replaced tomorrow. Every science, including economic science, has its weaknesses and internal contradictions, just as every Persian carpet has its deliberate mistake – for only God can create the perfect work.

"When economic systems fail, it is still important to keep a sense of proportion and a sense of humour. Let's go north, back to the United States of America. Pay attention to a different kind of meditation. This is a sixth story."

Story 36

Liquid Assets

On 26 July 2000, two friends, Jim and John, both received $1,000 bonuses at work. Jim and John were working for a very large telecommunications company in the US, and that year there was plenty of money for bonuses sloshing around.

Jim, being a diligent, sensible, financially conscientious person, put his whole $1,000 bonus into his company's stock scheme. With his $1,000, he bought seven shares at $138, paying a transaction cost of $35, and adding one dollar of his own. Having watched his company's stock soar in recent months, he felt very pleased with his purchase. He felt good about his future, and what it meant for his family.

John, being a more carefree and less conventional sort, took another route. He borrowed a friend's pickup and headed for the beer store. Here, he purchased 33 cases of his favourite beer. John, too, felt good about his investment: 33 x 24 bottles = 792 bottles of liquid nectar.

John calculated that he could drink fifteen bottles a week and not have to buy beer for a whole year. And that made a lot of sense to him.

Jim, however, was appalled by John's prodigality and lack of foresight. He missed no opportunity to let John know how he'd let himself and his family down. And for demon alcohol, too! As the months passed, Jim took to reading the stock prices in the newspaper, with excitement at first, and then with increasing nervousness as he saw the prices start to fall.

"It'll go back up," he'd say to John. And John, who'd be drawing on his own investment on a daily basis would reply, "Sure thing, just hang on in there, buddy."

Months passed and the stock value continued to decline. And the pile of beer cases was getting appreciably smaller, too.

Christmas came, and Jim's stock stood at about half its original value. But he was still confident. Surely this was rock bottom! So he continued to remind John every once in a while of his folly in investing in the wrong kind of liquid assets. "In six months' time you'll be right out of beer. Who knows what my stock will be worth?"

Summer comes and hard times in the telecommunications industry continue. There is plenty of bad news around. Both Jim and John have been laid off. Jim has just had to sell his seven shares to raise some cash to see him and his family through these hard times. He gets just $12 for each of his shares. That's $84. But, after paying the transaction fee of $35, he's left with just $49.

Later that day, Jim cycled round to John's house to commiserate over how bad things had become. By a happy coincidence, there were just two bottles of beer left, and John being a good friend, offered to share these last bottles with Jim.

Jim appreciated the gesture. A cold beer on a hot summer's day is always welcome, but a little bit of guilt nagged at Jim. "At the end of the day, at least I get fifty bucks out of this – you ain't got a darn thing now."

"That's life, I guess. Anyways, maybe you can give me a hand. I gotta take all these empties back to the beer store," John said as his other friend pulled into the drive with his pickup.

Off they went to the beer store, feeling quite a bit sorry for themselves. The beer store owner greeted them in a friendly way. "That's some celebrating you've been doing. Now let me see, thirty-three cases by twenty-four bottles at ten cents a bottle. By my reckoning that comes to exactly $79.20."

Jim was lost for words. How would you feel if you discovered that during the course of one year your $1,000 stock investment left you with less than $50, while you could have bought a whole load of beer for the same amount, drunk it and still had almost $80 in your pocket?

**Primary source: David Jones
Original source unknown**

* * *

Leading

It's hard to know what the message is here. Perhaps the story is just frivolous, which is also fine. Maybe the message to Jim is not to follow conventional wisdom without doing some research of your own. And the message to John is that sometimes it pays to think about yourself first. Either way, we could say that problems in the infrastructure, the habitat, affect everyone within it. So, if you are not in control of your habitat, it's likely that it will be in control of you.

Influencing

A powerful message here could be: do not completely trust what you don't completely understand. Or, as financial services experts say, markets may go down as well as up.

Motivating

The following systems might respond to this story:

RED:
will respond well to John's carefree live-for-today, to hell-with-tomorrow, instant-gratification attitude.

BLUE:
may well agree with Jim's criticism's of John's profligacy and his lack of making provision for the future.

ORANGE:
will be critical of Jim's failure to research the market and seek sound financial advice from an expert; and will be critical of John's lack of awareness of investment opportunities while admiring his free spirit.

My insights

- Make sure you know what you're doing before taking risks or making decisions.
- Don't accept what passes for conventional wisdom without challenging or researching it.

* * *

"Possibly.

"A great weaver is always looking for new ways to create better carpets, and looking to improve weaknesses in structure and limitations in existing practice. In a similar fashion, great thinkers and leaders always challenge and question existing wisdom, looking for the deeper truth below the surface.

"Let's go back in time, almost fifteen hundred years ago, to seventh-century Britain."

Story 37

Surface Tension

Hrethic the Warrior, commander of the Saxon armies, sat on a roughly sawn stool in the centre of his war tent. With a keen eye he scanned the sites of recent skirmishes, deftly drawn on deerskins.

Avenging recent raids, Saxon ships had swiftly sailed. They let loose their armies in the lands of Britons for British raiders, had kidnapped Cyntheow, consort of the king, and insult must be paid in blood and bone, with vengeance violent and vicious. The Saxon fighters sailed in force to wrack the raiders for their wrongs.

With Hrethic was his young son, Hrothulf. Lithe as an elm sapling, his father had brought him to learn the lessons and ways of warfare.

A captain came with news from the north. A Saxon army, helmed by Hrothmund, Hrethic's cousin, had sought and surrounded bands of the British local forces led by Wulfstan.

The bringer of news bowed before Hrethic, and delivered the deerskin. "Liege Lord of the Danes, before dusk this day we will butcher these Britons. On all sides we hold sway. Our men outman them six to one. Our weapons are whetted, our appetites abundant. Earl Hrothmund sends news our success is certain."

Hrethic glanced at the details drawn on the deerskin. He frowned and focused far in the distance, sitting as still as a hawk on the hand. Then stood. Action followed fast. Dismissing the messenger, he summoned his steward. "Go, gather what guards you can get. Speed without stopping to reinforce Hrothmund.

"A mess," muttered Hrethic. "Our forces will fail; our hearts will be humbled."

"How so, Father?" asked Hrothulf. "If our men and munitions are more by many, our swords and supplies superior by far, how should we suffer? How should we fail?"

Hrothulf felt the full force of his father's stare. Not a word was said. Silently, Hrethic signalled his son to follow his footsteps. He was led from the tent to a large, placid lake, a league from the camp. From the edge of the broad, Hrethic cut, with his two-edged axe, two equal strips of willow bark, and one of these he skimmed onto the smooth still waters of the broad.

Both father and son stood by the shore, surveying the willow bark well as it floated, still and stolid, motionless on the placid water's flat and fathomless surface.

Some considerable time passed in complete quiet, till Hrothulf became curious and questioned his father: "What is the meaning of your water-borne riddle? I have watched this willow for a while and more, yet I have no mastery of its meaning."

Hrethic stood silent, then signalled his son to follow his footfalls. Soon, Hrothulf was standing where water ran, rushing, tumbling and swirling, in a rocky ravine. In the swift-running river, Hrethic hurled the cut willow; sailing swiftly and deftly, with power and purpose, it was soon lost to sight.

"And now do you ken why my cousin will languish, and Wulfstan the Bold will pluck the great prize?"

The boy cast down his eyes and quickly confessed that he had no such knowledge of his master's deep meaning.

Hrethic held high the deerskin, the drawing of the death field, before his young son. "Observe our Saxon squadrons: like the lake, large and still, they are mighty yet immobile. Mark, too, on the map where my callow cousin lurks. In his arrogant overconfidence, he lacks the lust to fling the fight to the foe. See, he stands here, safe behind his troops, reclusive in the rear.

"Now watch how it is with Wulfstan the Battler. How boldly he leads his band of brave Britons. In the front ranks he stands, alongside his

spearmen, foursquare in the front. His rear ranks are here, ranged hard by the river, from where – no escape. The willingness of Wulfstan to perish in battle, to die if fate wills it, as he seeks to slay Saxons, will encourage his comrades. And they will each fight as fierce as ten champions since they have no choice but to do it or die.

"The bold ranks of Britons, like the rapid running river, flowing fiercely and furious, in determined direction, that carries the willow with force and with power, will sweep all before them and carry the day.

"And so, my young son, let the lesson be learned that in matters of business, in war or in peacetime, a company of fighters, though small in their numbers, when committed and courageous in planning and strategy, and firm in their purpose, will pluck the great prize."

In the late afternoon, when steward and soldiers reached the scene of slaughter, they found only buzzards, the bones of the Saxons, the stench of the slain.

Primary source: Nick Jones
Secondary source: There is a version of this story in
W. Chan Kim and Renee Mauborgne,
"Parables of Leadership"

* * *

Leading

 Leadership here is expressed in two ways. Wulfstan leads from the front and motivates his men by example. He is brave and fearless and galvanises his men into committed action. He will accept nothing less than victory or death. Hrethic is a different kind of leader. He is a strategist, a coordinator, a planner and a visionary. Both men use the environment, the infrastructure, to their advantage; both men value action and commitment; both men look to seize the initiative; and both men appear to have strong personal attributes and temperament.

Influencing

Influencing is achieved by example in Wulfstan's case, and his identification with his troops. Hrethic, on the other hand, influences his son by giving a natural demonstration of the situation as a metaphor in order for Hrothulf to learn for himself.

Motivating

While the story will appeal to all systems, perhaps it will particularly appeal to:

RED:	**ORANGE:**	**YELLOW:**
will appreciate the bravery, heroism and aggression of Wulfstan; they will also appreciate his gesture of fighting in the front line alongside the common soldiers; he is one of them.	will appreciate tactics and strategy; ORANGE may also consider how a small but committed organisation can overthrow a mighty but less disciplined one.	will recognise the expertise of both men and the economy and efficiency of their thinking; they are functional in approach and thorough in execution; they understand natural forces and work naturally with them.

My insights

- Commitment is essential to success.
- Metaphor is an excellent teaching tool.
- Natural systems provide excellent models for leadership and management.
- Avoid complacency and arrogance.
- Be proactive.

* * *

"Possibly.

"The Latin root of the word decision is *decidere*," said Al Sayyid. "*Decidere* literally means 'to cut off', and that's exactly what an effective decision does. It is like pushing a boat out into midstream with no way back. It is what Wulfstan does. Before you make a decision, nervousness and anxiety can exist. After you make the decision, and commit to it, you are locked onto a path of determined action.

"Decision and commitment go hand in hand like thread and needle, like warp and weft. Let us return to the twentieth century to somewhere in middle Europe and weave together a story of these and other themes. Sit tight, Young Master."

Story 38

The Messiah

A great monastery was heading rapidly towards its own dissolution. Many years before it had been a great seat of learning, it had been wondrously wealthy, and a hundred monks prayed and studied here. The learned brothers were sought out by princes and rulers for advice of all kinds: political, economic and practical as well as spiritual. But all living things decay. Perhaps through corruption, or subterfuge, or simple mismanagement, the monastery reflected a mere shadow of its former glory. And now just the abbot and four brothers, all in their twilight years, remained. All things considered it was, without a doubt, sorely in need of resurrection.

In a hidden valley near the monastery was a simple log cabin that an imam from a local town sometimes used as a retreat. The abbot and the imam had appreciated each other's company and wisdom for many years, so one day the abbot decided to pay his friend a visit. He asked the old imam whether he had any ideas about how he might save the monastery. The imam shook his head sadly. "It's the same thing everywhere. Hardly a soul comes to the mosque any more. There's no hunger for the mystical among the people these days." And so they talked together and prayed, discussed matters of spiritual philosophy and meditated on the parlous state of the world, religion and of the monastery in particular.

As he was taking his leave, the abbot said, "My friend, it is always a great pleasure to spend time with you. But I have not succeeded in my mission. Do you really not have a single idea that might help us save our monastery?"

The imam considered the question for a moment or two, and then replied, "I am so sorry, but I have no suggestion to offer you – except to say that one among you is the Messiah."

Now when the other monks heard about the imam's comment, you can imagine how surprised and amazed they were. It got them thinking. "One of us is the Messiah? Here in this monastery? Extraordinary! Who do you suppose it could be?"

They talked among themselves in dark secluded corners. "It must be the abbot, for he's a fine leader and very wise, too. Or could it be Brother Zdravko? He's a very fine healer, though he can be a little sharp-tongued sometimes. Surely, it's not Brother Bruno. He's got a memory like a sieve. But on the other hand he is wonderfully kind and loving. Or could it be Brother Vladimir? He's always around when you need him."

And sometimes, as they lay in their cots on the cold floor of their cells in the middle of the night, it was not unknown for each of them to consider just the faintest possibility. "Of course, he didn't mean me. No, no, no. But just supposing he did. Oh, God, no. That's not possible. Surely, not me. Surely not! I am not worthy of such a thing – could I be?"

And, as each monk's train of thought continued along these lines, a remarkable transformation began to happen. They began to treat each other with the utmost courtesy and respect just in case one of them might be the Messiah. And, in the very unlikely event that each monk himself might be the Messiah, they began to treat themselves with the utmost courtesy and respect, too.

Nothing happens by chance. All things have a reason and a purpose though the eye may not see beyond that which is apparent. So perhaps it was not completely by accident that the monastery had been built on the lower slopes of high mountains. The alpine countryside in which the monastery was situated was so beautiful that people would sometimes come in the summer months to picnic, or to walk along the panoramic pathways many of which overlooked the magnificent but crumbling edifice of the main chapel. And it was not unusual for these day trippers to meet the monks going about their business. Neither was it difficult for these visitors to sense the atmosphere of extraordinary courtesy and respect that surrounded these five old men, and the ambience of calmness and serenity that permeated their environment.

Word of mouth spread quickly about the aura of peace and wellbeing that seemed to pervade the monastery's grounds. People began to visit more frequently, and they brought friends. And these friends in turn brought more friends. Some of the younger men began to strike up conversations with the monks. After a while, one asked whether it might be possible to take his vows and become a member of their community. And, as it turned out, he was just the first of many.

Within a very short time, the monastery had once again become a flourishing, bustling centre of industry, study and worship. The imam had sown the seed of an idea. But it was the monks who found it in themselves to create the conditions for renewal. And it was all made possible through their fostering of mutual appreciation, courtesy, self-respect and the desire to make a real contribution.

Primary source: Sonja Stokic
Secondary source: Zander, R., and Zander, B.,
***The Art of Possibility*, Penguin**
General source: Jewish tradition

* * *

Leading

 What is the one thing you can say that will make the most useful change in another person's life? This is the contribution of the imam. It is a perfect statement because it is totally appropriate to the beliefs and values of the monks. As the monks fully reconnect with their beliefs and values, their personal attitudes and behaviours are transformed. And, as soon as this happens, they begin to create a transformation in their environment. As the monks become more personally conscious of themselves and each other, the world begins to notice, and the potential for change in the habitat is created.

Influencing

The monks were locked into a system that was disintegrating. They were trapped in their behaviours, and these old and "stuck" behaviours were contributing to the monastery's problems. The imam didn't attempt to change the system or the monks' behaviours directly. Instead, he looked for a way in which he could fit an idea into the system that would be compatible with the system's values and behaviours. The imam found leverage in an idea that fitted perfectly with the valuing systems of the monks. This creates a real WIN–WIN–WIN situation.

The imam's provocative statement made it possible for the monks to decide for themselves to change their behaviours, and connect with new ways of being and doing. And, as they began to live their lives with the same humility, compassion and respect for themselves and each other as the God they served, they were able, in turn, to influence others by the sheer force of their presence and integrity.

Motivating

The following systems may respond favourably to the story:

PURPLE:
the old traditions are preserved and maintained; the group is rebonded and begins to grow and thrive again.

BLUE:
will celebrate the preservation of the "one true way" and the monks' reconnection with right values; BLUE will also appreciate the imam's decency.

ORANGE:
will note the economy of the imam's strategy, and its efficiency in turning a failing organisation into a thriving one.

GREEN:
will welcome the interfaith support and the tolerance of difference; also the culture of mutual respect, tolerance and trust in the "workplace".

YELLOW:
will recognise the imam's use of "natural design" in using the monks' own value systems to create the possibility of change.

My insights

- True leadership starts with self-leadership and being completely aligned to one's values and beliefs.
- When personal consciousness, shared values and appropriate behaviours are aligned and in harmonious proportion, major change in the habitat becomes possible.
- When the habitat is right, everything within it can thrive and everyone can make a contribution.
- What is the one statement you can make or question you can ask that, by the implications embedded inside it, will cause the most change in the person or in the environment?

- All change starts from within.
- It is never too late to make a change

* * *

"Possibly.

"You know, this story reminds me of a Brazilian proverb," said Al Sayyid, "'For learning and for making love one is never too old.'"

Al Sayyid paused and the Young Magician thought he heard him chortle before continuing, "Although sadly for these old priests, they'll have to concentrate on the former."

The Young Magician had to think about that for a while, and then asked, "Where are we going next?"

"Let us return to the previous story for a moment and consider the imam's contribution. He had the courage and vision to go beyond a narrow view based on his own personal interests and beliefs to a wider, more embracing perspective that considered other points of view, and other belief systems.

"Most people have their own personal agendas – even prejudices – which prevent them from seeing beyond their immediate self-interest or present understanding of the world. This limits choice and possibility. The map they have of what they think the world is prevents them from seeing what it could be.

"An astute leader, like the imam, makes it possible for others to see beyond their own agendas, so they can listen to, and engage with, other possibilities and choices that before they had been blind or deaf to.

"Only when people become open to the possibility of other views, other choices and other opportunities can real change take place.

"So sit tight, hold on, and polish your sunglasses. We're going to an important meeting in a village hall somewhere in the middle of England."

Story 39

The Hat Trick

The speaker had arrived at the village hall to give a talk that people had eagerly awaited for many weeks. The talk was on a particularly contentious issue that touched on the lives of everybody in the village. There were many different points of view and some people had already taken entrenched views as they sought to establish where their own interests lay.

The speaker was just about to begin her talk when she noticed that everyone in the audience was wearing a hat. The butcher's hat was adorned with a string of sausages and two Viking horns made of black pudding; the baker was wearing a hollowed-out cottage loaf on her head; the kennel owner wore a bowler hat trimmed with Rottweiler teeth; the priest had a bright-red hat from which incense smoke wafted; the farmer's hat was hewn from tractor tyres; the estate agent wore a hat covered in elaborate sentences full of measurements and hyperboles; and the teacher's hat was made from a placard protesting against cuts in education spending. And there were as many other hats as there were people in the hall.

The speaker paused. She looked at the audience and told them she had never seen such a splendid collection of hats in her life. She complimented each one and wondered whether each person there might not hear better with their hats off.

One by one, they each put their hat on a table at the back of the hall. By the end of the talk, they were all surprised to discover how much more they had learned than they originally expected.

Primary source: Jane Revell and Susan Norman,
***In Your Hands*, Saffire Press**
Secondary source: Christina Hall

* * *

Leading

The speaker demonstrates respect for each of the people at the meeting, and then invites them to put aside their narrow views so they can listen better. As they do so, they can become more open to other views and values. Although the story does not explicitly say so, this openness is more likely to create more mature debate, and – in the longer term – a more viable and acceptable solution for infrastructural change within the community.

Influencing

The simple and respectful act of complimenting each person on his or her hat, without challenge or criticism, acknowledges and validates their right to hold their own point of view. Now that this is established, each person can more comfortably listen to other viewpoints and thus become more open to other possibilities and perspectives.

Motivating

The story could appeal to all the valuing and thinking systems:

PURPLE:
the whole community is acknowledged and recognised.

RED:
each one can express himself or herself; each one has been acknowledged and respected.

BLUE:
authority and order are established.

ORANGE:
things can get done because the meeting will be efficient; possibilities of sabotage to agreed plans are less likely, saving time, energy and financial resources.

GREEN:
everybody can contribute, everybody can be heard and listened to in a respectful consensual way.

YELLOW:
will appreciate the way that the speaker's simple but effective strategy satisfies the needs of all the valuing and thinking systems; YELLOW is also free to contribute its functional expertise and systemic understanding.

My insights

- Listen to people and show respect for their values.
- Acknowledge people and validate who they are and what they believe.
- Create and hold the space for a real discussion in which all views can be expressed and aired safely.
- Recognise and support the expression of all three aspects of perception:
  - First position: through one's own eyes;
  - Second position: through the eyes of others; and
  - Third position: looking down from a sufficient distance and seeing the whole pattern.
- First position is about being single-minded about what I want.
- Second position is about paying attention to what others want and how they experience the world differently from me.
- Third position helps me to get a more integrated, systemic view of what is really happening: the interconnected dance of reality.

* * *

"Possibly."

"Al Sayyid, is it better for a leader to go with the flow or swim against the current?"

"It depends upon the situation and what is required. The weaver needs to select the appropriate needle for a particular job. As we have seen, the influential leader motivates by working within the valuing systems of those he or she wishes to work with. But sometimes it will be necessary for a leader to do what is different or unexpected.

"Look inside my secret pocket by the chalice. Inside the library you will find a quotation."

The Young Magician fished around inside the library entrance until his hands closed upon a document. He took it out and read it.

"It's by the Irish writer, George Bernard Shaw. It says, 'The reasonable man adapts himself to the world as it is; the unreasonable man tries to change the world to what he wants it to be. Therefore, all progress depends on the unreasonable man.' But is it true?"

"As I say, it depends. Let us go back a short way in time to Vietnam for our next story."

Story 40

Illumination

An old farmer had to decide which of his three sons was worthy to inherit his land and manage it for the good of the extended family. So he gave each son a barn to fill. The first son stocked his barn with stacks of wood and the farmer was well pleased, for it was certain they would now survive the harshness of winter.

The second son filled his barn with hay. Again the farmer was pleased because now all the animals could be fed, and they would survive the harshness of winter.

The third son put a large candle in his barn, right in the middle, so that the light shone brightly into every hidden nook and cranny, so everything could be seen and nothing was hidden from the light.

The farmer decided to give his land to this son because the light would allow him to notice whatever was going on and be inspired to do the right thing.

When his other two sons challenged his judgement, the old man simply quoted an old proverb: "Ordinary people flow with the current. Wise people go against the current. A huge elephant is carried downstream. Tiny fish swim upriver."

Primary source: Benny Chia
General source: Asian tradition

* * *

Before writing his notes, the Young Magician looked at Al Sayyid and said, "Sometimes, working to explain, even to oneself, the meaning of a richly woven metaphor is rather like trying to unravel the significance of the designs and patterns in a skilfully designed carpet."

To which Al Sayyid replied, "That is indeed an art."

* * *

Leadership

 This story is very puzzling for me. Perhaps it means that the one who is the natural leader is the most far seeing, who has a deeper level of personal awareness, whose behaviours are most likely to deal with and predict challenges or dangers in the environment. The other brothers make their contribution, which is valued, but a strong work ethic alone is not sufficient. The story poses the question: What are the attributes of the effective leader?

Influencing

The last brother, whether intentionally or not, appears to match his father's values most closely. The father values the one with the courage to be different, the one who is not afraid to swim against the current, who sees things differently. Perhaps this is what is required by the particular conditions in which this family lives.

Motivating

The different systems may read very different messages into this metaphor. If I hazard some guesses they may look something like the following:

 **PURPLE:** may recognise the mystic wisdom of the elders.

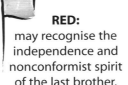 **RED:** may recognise the independence and nonconformist spirit of the last brother.

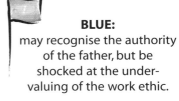 **BLUE:** may recognise the authority of the father, but be shocked at the under-valuing of the work ethic.

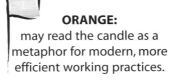 **ORANGE:** may read the candle as a metaphor for modern, more efficient working practices.

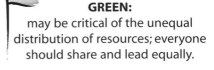 **GREEN:** may be critical of the unequal distribution of resources; everyone should share and lead equally.

YELLOW: may take the metaphor of the candle as representing a far-seeing, systemic, integral view of the universe so that wise decisions can be taken in favour of all living systems, and where more can be done with less.

My insights

- Sometimes it is necessary to break out of old, stuck ways.
- Effective leaders need to give others permission to be creative and "think outside the box".
- Everyone has a contribution to make but not all contributors have what it takes to be a leader.
- What kind of change is required in a given situation:
  - First-order change: change within the current system; more of the same with embellishments?
  - Second-order change: radical change of the system?
- A tiny fish can do what an elephant cannot.

* * *

"Possibly.

"And whenever buying a carpet, always turn it over and look at the other side, too. For every side has its equal and opposite, and every front has its back. Hold on very tight: we're going to visit a pig farm. For every weft there is a warp."

Story 41

It's About Time

A city woman on a weekend break is strolling along a country lane, when she sees a farmer in his orchard. The farmer is surrounded by piglets who are squealing excitedly. The farmer bends down and picks up a piglet so it can eat an apple from the tree. He puts this one down and picks up another piglet, lifting it high into the branches where the apples are sweetest. Then another, and another …

The woman watches this for some time and then can no longer contain her impatience. "What on earth are you doing?"

"Doin'?" says the farmer, "I'm feedin' my pigs. Tha's what I'm doin'."

"I can see that," says the woman, "but why are you picking each one of them up to eat?"

"Why? So's they can eat. They loves apples does my little piggies, and I's got loads'v apples on my trees this year."

"But that's so inefficient. You're making lots of work for yourself."

"Work?" says the farmer. "My little piggies ain't heavy."

"But, for goodness' sake," says the woman, "you could just shake the tree, and let them eat apples off the ground. That way you could save a lot of time."

"Time?" says the farmer, "Wha's time to a pig?"

Primary source: Eleonora Gilbert
Original source unknown

* * *

Leadership and influencing

Inhabiting different environments, the city woman and the farmer have developed very different values about the world and about time. The woman finds the behaviours of the farmer inefficient and incomprehensible, while the farmer cannot understand what the woman is talking about. Neither one is likely to influence the other or change their way of thinking and valuing because each is quite unable to experience the world from the other's point of view.

Motivating

There is a lot of resonance in the story for different valuing and thinking systems:

PURPLE:
will enjoy the farmer's close connection with his animals and the ritual of their feeding.

RED:
may look to gratuitously provoke a fight between the two.

BLUE:
will probably side with the farmer as the rightful authority on pigs.

ORANGE:
will recognise the woman's analysis of inefficiency but be critical of her appalling lack of strategies for rapport building.

GREEN:
will applaud the farmer's solicitous care and concern for his pigs.

YELLOW:
may be curious about how these two value systems can be brought together; will also value guardianship for all living systems; YELLOW will also recognise the different time scales at work.

Time scales

PURPLE:
looks to the past –
What would the
ancestors have done?
No sense of
future time.

RED:
lives in the present;
little awareness
of past history
and future
consequences.

BLUE:
connects past
through present to
future in a linear,
sequential
progression; makes
sacrifices today for
future gratification.

ORANGE:
aware of past and
present; main focus is
on future and can
handle many projects
at once.

GREEN:
inhabits a fuzzy
time sense of all
time as one time.

YELLOW:
can work through all
time zones, and
frequently
experiences "flow
states" where time
becomes suspended
through absorption
in activity.

My insights

- Sometimes, the old ways are just fine – even if they could be more efficient.
- People relate to time in different ways. For example:
  - as a commodity, something to be cut, deployed, apportioned, and put to use for the future;
  - as a space in which to notice what is happening in the present moment.
- Effective leaders need to recognise and respect how people value time differently.
- The piglets' perspective is as important as that of the farmer and that of the woman; they will thrive on attention.
- Hurry-up people may be prone to greater stress; they may need more balance in their lives.
- Leaders need to recognise their preferences in regard to work and time frames, and not be trapped within them.

* * *

"Very possibly," said Al Sayyid, before continuing: "Everybody has preferences. These are the values and behaviours we currently feel most comfortable with. The excellent leader realises his own limitations and may seek out excellent and able lieutenants to support him in the areas that are lacking. Just as every carpet is perfect in itself, and yet limited in its scope and function, the excellent leader will recognise her imperfections as well as her strengths. And the excellent leader knows she cannot be a leader unless others *choose* to follow her."

"Just as I would guess," added the Young Magician, "that the pigs would instinctively recognise that their welfare will be better served by the kindly farmer than the efficient woman. If I were a pig, I would certainly follow the farmer."

Suddenly, as if the idea of being one of the pigs had struck a chord in him, he swung his backpack in front of him, rummaged around in one of the pockets, fished out the apple the High Master had given him, and ate it.

"It's time for the sixth story," said Al Sayyid. "Let us consider the compassion of the inspiring leader a little more deeply. For the wise leader pays attention to all living systems, not just the human one, recognising their interconnectedness and the contribution they make to the health of the whole planet. Put your apple core where it will decompose easily. Put on your sunglasses, for it is time to travel back to southern Asia."

* * *

Story 42

Fate Non Accompli

The Master looked into the face of the young monk, and behind the eyes he could read that the boy's life would not stretch a month more. Illness would take him as the signs surely predicted.

With compassion and sadness, he sent the little monk home so he could at least die surrounded by his family in the gentle hills of his homeland.

When two months later the young monk returned in great spirits and rude good health, the Master's amazement was matched by his delight. And this time what the monk read behind the boy's eyes was that having overcome obstacles he would now survive into ripe old age.

The Master, curious to find how the little monk had cheated Fate, quizzed the boy with many questions about his journey home. The boy mentioned that, among other things, he had saved a colony of ants from a flood. He had carefully placed a stick across a swollen stream so they had access to an escape route.

"Aha!" said the Master. "That is what makes all the difference! If you're good to life, life will be good to you."

General source: Zen tradition

* * *

Leading

 An act of kindness or generosity can create real change in the world, both internally and externally. The young monk's action, though a small gesture in his own environment, makes a significant and lifesaving difference in the ants' environment. It may seem a leap to suggest that the value the young monk places on life rather then death, on others rather than self, saves his life. Yet there is much growing evidence that acts of giving, acts of loving and states of compassion cause us to vibrate with a different, more vital, energy. Perhaps this is enough in itself to bring us longer life.

Influencing

Influencing the environment depends on the combination of right attitudes, right values and right actions. Here is a WIN for the little monk, a WIN for the ants and the Master, and a WIN for the ecology of the system as a whole.

Motivating

The story is more likely to resonate with the *sacrificial* systems, the ones that focus on adapting the self to the values of the community.

PURPLE:
benevolent spirits will reward acts of kindness and compassion; karma; there is a fine line between the human world and the world of nature.

BLUE:
right ways of being and behaving will be rewarded.

GREEN:
compassion, harmony, the spirit of sacrifice and the sharing of resources realign healing energies; GREEN sometimes manifests PURPLE-like New Age attitudes.

My insights

- There is something magic about random acts of kindness, where a person gives without any particular reason, and without any expectation of reward.
- The Old Master thought the boy would die, but no one had passed the message on to him. Perhaps he just had no plans to die. He was so full of life, and making life possible for others, that perhaps he just didn't notice that death was an option.

* * *

"Possibly. Now please notice, Young Master, how the desire for survival is deep-rooted and hard-wired in every mind. Every crisis an individual faces is an opportunity to connect with their personal genius. In moments of crisis there is often little time to think. And it is this absence of time in which to suppress our genius that allows it to emerge. Learn, Young Master, to let your genius express itself freely, for it is always there for you, as it is in every living being, and waiting for its opportunity to show what it can do.

"Our coordinates are set. Italy, by the sea, in the mid-twentieth century."

Story 43

The Counterintuitive Route

A nine-year-old boy was floating in a leisurely fashion on his back in the Mediterranean Sea five metres or so from the shore. It was a typical scorching sunny day and the sea was flat-calm. He was enjoying the sense of support the water gave him, and thinking of not very much at all, just wrapping the coolness of the water around him in the heat of the afternoon sun.

Whatever made him glance around, he could not afterwards recall. Perhaps the pull of moving water, perhaps a sea bird's call of alarm, perhaps a sixth sense. Bearing down on him high and fast was a huge wave, perhaps four metres from tip to trough. It towered above him. Without hesitating, he swam towards it, into it and through it. He felt its pull, sucking him back towards the shore, but, swimming with all his nine-year-old strength and determination, he managed to emerge on the other side, his lungs heaving, his heart racing and adrenalin pumping through his small frame.

Another wave of the same size bore down on him. Summoning his strength and purpose he plunged once again through the base of the wave and emerged, gasping, the other side. A third huge wave was almost upon him, and with the last of his energy he disappeared into it.

It seemed to go on for ever, the sensation of being sucked backwards towards the beach, of being crushed by the force, and being caught up and rolled over disoriented and directionless in the backwash, and yet he managed to emerge once again. And this time the sea was calm again, as if the three mighty waves had never been.

No one really knew where those waves came from – perhaps an underwater earth tremor, perhaps the wake of a huge ship – but three people drowned on the beach that day. Where did that moment of genius come from that told a nine-year-old boy that sometimes it is better to swim towards danger, that often safety lies in the counterintuitive route?

* * *

Leadership

Every organism is programmed for survival, and in a sense every organism is pure intelligence. For we humans, it is often our self-talk that gets in the way. In this case, the young boy had no time to think, only to act. There was no time for negative interference to stem the flow of genius. Once the choice is made to commit fully to the course of action, every element of mind, brain and body is activated to achieve a successful result.

Influencing

The message here is that each one of us is always much more capable of achieving success than we think we are. But we have to trust our instinct, and our natural genius, as much as rational thinking.

Motivating

I didn't expect to use this, but I guess this is one story that deserves a BEIGE survival system flag.

BEIGE:
do whatever it takes to survive; outthink the natural forces in order to overcome them; to catch a fish, think like a fish.

My insights

- Do not be afraid to swim towards danger: it can be the safest route.
- Commit 100 per cent of yourself to every important decision.
- Genius resides in everybody; most people invest a lot of energy suppressing it.
- What could you do if you knew you couldn't fail?
- When you think about it, how many moments of genius can you recall having in your life?

* * *

"Possibly. Now consider, there resides in all of us, even in us old carpets, a real passion to survive – a real will and intention to survive. It's important to look at the other side of the coin, however, under the rug so to speak, to realise that sometimes we will have the time to think things through rationally and logically, and we will need to do so without panic or fear. While it is true that many important things cannot be fully explained, counterintuitiveness often has its foundation in things that can be understood. What is needed in these cases is knowledge.

"Lack of knowledge, or failure to think things through carefully, can lead to failure or tragedy, as our next story, from a swollen River Thames, illustrates."

Story 44

Go with the Flow

On a freezing winter's day, a man in a small dinghy underestimated the power of the river's current. His boat smashed on the stanchions of the jetty and he was carried over the weir. He bobbed up in that part just below the weir where the water seems flat and calm. And he tried to swim away from the weir, downriver and towards safety. But, hard though he tried to escape, the water pushed him back, trapping him in that flat, calm space. He couldn't perceive, in his panic, that the water that rushed over the weir, flowed below him on the river's bed, was soon forced upwards again by the mass of water downstream, and then flowed back towards the weir in a circular movement that totally trapped him. He was fighting against the current in a battle he could never win.

The water was icy. Soon the man's efforts flagged, and panic, despair and hypothermia took him. He went under for the last time. And in less than twenty seconds his body bobbed up downstream completely free from the maelstrom in which he'd been trapped.

Had he gone with the flow, had he acted systemically – though counterintuitively – and dived down to the bottom instead of towards the resurging current, he would have discovered safe passage. If you push against a system, the system will push back just as hard.

* * *

Leadership

 The swimmer's behaviours are contrary to the complex but natural flow of the water. To operate within any system, whether simple or complex, artificial or natural, it is more useful and efficient to understand how the system works, and work with it rather than against it. This is as true for patterns of water flow in a weir as it is for the valuing and thinking systems that we have been exploring throughout our journey.

Influencing

The etymology of the word "influence" is from the Latin *influere* – [*in* + *fluere*] *to flow in*. That is exactly what influence is: the ability to flow naturally and without resistance alongside another's preferences, values and beliefs. It doesn't mean you have to agree with them, but you can choose to respect and validate them wherever it is appropriate. The hard reality of the story illustrates the dangers of trying to force issues rather than work elegantly within the prevailing system, whether natural, social, cultural, political or technical.

Outcome: escape from the icy water.

Awareness: my current strategy is not working.

Flexibility: consider how water flows and behave appropriately.

Motivating

The drama of the story, and the potential learning from it, will appeal to all systems. But it will appeal particularly to:

YELLOW:
systems thinking, competence, knowledge, thinking and working elegantly and economically by modelling the patterns of natural design.

My insights

- Go with the flow.
- Drama and tragedy are powerful learning contexts.
- Practise appropriate thinking and behaviour in relationships and environments.
- Influence is about understanding and accepting *what is*, and working *with* forces rather than against them.
- A martial artist's graceful use of an opponent's energy against himself is a more useful metaphor for influence than, say, boxing.
- What you resist persists.
- The most elegant way to change a system is to understand it and work from inside it.

* * *

"Possibly. So think of this. In every enterprise of any importance it is necessary to know the environment in which you will be operating and the behaviours, value preferences and identities of everything in it. Not to do so is to court disaster. It would be like failing to knot the threads of a carpet sufficiently. Know your territory, or your enterprise can easily begin to unravel."

"And I guess it's also important", added the Young Magician, "to know about your competition, local conditions and the presence of predators."

"So let's revisit India to reinforce these points, but with a little more lightness than in the previous story."

Story 45a

Good Enough

The delegates at the World Business Leadership Conference were having a day off. Many of them had taken the safari option and were photographing animals in the reserve. Two had wandered off together, away from the group and the tour guide, to get a more authentic experience. Soon they found themselves eyeball to eyeball with a tiger.

The tiger licked his lips, grunted and smiled. The men realised they were stranded – the jeep was a couple of hundred metres away. One of the men took off his rucksack, dropped his camera, kicked off his heavy boots and got ready to run.

"Are you crazy?" hissed the other. "You can't run faster than a tiger."

"I don't have to," he whispered back. "I only have to run faster than you."

Various sources

* * *

Story 45b

Not Good Enough

The delegates at the World Business Leadership Conference were having a day off. Many of them had taken the snorkelling option and were pursuing brightly coloured fish around the reefs. Two had swum off together, away from the group and the tour guide, to get a more authentic experience. Soon they found themselves eyeball to eyeball with a tiger shark.

The tiger shark looked at them with curiosity. The men realised they were stranded – the boat was fifty metres away. One of the men, a strong swimmer, took off his mask and snorkel, dropped his underwater camera and struck out strongly for the boat, leaving the other stranded.

The shark flashed past the stranded snorkeller and made short work of the swimmer.

* * *

Leading

While it is necessary to know the environment and current conditions in which you are operating, it isn't always necessary to be the "best" or seek out the "perfect solution". Most of the time in business and in life the best is the enemy of the "good enough". To succeed in most walks of life you need to be only as good as, or a little better than, the "opposition". Not only is the search for perfection time-consuming and wasteful of resources: the chances are that, once you've found "perfection", time and circumstances have already moved on and your perfect solution has become an irrelevant solution.

However, this doesn't preclude knowing something about the environment and conditions in which you are operating, as the second story illustrates. Sharks are attracted to meals that move horizontally in the water and that exhibit signs of thrashing about. The snorkeller who stayed where he was remained still and quiet, and held his body vertically. Smart move! He got back to the boat.

Influencing

Outcome: survive in a dangerous climate.

Awareness: there are dangers out there.

Flexibility: know how to deal with local conditions by studying the environment and it's inhabitants; generate a range of options.

Motivating

The two stories may provoke the following reactions from the valuing and thinking systems:

PURPLE: in a world full of danger, how strange that intelligent people should expose themselves to such risk.

RED: will savour the juice of danger, the vitality of the moment and the egotistic desire to survive at another's expense in a dog-eat-dog world.

BLUE: may consider implementing rules to prevent people wandering away from the official pathways.

ORANGE: will recognise and appreciate the importance of operating more efficiently than others at the cutting edge in a fiercely competitive environment.

GREEN: will be shocked at the desire of some individuals to put themselves and their interests before the needs of others.

YELLOW: if the habitat is understood, we'll begin to appreciate how it works and how we can best work ecologically with and within it.

My insights

• The good enough is often good enough.
• Know your enemy.

- Take time to learn about the environment you swim in.
- What's the "shark" in your life?
- What unnecessary baggage are you carrying?

* * *

"Possibly.

"The ability to work within the natural patterns of others is a critical skill for anyone who wishes to be an effective and inspiring leader. Understand the habitat, recognise, validate and support the beliefs and value preferences with appropriate behaviours, and remain connected to your own personal integrity. These are the essential components of integral leadership."

"Can you show me an example to illuminate this?" asked the Young Magician. "Surely, if we can switch people on to this way of thinking, it will bring light where currently there is a lot of fog."

"Young Master, hold very tight. Our next stop is Brighton."

Story 46

Resistance

An electrician who lacked confidence went to a life coach for help. He wondered why other electricians did better than he did. He wondered why many of his classmates at school and college had more successful careers and lives than he had. He blamed the world for not giving him opportunities, and he supposed he didn't get opportunities because he didn't deserve them.

The coach asked, "What stops you noticing all the opportunities that exist around you?"

He replied, "Fear of failure."

"So what would you like instead?"

"Confidence."

"So what stops you feeling confident?"

"Fear of failure."

"And what would you like instead?"

"Confidence."

"Notice," said the coach, "how this loop in your thinking is creating your stuckness. Now may I ask you a question as an expert in what I do, to a man who is an expert with electricity?"

"Sure."

"First of all, I really need to know from you, do you really want to shine? Will you be OK with that? Can you fully commit to this switch? Or perhaps you really do prefer to live a life safe and protected, like a man in a darkened room?"

"Yes, I want to change. I want the confidence to make changes."

"On a scale of one to ten, how much do you want that?"

"Ten."

"Sure?"

"Absolutely sure."

"OK. So imagine a wooden board into which are screwed three light-bulb sockets. Each socket is connected to a common cable that is plugged into the mains. In the first socket is a ten-watt bulb; in the second is a hundred-watt bulb; and in the third a thousand-watt bulb. Switch on. Now what's the difference?"

"The first bulb glows the dimmest; the third bulb glows the brightest."

"Now considering that the same two-hundred-and-forty-volt energy cable brings equal power to each socket, how do you explain the difference in output between the three sockets?"

"Resistance."

The coach remained silent. Slowly a glimmer of recognition glowed in the electrician's expression, and then a huge smile spread across his face and illuminated his eyes. The coach looked at him with a quizzical brow. "Well?"

"Now I have an answer to your question about what's stopping me," he grinned. *The short answer is 'no one but me'. My life is like the ten-watt bulb. It's me who's* resisting *opportunity."*

"Yes, it used to be like that. And now?"

"And now it can change. First I'll plug in a hundred-watt version, then I'll go for a progressive upgrade."

"So before you generate some strategies for success, just remind your-self that life, like electricity, consists of pure energy. This same energy – or call it life force or spirit if you prefer – flows through all of us equally.

There is no end to this supply, and only you can cut this supply off through your own resistance.

"And now that you've stopped blaming the external world for your situation, and have accepted full responsibility for yourself and your actions, you can plug into the abundance, wholeness, beauty and completeness of the universe. It flows within us, and through us, every moment of every day."

* * *

Leading

 Top-quality coaches and therapists frequently use metaphor to generate change in their clients. Metaphor is a powerful and effective leadership tool because it works naturally within the habitat of the listeners and allows space for them to take ownership of the meaning of the message and *lead themselves* to the desired result. Once the electrician understands how the metaphor's message connects to his reality, a reality in which he is an expert, he can confidently repair the short circuits, change his behaviours, adjust his values and naturally deepen his personal consciousness and awareness.

Influencing

Matching the reality, values, and language of the people with whom we communicate is unbelievably powerful. When the coach matches the world of the electrician through the metaphor of power, light and resistance, change can be quick, easy and elegant. Now that's what I call a transformer at work! This is a real WIN–WIN–WIN!

Motivating

The following valuing and thinking systems will engage with this story:

RED:
will appreciate the creativity of the coach, and the new opportunities the electrician has to be more assertive.

BLUE:
provided the coach has the required qualifications, BLUE will appreciate a master at work.

ORANGE:
will note the elegance and efficiency of the strategy:"Could I use this strategy among all my other tools and techniques to get more of what I want more easily?"

GREEN:
will appreciate the new opportunities for growth and development, and the nonconfrontational methods of the coach.

YELLOW:
will approve of the elegance of the metaphor, and the systemic, integrative approach that works within the natural patterns and designs of both the electrician and of electricity.

My insights

- If you take the time to find a person's "buying pattern", you will never need to sell to them.
- All behaviours and all valuing and belief systems are patterned. Work naturally within these patterns for effective results.

* * *

"Possibly. Are you aware, Young Master, that the word 'therapy', from the Greek *therapeia*, means healing. Healing can take many forms: physical, mental, social, cultural, psychological and so on. The etymology of the verb 'to heal' derives from the old English word *haelan*, which also means 'to make whole'. And that is the job, ultimately, of all great leaders: to create a wholeness, an integrity, within the community over which they exercise their influence.

"We are travelling to the USA for our next story. You'll watch a master at work, one of the most influential therapists of the twentieth century, and a natural leader in his field. We met him earlier as a child on horseback in Story 17. Are you ready?"

Story 47

Drying Out

A man went to a therapist. He said, "I'm an alcoholic. It runs in the family. My parents were alcoholics, and their parents before them were alcoholics. My wife's an alcoholic, and her parents were alcoholics, too. I've had the DTs eleven times. I'm up to here with being an alcoholic. What can you do about it?"

The therapist asked what his job was. "I'm a journalist. It's an occupational hazard."

"Fine," said the therapist. "Now here's what I suggest. And maybe it'll seem a little strange, but this is what I want you to do. Go to the botanical gardens, and look at all the cacti there. Look at all of them, every single one of them. And just marvel at these cacti that can survive three years without water, without rain. And do a lot of thinking."

Primary source: Sidney Rosen, *My Voice Will Go With You: The Teaching Tales of Milton H. Erickson*, Norton (adapted by kind permission of Sidney Rosen) Secondary source: Milton H. Erickson

* * *

Leading

Just as in the previous story of the electrician, this story works through indirect suggestion applied metaphorically. The therapist asks the journalist, who clearly is an intelligent man curious about events and conditions in the outside world, to consider a phenomenon from the world of nature. The situation of the cacti exactly mirrors the change the journalist desires to make. The therapist creates a link in the journalist's mind between two habitats – his own and the desired one. He leaves space for the journalist to connect to his inner core and inner values, change his behaviours and make the change he wants.

Influencing

The use of a naturally designed system is an excellent "convincer" for an intelligent man. He can work out the connection for himself. Additionally, the therapist doesn't put pressure on the man: he simply tells him to go away and think very hard. This may not be the best strategy for everyone but it works with the journalist, it fits his value patterns.

Motivating

The story has resonance for all the systems:

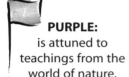

PURPLE:
is attuned to
teachings from the
world of nature.

RED:
may appreciate that the
therapist gives space
for the journalist to
decide for himself.

BLUE:
will respect the
therapist's authority,
especially the letters
MD after his name.

ORANGE:
will appreciate the
one best way
among many
possible ways.

GREEN:
will respond to the
ecological angle and
the absence of
directiveness or blame.

YELLOW:
will find the
approach delightfully
functional and
fit for purpose

My insights

- We can learn much from nature and natural systems.
- Change can be so easy when it fits the way a person or a group naturally is.
- Show a person a path and they can usually find their own way.

* * *

"Possibly."

"Al Sayyid, do you know how this story ended? Was the journalist successful?"

"Take a look inside my secret library. You'll find a book. Scan it and you'll find the answers you seek."

The Young Magician extracted a paperback volume. It was entitled: *My Voice Will Go With You: The Teaching Tales of Milton H. Erickson* (edited by Sidney Rosen).

He scanned it quickly for the information he was seeking, and then his magic pencil wrote the following notes:

- Milton H. Erickson MD was a brilliant hypnotherapist.
- Many of his techniques and methods were central to the formation and development of Neuro-Linguistic Programming (NLP).
- Erickson frequently stressed the importance of understanding what kind of person one is dealing with. And then dealing with the person in a way that *naturally fits* his or her unique problem.

The end of the story

Many years later, a woman came to see Erickson and said, "You knew me when I was three years old, and I came to see what kind of man you are."

When Erickson expressed curiosity, she continued, "Anyone who would send an alcoholic to the botanical gardens to learn how to survive without alcohol *and succeed* is the kind of man I want to take a good look at. My father and my mother haven't touched a drop of alcohol since that day."

"So now you know," said Al Sayyid. "Curiosity satisfied?"

The Young Magician nodded. And then continued, "So what's the next link? How do you propose to naturally weave together the next threads of our adventure?"

"I think a story about teaching and learning will be in order. All great leaders are teachers and coaches of others. And they are also learners, and constantly seek to improve the quality of their environments as learning organisations.

"Let's head for Denmark, in the early twentieth century. I think you'll enjoy this story."

"One moment, Al Sayyid. Are you not forgetting something?"

"And what would that be, Young Master?"

"It's time for another sixth story."

"In that case, Denmark can wait a little while. Instead, I shall give you something to think deeply about from the land of my birth. Prepare yourself for a Sufi teaching tale to chew on. Hold tight while we wind the clock back several centuries."

Story 48

Three Sheep

Three sheep were grazing in a field. One sheep said to another, "Now I know what true freedom is."

The second sheep raised an enquiring eyebrow. "What is it?"

"I can munch or I can bite."

The third sheep took six months to work out a meaning.

Primary source: Sandra Maitri
General source: Sufi tradition

* * *

The Young Magician was pensive as he thought about this story. He remained quiet for several minutes. Al Sayyid did not interrupt.

Finally, he said, "I don't have a clue what this means, either. I have every sympathy with the third sheep."

Al Sayyid remained silent for a moment or two. "I do not much care to overinterpret stories. As well you know, they mean whatever they mean to the listener, and mean different things in different contexts, just as a well-woven rug can be used for many functions in many different environments.

"However, your task is one of exploration and in this context it is appropriate to tease out some underlying possibilities of meaning, some hidden threads, some difficult knots, among all the others that may also exist. Speaking as a carpet, I might venture that one possible thread is that the freedom to choose is the only real gift that humankind possesses. But that is just my own view."

"Is it OK not to know and just think about it for a while?"

"Certainly, Young Master. Not knowing is perfectly acceptable. In fact, unless you leave inner space in your heart and mind for not knowing, you will never learn anything new. Not knowing is an essential step towards fulfilling your potential through the nurturing of curiosity."

My tentative insights

- A story that disturbs and confuses gets attention.
- Disturbance and confusion stimulate the brain and the natural desire to make connections between things.
- Disturbance and confusion resonate in the unconscious mind – I can't stop thinking about this story.
- Even if it takes me six months, too, I'm going to make some sense of it.

* * *

"Possibly.

"Now are you ready for that educational trip to Denmark?"

"Anything to give my brain some peace. Let's go."

Story 49

Peda-Stodgy

During the early years of the twentieth century the following question appeared in a physics-degree final examination paper at the University of Copenhagen: "Describe how to determine the height of a tall building with a barometer."

One student wrote,

> *You tie a long piece of string to the neck of a barometer, then carefully lower the barometer from the top of the tall building to the ground. The length of the string added to the length of barometer equals the height of the building.*

This short answer so angered the examiner that the student was summarily failed. The student appealed on the basis that his answer was indisputably correct and that it fully satisfied the information required in the question. The university appointed an independent external examiner to decide the case.

The independent professor ruled that the answer was indeed correct but did not demonstrate any discernible knowledge of the science of physics. He therefore ruled that the student should be required to attend a viva and allowed a six-minute period of time in which to offer an oral answer that should offer at least a modicum of familiarity with the laws and principles of physics.

The student was duly summoned and the question put to him again with the professor's required stipulations. For five minutes he sat in complete silence, his brow creased in thought, his eyes darting in different directions. The external examiner tapped his timepiece and reminded him that time was getting short. The student replied that he had a number of apposite answers and was trying to decide which one to use. On being told by the professor that he would be the judge of what was apposite or not, the student was advised to share his thinking promptly, to which he responded, "First, you could carry the barometer to the roof of the high building, drop it over the edge and measure the time it takes to reach the ground. The height of the building can be gauged using the formula H = 0.5g × t squared. Tough luck on the barometer, though.

"Another possibility – provided the sun is shining – would be to measure the length of the barometer, set it on its end, and measure the length of its shadow. Next, you measure the length of the tall building's shadow and then it is just a straightforward matter of proportional arithmetic to calculate the height of the building.

"A highly practical, but more time-consuming method, would be – provided the building had an outside staircase – to walk up it and mark off the height of the building in barometer lengths, then add them up.

"If you wished to use a highly complex scientific procedure, you could tie a short length of string around the neck of the barometer and swing it like a pendulum. Do this first at ground level, then at the top of the high building. The height can be calculated by the difference in the gravitational restoring force $T = 2\pi \sqrt{1/g}$.

"However, if you simply wanted to be boring and orthodox about it, you could of course just use the barometer to measure the air pressure on the roof of the building and on the ground, and convert the difference in millibars into centimetres to give the height of the building.

"But, as we are constantly being exhorted by our professors to exercise independence of mind, and to apply scientific methods the quickest, best and most elegant strategy would be to knock on the caretaker's door and say to him, 'If you would like a nice new barometer, then I'll give you this one if you tell me the height of your building.'"

The student was Niels Bohr, later to win the Nobel Prize for Physics in 1922.

Original source unknown

* * *

Leading

There are two strands to this story. The first concerns a combination of academic arrogance and linguistic vagueness. Bohr's examiner is guilty of both. He has fooled himself into thinking that his "authority" gives him ownership of interpretation. And he petulantly expresses hostility and outrage when his worldview is challenged. This is no way to demonstrate leadership.

By contrast, Niels Bohr in the story's second strand remains personally composed in the face of mediocrity and censure. Bohr demonstrates leadership qualities by having the courage to take on the establishment. As George Bernard Shaw has said, "All progress depends upon unreasonable people." But Bohr's ability to succeed in this is because of his familiarity with, and mastery of, the science of physics, his ability to demonstrate this in his behaviours at the viva and his commitment to the true values of scientific rigour, independence and experimentation.

Influencing

In some ways, Bohr's behaviour is somewhat – dare I say it? – boorish. Nevertheless, he influences his second examiner as well as the readers and listeners through the depth of his knowledge and the passion of his challenge to a self-regarding and mediocre system.

Motivating

The story may connect with the following valuing and thinking systems:

RED:
will enjoy Bohr's head-on assertive attack on the establishment; and his remarkable creativity and improvisational skills.

BLUE:
will be shocked at Bohr's temerity in taking on the establishment.

ORANGE:
highly approves of the successful and pragmatic application of knowledge, and will also applaud the successful demolition of mediocrity among the establishment.

GREEN:
may appreciate the attack on
privilege and divisive
educational hierarchies –
universities should be equally
available to all.

YELLOW:
may question the elegance of Bohr's
methods but applaud his expertise
and his desire for systemic reform,
independence of mind and
transparent scientific enquiry.

My insights

- Language is an imprecise tool; if you want to be precise, take great care.
- Authority can breed arrogance.
- Institutions can breed complacency.
- Avoid saying things unless you mean them and are willing to actively carry them out.
- It is easy to dismiss talent if you are not actively looking for it.
- YELLOW thinkers can easily be mistaken for RED thinkers.
- YELLOW thinkers have little fear.
- 4 = ? is a better question than 2 + 2 = ? because students can offer a wide variety of possible correct answers depending on their creativity and depth of knowledge of mathematics.
- Methodology matters.

* * *

"Possibly."

"It strikes me," said the Young Magician, "that one of the key roles of a teacher or professor, just as with other leaders, is to hold a space in which others can contribute and engage to the best of their ability and to the fullness of their potential. This means that, although the leader may be wise and knowledgeable, it is neither wise nor necessary to lead twenty-four hours a day. If the leader leads too much, he or she will create dependency and its counterparts, lack of personal responsibility and lack of independence."

"Well said, Young Master. And in such cases, especially when creativity is suppressed, or when personal exploration and mistake making are curtailed, watch out for sabotage and resistance. Revel in this story from Norman times."

Story 50

In Your Hands

Once upon a time there was a mother. She was a very good and conscientious mother and she did her very best to look after her two little boys and feed them, clothe them, clean them and answer all their many questions.

Perhaps you're wondering what happened to the father. Unfortunately, nobody told the storyteller what became of him. He just isn't part of this story.

Anyway, as the boys grew older and got bigger they became more and more difficult to handle. They were boisterous and demanding, as was quite natural, and above all they had many questions. As they got older and more streetwise they asked more and more difficult questions.

The mother did her best to answer them all with suitable explanations, but the time inevitably came when she realised that she didn't know all the answers. So she decided to send them, because that's what people did in those days, to the Wise One Who Lives on the Hill.

So on the appointed day, clutching her tearstained handkerchief, she sadly waved goodbye to her two little ones as they set off, clutching their tear-stained little hankies, hand in hand with the Wise One Who Lives on the Hill. Of course, she wasn't too sad because she knew they'd come back for their half-term holidays.

Anyway, things went very well for the boys and the Wise One Who Lives on the Hill. The boys had many detailed and intricate questions and they were impressed and fascinated by the answers the Wise One gave them.

But as time passed they began to become a little irritated by the apparent omniscience of their mentor. They became frustrated as they began to feel that there was no space for them to think, to question, to predict or hypothesise answers. Or even to learn through honest "misteak"-making.

So they decided to hatch a plot. They racked their brains for many weeks searching for a foolproof way to undermine and challenge the Wise One's wisdom. They rejected many possibilities and they learned many things in the process. As they did so a strong bond of friendship as well as brotherhood formed between them.

Finally, an idea formed in the mind of the elder little boy. He said to his younger brother, "Listen, I've got an idea. Why don't we catch a little bird? I'll hold it carefully inside my hands so no one can see it. Then we'll go to the Wise One Who Lives on the Hill and say, 'O Wise One, tell us, tell us, tell us do, is the little bird in my hands alive or is it dead?'

"And if the Wise One says, 'It's dead', I'll open my hands and let it fly away. And if the Wise One says, 'It's alive', I'll just squish it to death like this!" he said pushing his palms together sharply.

The boys were so excited. They made a trap to catch a little bird and waited patiently for days until their little bird was caught. And then, with barely concealed enthusiasm and excitement, they went to find the Wise One.

The elder boy said to the Wise One, "O Wise One, tell us, tell us, tell us do, is the little bird in my hands alive or is it dead?"

The Wise One looked deep into their eyes for a long time before speaking.

Finally, he replied, weighing his words with great care and compassion, "The answer to your question, my young friends, lies entirely ... entirely ... in your own hands."

Primary source: Jane Revell and Susan Norman,
***In Your Hands*, Saffire Press**

* * *

Leading

 This story questions the nature of learning and the relationship between teacher and student. To be sure, the teacher is skilful, wise and knowledgeable, and the boys are clearly impressed by that. But they feel they have no space to discover things for themselves, to test things out and make mistakes, to connect with and develop their inner identity. The teacher's values and methodology are in conflict with those of the boys. So they begin to feel impotent and frustrated. This is the result of poor leadership.

On the other hand, it could be argued that the Wise One is deliberately taking the boys on a journey through their different stages of development, and offering them different kinds of methodology. The Wise One creates a situation and an environment in which the boys are eventually "forced" to take control of their lives and to challenge authority. It is a key part of their learning process as they grow towards maturity and the levels of personal responsibility that are required.

Influencing

Frustration leads the boys to make mischief, to scheme and ultimately play God with the life or death of a little bird. So, while the teacher may be at fault initially, it is the boys who go too far at the end. And, while the boys are well behaved, courteous and respectful at the beginning, it is the Wise One who is well behaved, courteous and respectful at the end.

Outcome: Assist the boys to fulfil their potential.

Awareness: I am not giving them enough space. I have some responsibility for their scheming.

Flexibility: Change my methodology. Give them space to work it out for themselves. What is the one statement I can make that will reconnect them with their inner sensitivity and personal values?

Rapport: Match their values, give them space to explore, discover and take personal responsibility.

Motivating

The story may resonate with these thinking and valuing systems:

 PURPLE:
the family bond is strong; the teacher is paternalistic.

 RED:
will recognise the boys' creative desire to push boundaries, to challenge authority and to test to the limits.

 BLUE:
will respond well to the Wise One's teacher-centred approach; may also wonder whether the Wise One is strict enough.

ORANGE:
will empathise with the boys' impatience with the Wise One; but will approve of the ending, which shifts the boys towards personal responsibility and future planning.

GREEN:
may perceive a welcome shift in the Wise One's methodology from Teacher to Facilitator.

YELLOW:
may discern in the story a journey through appropriate methodologies for each of the systems.

Methodology

PURPLE, RED and BLUE require more teacher-centred methodologies.

ORANGE requires a mix of teacher- and learner-centred methodologies.

GREEN requires a learner-centred, humanistic methodology.

YELLOW requires autonomous learning.

Teaching style

PURPLE responds to a paternalistic teacher.

RED responds to a respected 'boss' who offers tough love.

BLUE responds to someone who is a qualified authority.

ORANGE responds to a well-briefed, worldly-wise colleague.

GREEN responds to a sensitive facilitator.

YELLOW responds to a collaborative consultant.

My insights

- A wise teacher adapts her style to suit the needs of the learners.
- Learners change their needs and styles as they develop and mature.
- If the learners can't learn in the way the teacher teaches, the teacher needs to learn to teach in the way the learner learns.
- Integral education is concerned as much with personal and social values, and inner personal development, as it is with skills and behaviours and the development of measurable capacities.
- There is an imbalance in most education systems favouring the right-hand boxes over the left-hand ones.
- Left-hand boxes are harder to measure but essential for individual and social health, maturity and consciousness.

* * *

"Possibly."

"It is becoming very clear to me," said the Young Magician, "that there are many kinds of leadership, all of which are appropriate according to whether they fit the purpose of a situation, environment or relationship. In some ways it is the art of making a difference, of holding a space in which others can make the changes they need. In others it is about taking initiative, through being fearless, or being creative and thinking in innovative ways. Sometimes it is important to go with the flow; other times it may be necessary to swim against the current.

"Above all, it is about making the right contribution, knowing the one thing that will make the most useful difference in any given situation."

"And this can be done by anybody, any time," interwove Al Sayyid. "Leadership has nothing to do with power, and everything to do with a balance and harmony between the wefts and warps of the inner and outer worlds. Give your sunglasses a clean – we're off to the Black Country."

Story 51

The Difference that Makes the Difference

As she stood in front of her fifth-year primary class on the first day of the school year, Mrs Evans uttered the usual platitude. She told her students that she liked them all equally and would treat them all the same. But that was going to be really hard because sitting in the back row, sprawled over his desk, was Sam Stone.

Mrs Evans had noticed Sam's progress throughout the previous year. She noticed that he did not mix easily with other children, rarely played with them, that his clothes were dirty, his hair unkempt, and he sometimes smelled less than fresh. He had a bit of a mean streak, too.

Things got to a point where Mrs Evans actually began to take a certain amount of vengeful pleasure in taking out her red chisel-tipped pen and writing big fat Fs at the top of his work.

It was a requirement at this school for teachers to review each child's past records. Mrs Evans put reading Sam's records off till last. When she finally got round to it, she gasped with a mingling sense of shame and shock.

Sam's first-year teacher had written, "Sam is a bright child with an engaging personality and a ready laugh. He is well mannered and works neatly and with concentration. He's good to have around."

His second-year teacher had written, "Sam is a very good student, and well liked by his classmates. However, he is troubled because his mother has a terminal illness, and life at home must be a struggle."

His third-year teacher had written, "His mother's death has hit him hard. He tries to do his best, but his father shows little interest, and his home situation is likely to affect him if steps aren't taken."

His fourth-year teacher had written, "Sam is withdrawn, passive and shows little interest in school. He has few friends and frequently sleeps in class."

Mrs Evans felt a sense of real shame. And when Christmas came and her students all brought her presents, neatly wrapped with ribbons and bows, she made a real effort to look especially pleased with Sam's gift. It was clumsily wrapped in creased, brown paper and he took it out of a plastic, supermarket bag.

When Mrs Evans unwrapped it, some of the other children started laughing and giggling. She found inside the parcel an imitation diamond bracelet, with some of the stones missing, and a bottle of perfume that was less than half full. But she silenced the children's laughter when she remarked on how pretty the bracelet was, and slipped it over her wrist. Then she dabbed some perfume on her neck. Sam Stone stayed after school that day just long enough to say, "Thank you, Mrs Evans, today you smelled just like my Mum used to." After all the children had left, Mrs Evans sat down at her desk and cried. She cried for quite a long time, and she cried for many reasons.

*She made a few resolutions while she was crying. And, when she'd finished crying, she quit teaching reading, writing and arithmetic. She began teaching **children** instead. She paid particular attention to Sam, and as she began to work closely with him he began to change. The more encouragement she gave him, the more he responded. His mind snapped out of its torpor and once again became quick and alive. By the end of the school year, Sam had achieved among the highest marks in the class. And Mrs Evans was very proud of him indeed.*

A year later, she found a note on her desk. It was from Sam saying she was the best teacher he'd ever had in his life – and thank you.

Seven years passed before she heard from Sam again. He wrote to say he'd finished secondary school, scored well enough in his exams to win a university place, and that she was still the best teacher he'd ever had.

Three years later, she got another letter. Sam said that things had been tough financially, but he'd seen it through, worked his way through college and was about to graduate with a first-class degree. And, by the way, she was still his best teacher ever.

Four more years elapsed, before Sam contacted her again. He explained that he'd decided to continue his studies after his first degree. She was still his favourite teacher, and, by the way, his name had grown a little longer. The letter was signed: Dr Samuel J. Stone, MA, PhD.

But that's not the end of the story. In the spring another letter arrived. Sam wrote that he'd met a girl and they were going to be married. He said his father had died a few years back, and he was wondering whether Mrs Evans would be willing to sit at the wedding in the place usually reserved for the mother of the groom.

And that's exactly what happened. And Mrs Evans wore that same imitation-diamond bracelet, with some of the stones missing, and she made sure she was wearing the same perfume that Sam remembered his mother wearing the last Christmas they were together.

After the ceremony, they hugged each other and Dr Stone whispered in Mrs Evan's ear, "Thank you so, so much for believing in me. Thank you for making feel I was worth something, and that I could make a difference."

"Oh, no, Sam" she replied, "you have it so, so wrong. You were the one who taught me. It was you who taught me that I could make a difference. I didn't know how to teach until I met you."

Primary source: Mark Hawkswell
Original source unknown

* * *

Leading

At the outset of the story, Mrs Evans is a teacher who operates in the two right-hand boxes. Her focus is on capacities, behaviours, skills and resources. In the course of the story she learns to develop and integrate her left-hand boxes – personal integrity and a sensitive awareness of, and respect for, others – into her professional life. As she does so, she evolves into a far more effective teacher and leader.

Influencing

Initially, Mrs Evans sees only Sam's antisocial behaviour and responds negatively to it. Not until she reads the notes does she begin to understand its systemic causes. Knowledge is an essential resource for leaders of all kinds, and once underlying causation is grasped useful action can be taken. Mrs Evans creates a space and structure in which Sam can begin to connect with his inner resources. Mrs Evans creates an environment in which Sam can contribute and thrive. As she does so, she no doubt begins to influence her other students and, above all, herself. A WIN for Sam is a WIN for her and a WIN for the whole system.

Motivating

The story connects with the all the valuing and thinking systems:

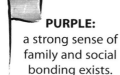

PURPLE:
a strong sense of family and social bonding exists.

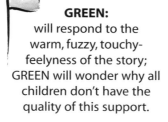

RED:
will recognise Sam's inner strength and sense of alienation, as well as the hostility of the system and its lack of understanding of his needs.

BLUE:
will applaud the quality of record keeping, as well as the basic goodness and decency of Mrs Evans, especially in recognising her own failings.

ORANGE:
will recognise Mrs Evans's sponsorship of Sam to express himself and create the future he wants.

GREEN:
will respond to the warm, fuzzy, touchy-feelyness of the story; GREEN will wonder why all children don't have the quality of this support.

YELLOW:
will recognise Mrs Evans's capacity and potential for development as much as Sam's.

My insights

- Search below the surface.
- Look for the causes of things.
- Life is a learning programme – make sure you enrol in the course.

- The concept of learning does not exist in the word 'teacher'; teachers have to add it.
- The difference that makes the difference is often a very small one.
- A person has the right to be who he or she is.
- A thought: I wonder how many former employees phone up or write to their ex-managers to tell them how they are doing or what a great leadership job they did.
- What would happen if leaders created habitats and relationships where this was the norm?

* * *

"Possibly."

"Going the extra mile seems to be important," said the Young Traveller. "Mrs Evans didn't have to go to the lengths she did, but it made all the difference. Not only to Sam, but to Mrs Evans herself."

"Not only that," said, Al Sayyid, threading his own thoughts into the conversation, "who knows what differences Sam may make in the world with all his qualifications, skills, energy and personality?

"In the way that a weaver is rewarded the more he puts time and skill into his work, the more people are rewarded for the time, energy, kindness and other resources they put out into the world. Now, polish your sunglasses and pack your sunblock: we're going to the Caribbean.

Story 52

Random Acts of Kindness

The storm came in the night. The waves crashed, the wind howled and the palm trees creaked and cracked. As dawn broke the sea-salt smell of the ocean hung powerfully in the humid tropical air.

First light revealed the extent of the sea's destruction. The grey waters heaved and boiled, hissing and angry. Along the beach, trees lay cracked and broken, their fruit spilled across the sand.

And along the length of the beach, left high and dry on the sands, with no hope of return to the water, thousands of starfish awaited the unforgiving embrace of the tropical morning sun.

A tourist, taking an early-morning walk, picked her way over the broken trees and considered the imminent doom of the starfish. Without knowing quite how, her attention was drawn far up the beach. At the far end of the bay, she could barely make out a movement, nothing more than a disturbance of the early-morning heat shimmer: down, up and out to the sea.

The shimmer moved slowly in her direction and a pattern began to emerge: forward, stop, down, up and out to the sea.

After a while, colours became apparent through the early-morning haze: yellows, oranges, reds, browns, blacks. And then it took on human shape. A young boy with matted hair took form, wearing a ragged multi-coloured shirt, and carrying a net over his shoulder. And every so often he would stop, bend down, stand up and sway out in the direction of the sea.

Ah, now she began to see what he was doing. He was stopping, bending down, picking something up and throwing it out into the sea.

And as he finally drew close to her, she saw what it was. It was starfish he was throwing into the sea. Stop, bend down, pick up and with a lazy

243

curving swing of his arm he would throw another starfish far out into the ocean from where it had come.

"But what's the point?" she said to him. "What's the point? There are thousands of these starfish washed up on the beach. What possible difference can it make?"

The boy said nothing. A broad smile lit up his face. He bent down, picked up another one and in a long lazy arc sent it on its way back to the ocean floor.

He turned to the tourist and held her gaze for a moment.

"Made a difference to that one, ma'am."

And then he moved on.

It was then that she saw the sack on his back filled to the brim with starfish. "And what will you do with those?" she shouted after him.

"Ma'am," he replied, his eyes sparkling, "as me mother never stops sayin': take what the good Lord gives. These is goin' to be sold on me gran's market stall to tourists so's they can decorate they bathrooms back home."

"So why did you throw some back to the sea?"

The lad considered his answer for some moments. "To say thanks for the present." Then, as an afterthought, he added with a smile, "And also for the future."

Primary source: Peter McNab
Secondary source: There is a version of this in Canfield and Hansen, *Chicken Soup for the Soul*, HCI

* * *

Leading

 The boy works easily within different infrastructures. He pays attention to the economy of the sea, taking from it and giving back to it. He doesn't have to throw the starfish back but has an intuitive understanding of the systemic relationship between today and tomorrow. He pays attention, too, to the tourist economy and knows how to operate effortlessly within it. There is an economy and sense of pleasure in his life, similar to the Mexican fisherman in Story 35: "MBA" (see page 177).

Influencing

There is a symbiotic relationship between the boy, the starfish, the sea and the local economy. They all depend upon, and in turn influence, each other. It is not a highly developed economy, but it does appear to be appropriate and ecological. Whether the tourist and the new economy will influence this for better or worse is not discussed.

On a deeper, more metaphorical level, how many leaders can say they are so systemically attuned to their habitat, and the people and resources within it, as this lad is to his?

Motivating

The story touches on the following systems:

 PURPLE: will appreciate the boy's easy give-and-take relationship with natural systems and the forces of nature.

 RED: will respond to his independence and free spirit.

 BLUE: will wonder why he isn't in school and whether he has a licence for starfish collecting; BLUE will also appreciate the lad's good deeds and the provision he makes for the future.

 ORANGE: will look for more efficient ways to exploit local resources.

 GREEN: will appreciate the lad's ecological awareness, and his concern for his fellow creatures.

 YELLOW: will appreciate the balancing of systems within a natural habitat.

My insights

- Big differences are made by taking small first steps.
- Attend to small matters as well as big ones.
- Make a contribution, however small and seemingly insignificant, whenever and wherever you can.
- Random acts of kindness satisfy the giver, and surprise and delight the receiver.
- Reinvest for the future whenever possible.
- Take no more than you need.

* * *

"Possibly.

"Tell me, Young Master, what would a perfect carpet look like?"

"I have no idea."

"Because in one sense there is no such thing. Every carpet like myself has a deliberate mistake built into it for fear of offending the Creator, the Maker of All Things, who alone is perfect.

"And yet it is also possible to say that there is perfection in every living and nonliving thing if we are prepared to seek it out.

"Everyone and everything has the potential to make a contribution in its own way. The great leader searches for ways to discover this potential and let it express itself.

"The story you are soon to hear originates from Sri Lanka, but we are going to hear it told to a class of twelve-year-olds in a multi-cultural, multiracial school in a poor and underprivileged part of London. Hang on tight."

Story 53

The Cracked Pot

Once upon a time there was a person — and this person was a water carrier. She carried pots, two pots to be exact, across her shoulders, on a pole.

One of the pots had a crack in it. The other was perfect.

Every day the water carrier would make the long walk from the stream to her house in the village. By the time she reached her house the cracked pot was half empty, while the perfect pot was still full to the brim.

For many moons this same story continued: for every journey the water carrier made she would deliver a pot and a half of water.

Naturally, the perfect pot was proud of its accomplishments, fulfilling perfectly the function for which it had been made.

But the cracked pot was deeply ashamed of its imperfection, and felt its own failure deeply, achieving only half of what it had been made to do.

Eventually, the cracked pot could contain its shame no longer. One day by the stream it spoke to the water carrier.

"I am so sorry and ashamed. I have wanted to apologise to you for so long. You see, I am able to deliver only half my load to the house because of this crack in my side. And because of this imperfection much water leaks out and is wasted along the way. I feel so bad because you work so hard and you don't get full reward for all your effort."

But the water carrier smiled and gently said, "Have you not noticed how beautiful flowers grow in abundance on your side of the path, while on the other side there are none?

"You see, I have always known about your flaw. So I sowed seeds along your side of the path many moons ago, and every day, as we walked back together from the stream, you have watered them.

"And for all these months I have been able to pick these beautiful flowers to decorate our house and brighten our lives. Without your being just the way you are, there would not be this beauty in our world. Without your contribution, the world would be a far poorer place.

Primary sources: Mark Hawkswell/Margaret Geissbuhler
General source: Sri Lanka

* * *

The Young Magician watched as the magic pencil wrote the following notes in his never-ending notebook:

> I listened to the teacher tell this story to the class. The change in the atmosphere of the room after the teacher had finished was extraordinary. Many of the children had tears in their eyes, and they looked at each other in a new way, with a new sense of respect and curiosity in their eyes. Several children in that class that day would look back years later and realise it was a day that changed their perspective on how they looked at life, at others and, most of all, at themselves.

Leading

 The story connects all four boxes. The personal integrity of the water carrier and her values and beliefs about what the fractured pot can do enable the pot to believe in itself. The pot realises it can make, and already has made, a contribution, and this sense of purpose and value allows it to feel whole and complete. Consequently, the habitat benefits from the greater range and variety of quality input.

Influencing

Metaphorically, the water carrier could represent the giver of life with all its possibilities. This could be God or it could be each one of us. If we can recognise goodness in others, then so we will recognise its existence in ourselves. The water carrier influences others through her compassion, and her search for possibility and contribution. From her perspective there will always be a contribution that each and everyone can make. There can be a WIN for all.

Motivating

All systems will respond to this story:

PURPLE:
all things whether animate or
inanimate have a life and a soul.

RED:
may respond to the respect shown
for its flawed inner nature and its
longing for recognition.

BLUE:
will recognise the
authority of the water
carrier, her goodness,
decency and good
husbandry.

ORANGE:
will note that the pot can make a
contribution, but will wonder if a beautiful
garden is really essential to its core business;
ORANGE may be cynical about the GREEN
sentimentality of the story.

GREEN:
everybody is important
and everybody has a
contribution to make; this
is above all a GREEN story.

YELLOW:
will appreciate the systemic relationships
within the story, and recognise that, while
the pot's contribution is perfect in this
context, it may be an indulgence in others.

My insights

- Each of us has his or her own unique flaws.
- It is our flaws that make us special and unique.
- Our flaws allow us to make our special contribution – even if we are not aware of it.
- Our cracks and flaws make our lives *together* so fascinating and rewarding.
- Take each person as they are, recognise them for what they are, and seek out what is good in them.
- Everyone has a contribution to make.
- Appreciate difference in life – thank goodness we're not all the same!

- Remember to say well done and thank you to the perfect pot.
- When things aren't perfect, take time to consider the wider perspective – what else could it mean? Reframe, if necessary.
- Avoid pride, develop humility and gratitude, especially if you're naturally good at things.
- Is this how beauty came into the world?

* * *

"Possibly. Think on this, Young Master, different storytellers weave the threads of their narrative in different ways, just as weavers do. Carpets can be spaces for travelling, praying, socialising, taking action, reflecting and meditating. Stories can be, too. It is time once again for our sixth story. Let us continue with our themes."

Story 54

Wake Up!

A man dreamed that he was walking along a beach with the Creator of the Universe. Across the screen of the sky, sketches of his life flashed by. In every scene, two tracks could clearly be seen etched in the sand, one belonging to him, the other to his Maker.

As the final scene of this celestial movie unfolded, he pressed the pause button and took time to look back along his timeline etched as footprints in the sand. As he did so, he noticed that there were several occasions along his life's journey where only one set of footprints could be seen. And these were usually at the very lowest and saddest moments of his life.

He felt puzzled and somewhat let down by this realisation. So he questioned the Maker of All Things about it. "My Lord, you promised that once I had chosen to follow your Way you would always walk beside me. But now that I look back upon my life's journey I see that during my most challenging and troubling times, only one set of footprints appears. Why, when I needed you most, did you forsake me?"

And the Source of All Life replied, "My son, my precious child, I love you and would never leave you. During your times of trial and suffering, where now you see only one set of footprints, it was then I carried you."

Primary source: Paul Scott Priestly
Original source unknown

* * *

Leading and influencing

The leadership skills described in the story are perhaps more associated with the contexts of parenting, or teaching young children, or intensive-care nursing. The concept of a nurturing, compassionate leader is alien to many business and professional contexts. But does it have to be so? There may be many times and contexts when an organisation, or when colleagues, or when a manager or leader "carries" an individual or a group. If this were more widely recognised, how influential might that be to the organisation as a whole and its sense of vision, purpose and mission?

Motivating

The story will probably appeal more to the sacrificial, cool colour systems:

PURPLE:
will respond to
the mystic
elements and a
paternalistic God.

BLUE:
will respond to a just
God that supports
weakness and right
behaviour; it will
clearly be 'our' God.

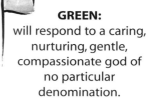

GREEN:
will respond to a caring,
nurturing, gentle,
compassionate god of
no particular
denomination.

My insights

Take a look around the environment in which you currently find yourself. Take a moment to notice all the wonderful inventions that you take for granted. Notice that so many things that make your life easy and bearable, once started as a never-before-thought-of idea that someone had the genius to see as an opportunity. And notice how often, or how rarely, you give thanks for the gifts of electric light and clean water, of heat and refrigeration, of books and computers, of recorded music and communication. And take a moment to thank those spirited minds that made these things possible. In a multiplicity of ways we have been 'carried' all our lives.

How often have you thanked your heart for beating, your brain for thinking, your lungs for breathing and all the other parts of your body that perform miraculous functions. Wake up! Thank them now. And whatever *chi* you follow, whatever god you serve, recognise how the universe has always carried you, and how much more so when you give your full, wholehearted trust to it.

* * *

"Possibly.

"And there is another, equally important, side to this vision," said Al Sayyid. "You cannot help anyone unless they are prepared to help themselves. Action and intention must come from within. It is not enough just to dream about what you want. Dreams, like beautiful carpets, are brought to fruition through rigorous planning and action, through awareness of the impact of your behaviours or lack of them, and the flexibility and creativity to see challenges from multiple perspectives.

"It is a sad reflection on the human condition that so much of the pain, grief and lack of personal and social responsibility that exist in the world today are due to the cages that humans build for themselves out of their own mistaken thinking. Are you ready for the plains of Wyoming, Young Master?

Story 55

The Prisoner

A wild mustang was captured and put in a fenced paddock bordering the open country where he once ran free.

During his first week of captivity he demonstrated all the vitality and spirit that he had possessed in the wild. But, as the weeks passed, his rage and wilfulness abated. The hay and other fodder previously ignored became not only tolerable but agreeable. No effort was required, and food and drink were plentiful.

And, while it was true that he was a prisoner in his paddock unable to escape, nothing could enter, either. So those old days when he used to fear constant attack from predators were nothing more than an almost forgotten nightmare. His new situation seemed to him a kind of pragmatic trade-off and – all things considered – a pretty cushy one, too.

Some months into his incarceration, a wild mustang passed nearby and spotted his fat, captive cousin. With caution, he approached the paddock. "What on earth are you doing here?" he asked, checking for any signs of danger.

"I'm stuffed," said the captive mustang between bites of hay.

Outside the paddock, the wild mustang took stock of the situation. He considered the state of the paddock's woodwork. "This gate doesn't seem all that strong. If we both lean hard on it together, it's sure to give. You'll be free. Come on, let's go for it."

"Don't bother. I've already tried." He was pawing the ground, arranging his bed of hay for a nice afternoon nap.

"Come on!" snorted the mustang, his eyes wide and white, and his nostrils flaring. "This wood's half rotten. Let's do it."

"Thanks, but no thanks." The penned mustang sighed as he lay down. "Believe me I've tried so many times to break out. If anyone knows the state of the woodwork it's me. Trust me. It's just a waste of time. Save your energy."

The fire and spirit of freedom surged in the wild mustang's veins. He reared high on his hind legs and brought his hoofs crashing down on the rotten woodwork. He smashed through three of the gate's five wooden bars, leaving the path to freedom open. With contempt he roared, "When did you last test this gate's integrity? Or your own?"

But the penned mustang wasn't listening. He'd already slipped into a pleasant doze, dreaming once again of freedom, of running over open landscapes, grassy plains, wherever his strong heart chose …

Primary source: Guy Finley website, www.guyfinley.com (adapted and reproduced with permission)

* * *

Leading

Choose which of these two you'd prefer to have as a leader, coach, teacher or parent? One is already living the dream with all its challenge, excitement and risk. The other is merely dreaming about living the way it thinks it wants. Action and intention are crucially missing. The wild mustang's personal integrity, values and behaviours contrast markedly with the one that has become seduced by all the many things the paddock may metaphorically represent: success, material pleasure, playing safe, routine, creature comforts and so on. The wild mustang, fully present to the whole habitat, has far greater awareness of the true state of the environment and the quality of its resources. It recognises the weakness of the fencing while the prisoner is blind to it. And, even when there is a route to freedom, the prisoner refuses to see it.

Influencing

Neither mustang appears able to influence the other. Their values have become too far apart. Neither makes any attempt to understand and appreciate the other's point of view. Communication and dialogue have become impossible.

The wild mustang cannot appreciate how seductive "captivity" and "civilisation" can be. The prisoner cannot understand why anyone would choose to live a life full of risk, danger and deprivation.

The reader or listener may appreciate that there is another way that is not either/or but both/and. The question then is: what balance?

Motivating

Perhaps this story doesn't appeal to particular systems but to the very different approaches of the sacrificial, communal systems and the expressive, individualistic systems.

Sacrificial systems:
PURPLE, BLUE, GREEN
tend to gather together for protection and safety, for easier organisation and administration, and to share and distribute resources more equitably.

Expressive systems:
RED, ORANGE, YELLOW
tend to be more individualistic and personally assertive; they prefer to defy fear, challenge fear or simply accept it as a necessary and inevitable condition of life. They are more likely to welcome risk, challenge and danger.

My insights

- It is very easy to become seduced into an acceptance of dependence based on expedience.
- Negative acceptance of 'reality' can take many forms: slavery to the god of material things, acceptance of political, social or economic injustice, or sheer laziness.
- The free mustang could represent many things: creativity, independence, freedom of spirit, choice, resourcefulness, determination, sponsorship, human potential and so on.
- Wake up! It is never too late to make a fresh start in life.

* * *

"Possibly."

"The theme of the importance of taking personal responsibility for one's own life recurs throughout many of these stories," said the Young Magician. "The question is: How can leaders and influencers get this message across to others? If more people took personal responsibility for their lives, it strikes me the world would be a lot healthier.

"I remember reading that Gandhi once said, 'You must be the change you want to see in the world.' That's totally about taking personal responsibility. Aha! And do you know what's just popped into my mind? My dream. And that Inuit proverb: 'There's no such thing as bad weather, only inappropriate clothing.' Don't blame what's outside: take time to find the right resources to deal with this situation."

"Precisely. Responsibility is absolutely about cause and effect."

"How so?"

"You have a simple choice. You can be at cause for your life. Or you can put yourself at effect. Either you operate on the world, or it will operate on you."

The Young Magician was curious.

"Slip your hand inside my library pocket. Choose any one of the titles from the body of knowledge called Neuro-Linguistic Programming, or NLP for short, and look under C > E."

The Young Magician settled down to read and soon his magic pencil was making notes:

C > E

Cause is greater than Effect

Results > Excuses

Act to achieve results you want rather than find reasons and excuses for failure

Responsibility > Blame

When something unwanted or negative happens to you, even if it is not your fault or responsibility, ask yourself: Who is going to have to deal with this? Chances are there's only one answer: *Me!* So you might as well get on with it and use your energy in a positive way.

Consider for a moment how enjoyable and cathartic blame can be. It's a negative energy dump. Now ask yourself: What does blame achieve? And what does it change? The probable answer is: *Nothing!* So why not take responsibility for dealing with it and move on in your life?

Blame is always *out there*. And whatever is *out there* you can't directly change. But if you *change yourself*, the one thing over which you do have power in this world, you will act upon all the systems in which you operate: friends, family, sports, work etc. And, as you change your contribution to the system, the system will begin to change, too.

Actor > Victim

Imagine your life as a movie. Are you the star in your movie? Do you make sure you take a lead role in achieving your dreams and desires? If you are not a lead actor in your life, the only other role that exists is victim. That's the hard choice.

"So the wild stallion is the actor, and the imprisoned one the victim?" asked the Young Magician.

"A victim very much of its own making, I think you will agree," said Al Sayyid silkily. Let's travel south and east, back to Europe, to the beautiful island of Sicily for our next story on this very same theme."

Story 56

Wistful Thinking

In a large auditorium at a conference centre in Sicily, a speaker was delivering a presentation on "Using Storytelling in Problem Solving". There were perhaps a thousand seats in the hall and about nine hundred people in the audience. Quite a number of the seats nearer the front were empty. Many Italians like to arrive just in time and sometimes a little after that.

Because of the size and shape of the auditorium, the speaker was wired up. He had a small radio microphone clipped to the lapel of his suit, powered by a discreet battery pack attached to his belt.

Not long into his talk he was interrupted. "We can't hear you," called a voice from the back on the left-hand side. "The loudspeaker isn't working."

"How many of you can't hear well?" asked the speaker. About fifty people raised their hands. Clearly, it was just one faulty speaker that was causing the problem, and there was nothing that could be done right then to fix it. "So why don't you come and sit nearer the front. There are plenty of seats down here or you can sit on the steps in the aisles."

Nobody moved.

The presenter continued his talk. Within half a minute he was interrupted again. "We can't hear you," shouted the same voice from exactly the same place at the back.

The presenter paused, and considered what to do. It would not be respectful to suggest directly that they move again. He was mindful of the topic of his talk and decided to go off script. He walked up the aisle towards the people sitting near the malfunctioning speaker so that they could hear his natural voice, while addressing the rest of the audience through the microphone. And he said, "When I was a young boy, about fourteen years old, I began to develop an interest in girls. And as chance would have it, my family lived in a big house quite near a girls' school.

"Sometimes I would get home from my school before the girls left their school and quite a lot of them would walk down my road and past my house. I used to stand in the bay window on the ground floor watching them, wistfully thinking how nice it would be if one of them, especially one of the ones I found more attractive, would turn left at the gate, walk along the path, ring the doorbell and invite me out. And do you know something? Not one of them ever did!

"And I began to realise that, if I wanted certain things in life, I was not going to achieve them by waiting for the world to change to suit me. I would have to change what I was doing in order to get the results I wanted.

"So I'm not suggesting for one moment that if you want to hear what I have to say during the next forty-five minutes, you will find the seats at the front very comfortable and ideal for that purpose."

The speaker then returned to the stage and resumed his presentation. Waiting only until about fifty people had settled into their new seats at the front.

* * *

Leading

The speaker makes use of an authentic story about personal responsibility to influence a section of the audience to recognise that no amount of complaining can change a malfunctioning speaker, so it is pointless to complain about it. However, what they can do is change their "stuck" behaviour because they have more flexibility than the hardware.

Influencing

The speaker works hard to maintain rapport with everybody by demonstrating respect, politeness, humour and patience. Having already suggested that they move, a suggestion that didn't work, the presenter elegantly illustrates the power of story to problem-solve – which is the topic of his talk – to indirectly shift "stuck" thinking without making the listeners feel pressured or disrespected. The speaker allows the group to feel free to make their own decision by using the phrase, "So I'm not suggesting for one moment that …" and then follows this directly with two embedded commands to make compliance more likely.

Motivating

The story resonates with all the valuing and thinking systems:

PURPLE:
The small group is respected and made to feel OK and then reintegrated into the bigger group.

RED:
will appreciate the speaker's assertiveness, and authenticity.

BLUE:
order is re-established, the challenge to authority is satisfactorily dealt with.

ORANGE:
will pay attention to how the challenge is dealt with in a way that deepens understanding of the presentation's core message while not jeopardising the relationship; ORANGE will see advantages in this.

GREEN:
will feel comfortable with the way the challenge is dealt with: respectfully and politely.

YELLOW:
will appreciate the elegant functionality of demonstrating the topic of the talk in action, while deepening the quality of the relationship with the whole group.

My insights

- Be structured and free to leave your script when the situation demands it.
- Focus on task *and* relationship.
- Be aware of the power of well-chosen language.
- Stories are an effective way to get across an idea or concept in experiential terms.
- Stories are a natural way to convince people of their "truth".

- Stories are an indirect way to give powerful messages and feedback that is polite, respectful and nonconfrontational.
- Personal stories are an effective way of demonstrating personal authenticity and transparency.
- The structure of influence:
  - know what you want;
  - be aware of whether you're getting it or not;
  - have the flexibility to change what you're doing so you get what you want; and
  - build and maintain rapport.

* * *

"Possibly."

"I guess", said the Young Magician, "that shifting people from their stuck patterns is one of the hardest tasks for those who wish, or need, or have been asked, to lead, influence or motivate others. And of course there are many leaders, influencers and motivators who are themselves stuck in old ways and patterns of thinking. They are too fond of finding old solutions to new problems. Too set in their ways, too blind to the need for change, too arrogant to think they have more to learn."

"Every great weaver begins each new project with an open mind," said Al Sayyid. "Of course, he has a design, a plan, but he will also let the thread, the yarn, the wool, the silk, the needle and the frame, speak to him. He starts afresh each time. Every new child is different. Let it be itself, not the image of its parents.

"We shall return to India for our next experience. I believe you enjoy a spicy curry."

The Young Magician nodded vigorously.

Story 57

Stuckness

A pilgrim longed to find a Teacher who could help him truly discover the One Great Truth.

One day he heard there was just such a Teacher, so he set off to find her.

He found her simple retreat hidden deep in tangled woods. The door was open but nobody was around. He looked inside and saw a small round table, a pot of tea and two delicate teacups. He waited for some time. But he was thirsty, so he poured himself a cup of tea.

Just at that moment, the Teacher appeared. She looked at the man, looked at the cup poised in his hand, shook her head, and left without a word.

The man waited but the Teacher didn't return.

Next day he came back to find that everything was exactly the same: the table, the teapot, the teacups. He waited. He was thirsty, so he poured himself a cup of tea. The Teacher appeared. She looked at him, at the teacup, she shook her head and left.

The same pattern continued for days until finally the man begged her, "Please, I have travelled many miles to seek out the Great Truth. Teach me so I may learn from your wisdom."

The Teacher paused, walked to the table, picked up the teapot and began to pour it into the man's already full cup. The man retreated quickly as the tea poured over the lip of the cup, over the saucer, over the table and on to the floor.

The Teacher said, "Your mind is like this cup of tea. It is already full. If you want to learn something new, first you must empty your mind."

General source: Zen tradition

* * *

Leading

 I read somewhere, "Minds are like parachutes: they work best when they are open." It is so hard to approach anything new or different without preconceptions and assumptions based on our previous experience. And yet learning requires us to be willing to break the generalisations that hold the current learning in place. To achieve the knowledge and personal integrity he seeks, the pilgrim must break free from his stuck patterns of behaviour and values, and be open to possibility.

Influencing

The Teacher elegantly uses the same teacup as a metaphor for demonstrating what it is the pilgrim must do. Within the stuckness of the old pattern lie the seeds for personal change and transformation.

Motivating

The story is a challenge for each individual, whatever systems he is operating within, to look inside himself and question his openness to learning and to change.

Are you *open* to change and transformation?

Or are you temporarily *arrested* and not yet ready to move ahead?

Or are you *closed* to all possibility of change and growth?

My insights

- In order to learn easily, put aside all your assumptions and prejudices.
- Open your mind and open your heart, to new challenges.

- See things in a new light.
- Tune into new voices.
- Enjoy deep feelings of confusion and wonder.
- Make sense of new possibilities.
- Be in a state of readiness to receive.
- The learner has as much responsibility as the teacher.
- The wise teacher may refuse the pilgrim who is not fully committed and prepared.
- Only when the student is ready will the teacher truly "arrive".

* * *

"Possibly.

"There is a natural beauty", said Al Sayyid, "when things happen as they are ordained to do, in the correct sequence of things. The acorn precedes the oak, the design precedes the carpet, the needle precedes the thread. In the Eastern traditions of Zen and Tao, the route to happiness is to pursue the Natural Way. It is of no value to stand in contradiction and opposition to the way things flow. Give yourself to the flow, enter into it completely, trust the universe to assist you in navigating through life. Why seek out complexity and what is difficult, when so often these paths give so little in return? We shall stay in Asia to discover more about this tradition, the Way of the Tao."

Story 58

The Sequence of Things

A powerful duke visited a Zen master and asked the wise man to create for him a work of art encapsulating the secret of happiness.

The master told him to return in a week.

When the duke returned, the sage gave him an exquisite sheet of parchment upon which beautiful calligraphy expressed the wisdom the duke had required.

When the duke unfurled the parchment it simply read:

> **Father dies.**
> **Son dies.**

The duke is livid. "What kind of happiness is this!" he demands.

The master remains silent. He turns to his brushes, picks one up and dips it into his inkpot. He writes:

> **Son dies.**
> **Father dies.**

"Would you prefer it in this order?"

Primary source: Mark Forstater, *The Spiritual Teachings of the Tao*, Hodder & Stoughton
General source: Taoist tradition

* * *

Leading

According to the Tao, humankind's ideal state consists of freedom from desire, effortless simplicity and the acceptance of life as it is, and in its natural flow and order. This may be a long way from the general conception of the modern leader, but the sage's imperturbable faith and confidence in the validity of his worldview is impressive. He has the ability to operate within complexity and express it simply, elegantly and powerfully. He does not trivialise the message but actually enhances it and connects it to a deeper truth. He is completely at one with his environment and everybody and everything within it. The duke may be powerful, but the sage treats him as an equal.

Influencing

When challenged, the sage remains calm, and counters the challenge both respectfully and in a way that serves to reinforce his message and convince others of his truth. Above all, he seems to be absolutely free from negative stress, and completely and utterly congruent in everything he does and says. He is at one with his universe. This is the secret of influence.

Motivating

The story offers a message to all the valuing and thinking systems:

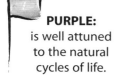

PURPLE:
is well attuned to the natural cycles of life.

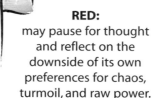

RED:
may pause for thought and reflect on the downside of its own preferences for chaos, turmoil, and raw power.

BLUE:
will respond to the themes of order, structure, sequence and everything in its proper place.

ORANGE:
may find this simplistic – the world is more complex than this. ORANGE spends much time attempting to exploit the universe not work within it. Nevertheless, ORANGE may be attracted to the need for a firm foundation and the logical force of the argument.

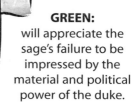

GREEN:
will appreciate the sage's failure to be impressed by the material and political power of the duke.

YELLOW:
will once again appreciate the elegance of working within
natural systems, and the use of natural designs as solutions for
complex problems.

My insights

The Hedgehog usually outwits the Fox.

The habitat is as it is. The natural patterns of life are as they are. Should we work within these patterns and rhythms? Or should we attempt to change them? No amount of power or wealth can prevent what is inevitable. What are the benefits and dangers, in the short and longer terms, of changing the natural and ecological balance within the ecosystems of the universe?

* * *

"Possibly."

"Great leaders create an environment in which others can thrive, can grow and can reach their full potential in order to achieve certain objectives," said the Young Magician. "They have very little need to seek attention for themselves, and do not crave attention or adulation."

"Precisely! Like a functional carpet that blends perfectly into the interior design of a room, you may not even notice their presence. Or, when you do, you will express surprise at the elegant economy of their contribution.

"They put their skills and resources at the service of their organisation, or their institution, or team, or family, or client. They desire to make a contribution that will give more to the world than they take from it, and their concern is to hand over their stewardship to the next generation, so it may succeed even better for the good of the community and the habitat as a whole."

"Can you give me an example of this?" asked the Young Magician. "As a story or metaphor, of course."

"Then let us wind the clock backwards to Europe in the eighteenth century."

Story 59

Out of Thin Air

As an experiment, an eighteenth-century botanist planted a sapling in a large clay pot having first weighed the soil and the sapling. Some five years later he weighed the tree and found that it had increased in weight by 195 pounds. But when he weighed the soil he was amazed to discover it had diminished in weight by only thirteen ounces.

He thought about this. Where did the tree's extra 195 pounds come from if not from the soil? The answer of course is out of thin air.

Trees absorb carbon dioxide through their leaves. Then, during the hours of daylight, by the process of photosynthesis, the carbon dioxide molecule divides into one carbon atom and two oxygen atoms. The oxygen is released back into the atmosphere, while the carbon atoms are transformed into a six-carbon simple sugar ring, known as glucose, which in turn forms a building block for cellulose.

The miracle of this process is the breaking down, releasing and recombining of essential elements from one structure to another. The growth and development of the tree is the result of this remarkable transformational process.

Primary source: David J. Grove, quoted in James Lawley and Penny Tompkins, *Metaphors in Mind*, Developing Company Press

* * *

Leading

Leadership is like the soil. It is the environment that nurtures the plant. It makes it possible for the processes of growth and transformation to take place but trusts that the sapling will naturally do so for itself. It doesn't have to busy itself being a leader. It is enough to provide the context and support the process. The great leader develops a sense of "chemistry" with his staff, with the "plant", with the resources and with the habitat. The great leader wears his knowledge lightly.

Influencing

The soil forms the environment in which the tree can thrive and develop. But it is the invisible process of photosynthesis that transforms solar energy into food that allows the sapling to grow without cost to its host environment, the soil.

And so it is that many of the best change agents – whether educators, therapists, thinkers, philosophers, parents, business leaders or simple storytellers – support major change in others while leaving little or no footprint on the ground. They create WIN–WIN–WIN scenarios.

Motivating

All systems will find something to wonder at in this metaphor:

PURPLE:
will be amazed at how "magic" takes place.

RED:
will be awed by the power of natural forces and the creativity of nature.

BLUE:
will celebrate the excellence of God's creation.

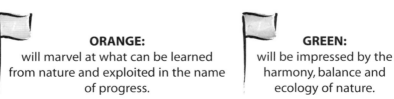

ORANGE:
will marvel at what can be learned from nature and exploited in the name of progress.

GREEN:
will be impressed by the harmony, balance and ecology of nature.

YELLOW:
will note the primacy of natural systems, and note how the natural design
of this system can be replicated again and again in solutions to other
problems; less is more.

My insights

For some reason this metaphor reminds me of something that Lao Tse, the
Chinese sage, is thought to have written many centuries ago:

> Go in search of your people:
> Love them;
> Learn from them;
> Plan with them;
> Serve them;
> Begin with what they have;
> Build on what they know.
>
> But with the best of leaders
> When their task is accomplished,
> Their work is done,
> The people all remark,
> "We have done it ourselves."

Have we really changed all that much in the last two thousand years? I wonder.

* * *

"Maybe and maybe not."

"Hey! That's a shift."

"Indeed, Young Master, it is, even if a small one. And it's time for
our sixth story, which is also the final story of your journey. Soon
it will be time for you to reflect on the meaning of your journey,
what you have learned and whether you have the answers to
explain your dream. But just for now, relax, sit back and meditate
on the wise words of my countryman, Jalal ud-Din Rumi. Turn
back the clock another five hundred years to thirteenth-century
Persia, and imagine one of the greatest poets of any age sitting
cross legged on a carpet just like me, and penning these timeless
words."

Story 60

Absence or Presence?

A man hears footsteps in his house at night.
He reaches out for flint to spark and make a light.
But the thief squats down beside him,
And when the tinder starts to catch,
The thief snuffs it out.

The man thinks
The fire is dying by itself,
"Perhaps it's damp."

Often we never see what snuffs out our light, our love.
Something in the dark does it.
Something we do not see.
It's like saying that day sparkles and fades, then on comes night.
And that nothing happens in those changes.
Whatever happens, or doesn't happen, a presence is helping.

Primary source: Eleonora Gilbert
Secondary source: Jalal ud-Din Rumi

* * *

Leading

The haunting beauty of this poem invites another dimension to my thoughts on leadership. It is a poem about God and Spirit, about absence and presence, about why things happen or don't happen, and about how we lead and take responsibility for ourselves, or fail to do so. To me it suggests the presence of a power greater than ourselves that we would be foolish to ignore. Call it Spirit, or Vision, or God, or Energy, or whatever you wish. It raises the question: Who leads the leaders? And in this way it connects the ethics of leadership with the questions: Who am I as a leader? Whom do I serve? What are my skills and competencies? What is the environment with which, and in which, I engage? What presence is helping me as a leader? And how does my presence serve those who have chosen to trust and follow me?

Influencing

A person who appears to be centred within himself, and whose personal identity, values, beliefs and behaviours are totally aligned and in tune with each other, is far more likely to demonstrate those intangible characteristics that others label *presence* and *integrity*. It is the perception of presence and integrity in an individual that encourages others to have the confidence to believe in, trust and follow this person. You become an effective leader because others choose to follow you.

But the sense of presence and integrity is even more greatly enhanced when a leader seems somehow to be connected to a higher power – whatever that might be. It's not the sort of thing I can explain, yet I'm sure many people will know exactly what I mean.

Motivating

The complexity and richness of metaphor in this poem really defies interpretation. But that hasn't stopped me before from offering my very limited perception about what a story means for me. While the more expressive systems may be impatient with the oblique and meditative aspects of the writing, it may well appeal to:

PURPLE:
will respond to the mystic elements and feel at home with the homely allusions and metaphors.

BLUE:
will respond to the confirmation of a powerful and omniscient god who sees all things and is behind all things.

GREEN:
will respond to the gentleness, meditativeness and New Age spiritual resonance of the writing; and the expression of how different communities and faiths, from different periods in world history, can join together with shared ideas.

YELLOW:
will appreciate the need for deeper reflection of why things are as they are, and turn out as they do. Also, YELLOW is aware that rational, logical explanations are not enough for many contexts and that presence may take many forms.

My insights

- How rich the power of thought and expression was so many centuries ago.
- What is it that sometimes extinguishes my light, my love?
- What is the presence that so often helps me?
- Why is it not always there? Or is it?
- What is the *presence* that makes for great leadership?
- How do you know when it's there?
- How do you know when it's not there?

* * *

"Al Sayyid and the Young Magician looked at each other and smiled. Then together they both said, "Possibly!"

Section 5

Homecoming – Change, Learning and Transformation

The Young Magician was kneeling on Al Sayyid and feeling pleasantly full after a good lunch. Around them on the grassy slope lay what was left of their picnic. Far below, at the foot of the mountain was the lake, lying calm and placid in the summer sunshine, the very same lake into whose depths some months before the Young Magician had hurled his golden coin, and begun his long voyage of discovery. And beyond that, just discernible in the haze of the midafternoon sun, stood the town and the vague, shimmering outline of The Academy.

"Congratulations and welcome back," said the High Master. "I've read your stories and the notes you made, and I'm looking forward to the presentation that you'll be making to the Panel of Wizards and Magicians next month. In the meantime, I'd like you to tell me about the interpretation of that dream of yours. And, afterwards, tell me what you consider to be the key attributes of an excellent leader."

"You know well, Master, that my dream both disturbed and intrigued me. It made me curious to discover its meaning. I knew there was a message in it for me, and my whole journey has been, in part, a quest to discover what that message was. I have not been disappointed. What I've learned on my journey is exactly what the dream and the sixty stories have taught me.

The Young Magician collected his thoughts. And then he said, "Al Sayyid, may I use your central panel to map out my main points?"

"Go right ahead, Young Master."

The Young Magician smoothed the surface of the carpet and then wrote,

Fish and Water

"Master, do you remember how puzzled I was when you said to me, 'I don't keep fish, I keep water'?"

The High Master nodded.

"Of all the things I have learned, this metaphor has been the greatest and most powerful. It teaches me that unless I have an understanding of the habitat in which human and other life forms exist, I cannot possibly make sense of the extraordinary richness, complexity and systemic nature of this world of ours."

"Correct," said the High Master.

"If we look after the water, everything within it will thrive. But it has to be the right kind of water. For example, some fish are tropical. They need warm seawater kept at a certain temperature, with the right kind of minerals and plant life present in order to sustain them. Other fish prefer freshwater. And, if the water is right for them, it will provide the conditions these fish need, too."

"Exactly so," said the High Master, "and this is precisely what you have learned from the colour-coded valuing and thinking systems of Spiral Dynamics. Work with people's *natural* systems. When the habitat is appropriate everything in it can thrive, and everything in it can make a contribution."

Habitats
"And," added the Young Magician, "if we also add the four-box model to the valuing systems, we can see that it's quite possible for the wise leader to create and nurture a healthy, balanced, appropriate habitat in which her family, or client, or patients, or team, or students, or employees, or business, or organisation, or nation can thrive."

"So how might an effective leader achieve this?"

"These questions might be useful." The Young Magician turned again to Al Sayyid's central panel, and wrote:

> What habitat will *naturally* encourage everything in it to thrive and fulfil its potential?
>
> How can I most appropriately provide it and then nurture it?
>
> How can I ensure the result is a WIN for me, a WIN for others and a WIN for the system as a whole?

"Good," said the High Master. "So wise leadership isn't so much about busying oneself with fragmented tasks and specialisations, but developing an integral awareness of how the whole system fits together with appropriate balance and harmony."

"Exactly. That's what my journey and the dream have taught me."

Integral awareness
"So tell me, how can one develop such an integral awareness? How does one move beyond a fragmented view to a more holistic one?"

"Al Sayyid, do you remember, many months ago, when you helped me work out the four elements of the four-box model, that you also used the word 'integral'. You described a leader who consciously worked with all four of the boxes as an 'integral leader'."

"Indeed I did, Young Master."

The Young Apprentice drew a design in Al Sayyid's rich pile, and wrote one word in each of the boxes.

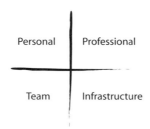

"Al Sayyid introduced me to this way of organising my thinking. It's based on the work of the Wizard Ken Wilber.[1] Everything can fit into one or more of these four boxes. An integral or holistic view of the world, or of business, or of education, or of medicine, or of politics, or of anything else would aim to have some kind of balance or harmony existing between these four elements.

"An integral leader seeks to blend all these elements together in ways appropriate for any given situation and habitat. She'll want to keep in mind the personal valuing and thinking systems of the people who she leads – UL; their knowledge, skills and capacities for professional development – UR; the organisational culture in which they operate – LL; and the infrastructure – the material, technical and natural resources that are available to them – LR. And then ask herself: How do all of these best fit together?"

"Excellent. Now relate all of this to your dream?"

"Then let me start with this Chinese proverb: 'The last things to know about the sea are the fish'."

The Young Magician drew another diagram on Al Sayyid's surface before continuing:

"Fish aren't aware they swim in water until you take them out of it. In the same way, we humans aren't aware we live in air until we're deprived of it. What we notice are walls, shapes, objects, boundaries, and we fail to notice the space that holds these things apart. We take the space for granted. That's why the integral leader carefully considers the infrastructure in which she operates, and knows what resources, methods, techniques, processes and systems are available to her within it."

"Exactly," said the High Master. "The integral leader takes time to get to know and understand the operating space. When we know about the sea, we will be able to work within it much more effectively."

The Young Magician rubbed out the proverb, and now wrote, "Metaphor: the right brain's unique contribution to the left brain's language capability".

"Ah yes, Leonard Shlain,"[2] said the High Master. How do you interpret this part of your dream?"

The Young Magician sketched another diagram and continued:

"The two right-hand boxes represent aspects of the objective, external world that can be observed and measured. The brain, and the brain's functions and capacities, belonging to the Upper Right box, can be measured too. So this quotation reminds us that using and developing the skills of both hemispheres of the neocortex, the upper part of the brain, is highly desirable.

"In my journey through sixty stories, I discovered many times the power of metaphor to take complex ideas and make them easy to grasp, to take challenging concepts and translate them powerfully and memorably into everyday tangible, lived experiences that anyone could relate to and understand. This is an important part of the magic of metaphor."

"May I?" said the Master leaning across and adding a new diagram:

"As we pay attention to these metaphors, they invite us to consider how the environment in a story is similar to, or different from, the environment in which we live. Metaphors invite us to relate to the *values* that are presented in the story and compare them with our own, or our *culture's*. And, of course, metaphors invite us to look *inside ourselves* and wonder how we ourselves might deal with the issues that the characters in the stories face.

"The marvellous thing about stories is that they challenge our own perceptions and levels of awareness. When metaphor and right-brain thinking are connected to language and left-brain thinking, we experience the power of whole-brain thinking! Excellent, go on. What's next in your dream?"

The Young Magician wrote on Al Sayyid's panel again: "There's no such thing as bad weather, only inappropriate clothing."

"This Inuit proverb asks us to think about the role of personal responsibility. Are we putting ourselves *at cause* for our life, or are we putting ourselves *at effect*? If we're cold and wet, it's not the weather's fault, but our own for not choosing appropriate clothing from our wardrobe!"

"Absolutely, Young Man, if we're *at cause* we choose to be the central player in our life, and make things happen the way we want them to, taking full responsibility for our decisions, and for the way we handle whatever happens to us. On the other hand, if we place ourselves *at effect*, then we choose to make ourselves victims, helpless bit-part players in an obstructive world where everything and everyone is to blame except ourselves."

"On my travels, I found many stories that stress the importance of taking personal responsibility. It seems that, without a really strong sense of responsibility, it's almost impossible to develop the levels of personal awareness, consciousness and integrity that are necessary for one to be thought of as a great and influential leader. Integral leadership begins in this box, the Upper Left. Leadership starts with the way we each lead ourselves."

"Good," said the High Master. "Now what happens to a leader who lacks the ability to work across the four boxes, who lacks the ability to take an integral view?"

All miracles require a shift in perspective

"Stuckness is what happens when leaders get trapped in old ways of doing, seeing and thinking," said the Young Magician. "What used to work so well, no longer does. Technology fails, relationships fray, skills are inadequate, confidence suffers. Stuckness can happen in any of the four boxes. It usually means that the world has moved on but nobody has noticed.

"A shift in perspective is required. Not just seeing the world from your own point of view, but from other points of view, too. In particular, seeing the world from a much wider perspective, so you can experience the points of view of everyone and everything that is affected by the situation.

"The ability to make shifts in perspective brings creativity into play. Creativity is simply the art of seeing things from new, unusual or unexpected perspectives. It's creativity that generates new solutions that can be applied to new issues or challenges."

"Excellent," said the High Master, "and this is exactly what the metaphors and stories that you've collected do. They shift perspective, and offer different ways of experiencing what is and what might be. They offer creative insights into new possibilities: escape routes from stuckness, and pathways towards change."

"Right," said the Young Magician, "and, above all, they're so immediate, so real and, above all, so simple.

Make it as simple as you can but not any simpler – Einstein

"There's a real art to taking a complex idea and making it easy to grasp; in taking an abstract notion or concept and making it come to life so that others can identify with it in a concrete way. Stories and metaphors are really good at making their point with great power and surprising economy.

"It was Al Sayyid who really helped me to understand what Einstein was getting at. He helped me realise that it was possible to work with a model that could divide the key elements of leadership into four interrelated boxes. This is a really useful and effective way of taking what's complex and making it simpler, and easier to understand, by focusing on the underlying patterns rather than the surface details."

"It is, of course, not true," said the High Master. "It's a model, and a model is simply a way of testing a theory against experience. But if this model helps us to analyse and make more sense of the world of experience without in any way trivialising or distorting it, then it's a useful model."

"The colour-coded flags based on the Spiral Dynamics model are also very useful. With this division of the world into eight waves of thinking and valuing that exist within people I can begin to ask why do I behave as I do in different sets of circumstances? Why do others behave as they do? What are the underlying conditions of existence that support different kinds of responses and value sets within people? Knowing this, perhaps it's possible that I can begin to have a better understanding of myself and others, and begin to recognise some underlying patterns beneath the apparent complexity of the human condition."

"Exactly! The simplicity and accuracy of these models are useful for leaders who want to create the most appropriate habitats for their 'fish' to swim in. If they know what environments are most appropriate for the 'fish', what motivates or demotivates them, what they value, and what they believe, it will be much easier to create the most conducive conditions for thought and action, and to adapt their own behaviours and strategies, if necessary, to suit the needs of the 'fish'."

"And I suppose," chipped in the Young Magician, "there's no reason why the 'fish' can't learn about and use these models for themselves. In fact, that's what I am – a 'fish'! And I'm quite capable – most of the time – of making sensible and responsible choices in complex situations."

"Well said. Now explain to me please why you've put a set of coloured flags inside each of the four boxes at the top of this section?" asked the High Master.

"Because each of the valuing and thinking systems can be observed in people individually in the Upper Left Box, in their skills and behaviours in the Upper Right Box, within the cultures in which individuals operate in the Lower Left Box, and in the levels of development of the infrastructure in the Lower Right Box. Are the boxes developed to similar levels? Or are there mismatches?

"It can be very useful to think about the balance and relationship between the levels of development in each of the boxes when analysing the effectiveness, or lack of it, of any group or organisation."

The people – transformed into butterflies
"This final part of the dream refers to the fact that change is constant and ever present, and that we all have hidden potential that is awaiting the right conditions to be unlocked. The fact that some butterflies fly up, some straight, and some crash to the ground refers to the fact that as conditions change, some people return to previous valuing and thinking systems, others continue in their present systems and some develop greater levels of complexity and move into the next system.

"Whichever direction they move is neither good nor bad in itself: it depends on what is appropriate for the conditions in which they find themselves living. There is no point developing great complexity when the habitat doesn't require it. In fact, it can be downright dangerous."

"Excellent. It seems that there is much to say in favour of the thoughtful interpretation of dreams. Now, based on the stories you've collected and your research, I'd like you now to give me an example of how the four-box model might work in practice. How would an integral leader begin to think about making sure his or her organisation or institution is functioning effectively?"

The Young Magician thought about this for a moment, then wrote on Al Sayyid's central panel:

Applied leadership

"Suppose," he said, "you decided to take an inventory of The Academy, of which you are High Master, based on the relative health and strength of these four boxes. You would quickly begin to realise how systemically these four areas fit together in a balanced and integral way – or not!

"Do you have a good balance between the four boxes that encourages the smooth and efficient running of The Academy and its continuing development? Or do serious imbalances exist that create breakdowns in communication, poor delivery of resources and other problems that weaken the effective functioning of The Academy?"

"Be more specific."

"Let me start with the two left-hand boxes: **Personal** and **Team**. Imagine a school where every student is encouraged to develop a good temperament and an open and curious attitude towards learning. Additionally, there is a real sense of shared mission and purpose in the school that supports the learning, growth and development of every student and teacher, and of the school itself.

"In the Upper Right box, each student develops the intellectual capacities to learn easily, the teachers benefit from regular in-service development programmes, and students and teachers alike demonstrate skills and behaviours that will reach and surpass the desired standards of achievement.

"And in the Lower Right box there are sufficient resources available to provide technical and material support, there are appropriate and effective systems of administration and organisation in place, and teachers can offer a range of methodologies suitable for the needs of each different student."

The High Master held up her hand to stop the Young Magician for a moment. "If all these elements were in place that would indeed create the foundations of a very effective centre for learning and study."

"On the other hand," responded the Young Magician, "imagine a school where an individual student deliberately chose not to work, study or learn. No amount of excellence in the other boxes will make a blind bit of difference unless the individual student chooses to change his or her attitude.

"Or you could imagine an institution where every student wants to learn, there is fantastic support in the community, and each teacher is an expert. But, in the Lower Right box, the headteacher decides that a certain teaching methodology will be applied throughout the school whether it is appropriate for the students or not. This will inevitably impact upon the natural motivation of many of the students and teachers."

"In other words," said the High Master, "the successful running of any organisation depends on the quality and balance of the relationship between the four sectors. Attention needs to be given to each sector for itself and in relation to each of the other sectors."

"That's it," said the Young Magician.

"And suppose I were to consider a different situation," said the High Master, "let's say a medical context, we could imagine the following scenario.

"A patient is diagnosed with a serious illness. In the Upper Right box, the patient is prepared to consult the doctor, accept the treatment, eat healthily and rest properly. In the Upper Left box, the patient is optimistic, has the will and desire to overcome the illness, and is willing to engage actively in the recovery process. In the Lower Left box, her family, friends and the community offer her huge moral support. And in the Lower Right box, the doctors say they have the skills and techniques to cure the disease, and the health service has the budget to afford hospital treatment, the necessary drugs, and the appropriate aftercare. If all these elements are present, the prognosis for the patient will be extremely good.

"But if, on the other hand, there is no budget available, or the doctors are untrained, or lack the requisite skills or knowledge, the patient may not survive. If the patient is despondent and pessimistic, it will affect her chances of recovery. If community support is lacking, the patient's strength of spirit may suffer. And if the patient refuses to comply with the treatment, continues to behave in unhealthy ways, and refuses to take responsibility for her own recovery, then the patient's chance of survival is that much slimmer. If any of these four elements is underrepresented it may seriously undermine whatever excellence is present in the other sectors."

"And the same will be true in any business context too," added the Young Magician, keen to get back into the conversation. "Just as an integrally organised health service will seek to develop all four of the boxes in a sympathetic and balanced way, so a well-informed business leader will ensure he or she does the same."

The High Master laughed. "The problem is that in most schools, health systems and businesses, in my experience, far too much attention is put on the right-hand boxes because they are measurable and definable, and politicians, accountants and shareholders like that."

"Exactly," said the Young Magician. "Putting one's attention only on external factors while ignoring the interior ones is like, is like ..." – he searched hard for a suitable analogy – "is like training a top-class athlete's body and not his mind. Everyone knows that at the top level it's the athlete's attitude and mental preparation that makes all the difference."

"It is exactly the same in all forms of performance," said the High Master. "It is the interior attributes that give performance the cutting edge it needs to survive, succeed and develop. The wise leader naturally pays attention to the measurable factors in the right-hand boxes such as appropriate skills and training, effective recruitment, profits and investment in modern plant and machinery. But she also pays an equal amount of attention to the non-measurable factors in the left-hand boxes such as an organisational culture to which all feel they can belong and contribute, and to the individual personal development of each and every employee."

"That's just what I wanted to say. You just had better words."

Change, learning and transformation

"Fascinating," said the High Master. "Now what can you tell me about change, learning and transformation?"

"You set me two questions to think about and, if possible, find answers to: 'What is it that inspires people to change, learn and transform?' and 'How can a leader influence them *to want to* change, learn and transform?' Here are my notes." The Young Magician passed a loose-leaf file to the High Master.

As the High Master opened the file, the Young Magician added, "While it's true that you can't *make* people change, you can influence them to do so *provided* you create and nurture the right conditions."

The High Master began scanning through the pages for the main points. Among other things she noted:

Six key conditions necessary for people to change, learn and transform:

- People won't change unless they appreciate a pressing need to do so.
- People need to have the will, ability and potential to make whatever changes are necessary.

- People need to have some idea about why there is a problem and what alternatives exist to do things differently.
- People need to know how current problems can be resolved so they can move on to new challenges with confidence.
- People need to know how to deal with resistance to change: resistance may be internal, such as personal fear of the unknown; or external, such as lack of promotion opportunities.
- People need to be given support and consolidation so they can learn new skills in a relatively safe environment with plenty of encouragement.

"Excellent," said the High Master. All effective change comes from within. If you want people to go through any change or transformation process, including learning, then these six conditions are really important."

"In my experience," said the Young Magician, "the effective leader recognises these six conditions and supports them *from the perspective of the person going through the change process.*

"Also, there's no reason why a leader who wants to accelerate change can't actively intervene in providing any individual or group with the support and resources they might need. A leader might even deliberately create some dissonance too if that might be helpful."

The High Master gave him a long look, and then continued reading.

Five steps to influence people *to want to* change, learn and transform:

- Create environments and situations in which the six conditions above can easily and *naturally* occur.
- Find out, and work through, the ways people *naturally* get motivated:
  - Motivate PURPLE with PURPLE goals, thinking and behaviour.
  - Motivate RED with RED goals, thinking and behaviour.
  - Motivate BLUE with BLUE goals, thinking and behaviour.
  - And so on …
- Align your own outcomes as a leader with the outcomes of those who choose to follow you, and support them to get what they want.

- Make sure there's not only a WIN for yourself as leader, but also a WIN for each person, and a WIN for the system or habitat as a whole.
- Make sure that people feel safe to make changes, that they have complete trust in you and know that you have their interests at heart.

The High Master returned the notes to the Young Magician.

"What makes you so sure your ideas will work?"

"First, because there's plenty of research to support it. Second, I have my own personal experience to back me up."

"And what experience is that?"

"What I've described above is, more or less, the very process you have guided me through. All the conditions that I have mentioned in my notes relate either to me or to my situation in some way. Although I chose to undertake the journey, it was you, Master, who created the conditions in which it could happen. And, although you were not there personally on my journey, you somehow arranged things so that Al Sayyid could give me all the support I needed to consolidate my learning and development."

"True. The habitat was ideal for you and, as you know, the best learning happens when you take the opportunities that are available to discover things for yourself."

There was a pause in the conversation as both men gazed across the valley into the hazy late-afternoon distance.

Notes
1. K. A. Wilber (2001), *A Theory of Everything* (Gateway).
2. L. Shlain, L (2000), *The Alphabet versus The Goddess* (Penguin).

Section 6
Attributes of Great Leaders, Influencers and Motivators

After a while, the High Master said, "We've discussed how the integral leader *keeps water, not fish.* How she pays attention to the balance and relationship of the elements within the four-box model, and also the valuing and thinking systems of Spiral Dynamics.

"So what else have you discovered after all your travelling, your gathering of stories and metaphors, your research and your reading? What conclusions, if any, have you come to about the key attributes of effective leaders? What makes really effective leadership, or integral leadership, possible?"

"In my view, the best leaders don't appear to lead twenty-four hours a day," replied the Young Magician. "In fact, you wouldn't know some great leaders are leaders at all because they don't have to go round making it obvious. Excellent leaders feel the responsibility to lead only when certain factors come into play. Very often, it seems to be circumstance that brings out the qualities in a great leader.

"On my journey, I made a list of all the attributes of leadership that I came across. Each of these attributes has a contribution to make, but, while some of them are specific only to a few particular contexts, others are more general and more widely applicable.

"Nevertheless, among the many attributes Al Sayyid and I discovered on our travels, it's hard to find any *one* attribute that stands out above the rest.

"I've also looked at many books about leadership in Al Sayyid's extensive library, to see what other researchers have had to say. But none of them seem to have much agreement as to whether it was this thing or that thing, this attribute or that attribute."

"But if you had to stick your neck out," said the High Master, "if you were really put on the spot and asked what is the difference between a great leader and an average one, what would *you* say?"

"Well, if I were really pushed, I would have to say that there are a small number of key attributes that appear to cluster around the very best of leaders."

"Excellent. And what would they be?"

The Young Magician smoothed out Al Sayyid's central panel and wrote:

- integral
- pragmatic
- presence and awareness
- integrity and inner alignment
- personal responsibility
- contribution
- change agent

"Put these together and you've got something special. If you don't mind, I'll refer to my notes as I go through these."

He opened the file and began to read.

Integral

Integral means having the breadth of vision to pay attention to what's happening within the *whole* context, and recognising how all the elements within it fit together. It demonstrates an ability to consider the relationships between the *biggest picture* and the smallest *detail*. It's about keeping the water healthy so the fish can thrive.

Pragmatic

The excellent leader combines integral thinking with pragmatism. These leaders pay close attention to practical requirements, and to the consequences of the decisions they make in each of the four boxes individually and as a whole.

Depending on circumstances, they are prepared either to flow with the current or swim against it. They have developed a range of practical skills and behaviours, and will not be distracted from their clear sense of vision, mission and purpose. They are able to work both within and beyond the immediate environment, and take time to discover what needs to be known about the infrastructure and the environment.

Presence and awareness
Presence means being right here, right now, totally present in the moment. Presence is essential for awareness. Presence allows the Aware Leader to notice what really is, rather than what could be or might be. Presence is an antidote for making assumptions.

Being present allows the Aware Leader to focus the full force of his or her attention on what needs to be done, and to gather quality information about what is actually happening. Quality information allows more effective planning for the future, and more useful learning from the past because it is done with the full attention of the present moment.

Being present channels the flow of personal energy to sometimes make it appear that the leader who has *presence* is connected to a higher power.

Integrity and inner alignment
Integrity appears to possess the Aligned Leader. While integrity does have a sense of moral uprightness and honesty, it is much more than this. It's a sense of oneness with the self, of inner alignment, of being *all of a piece* and true to oneself, one's beliefs and one's values. In the Aligned Leader, integrity is *tangible*, a factor that also contributes to his presence.

The word "integral" derives from the same etymological root as "integrity". Integrity deals with the interior reality, the Upper Left box. Integral deals with both the inner and outer realities, seeking to interconnect the four boxes with each other, and the habitats upon which, and within which, they operate.

Personal responsibility
The best leaders are prepared to take personal responsibility. They put themselves *at cause* for their lives, and make things happen the way they want them to happen. They accept that leadership starts with themselves and they make sure they put their talents and resources to the best possible use.

Responsible Leaders are clear about their vision, mission and purpose in life; they know who they are, what they believe and value; and do what it takes to get things done, wherever they are, whoever they're with.

Contribution
The Excellent Leader is more concerned with giving than taking. These leaders ask themselves:

• What does this situation demand of me?

- What talents and resources do I have to make a difference here?
- What contribution can I make?

They wish to hand on to their successors something more, something greater, something healthier and more vital than they themselves inherited. They are far more concerned with developing the organisation for which they are responsible than developing their personal ego and status. They take on the roles of stewardship and guardianship over all that is good in the organisation, both human and technical.

Change agent
The best leaders make change possible, but only when it is necessary and appropriate. They create the conditions for change, they sponsor change, they support change, and they ensure that it is consolidated through space and time. They endeavour to synchronise change across all four boxes so that development meshes smoothly. They gather up the threads of the past and, through the loom of the continuous present, weave them into future designs for others to complete.

* * *

Al Sayyid, who had been listening with great concentration for so long, could no longer stay silent.

"Young Master. It seems you really have learned something about carpet metaphors, after all."

The Young Magician paused for a moment, and then replied, "Possibly." There was a smile in his eyes.

He was silent for a moment, as if weighing up exactly what to say, and then he continued.

"Al, Sayyid, I have learned so much from you. There are two qualities in particular that I shall never forget; two attributes of leadership that have really helped and encouraged me to learn and grow.

"First, you're an excellent coach. You've coached me all the way through our journey. You've been patient, you've never been directive, and you've never been judgemental. You've always given me space, or asked the right question so I could find out for myself.

"Every time I lost sight of my goal, you reminded me of the way. Every time I achieved something, you raised the height of the bar and challenged me to stretch even higher. You have shown me that the art of coaching and the art of excellent leadership have much in common.

"Second, you're a great example of the servant leader. At every stage of the journey you made sure everything I needed was to hand. You gave me space to become who I can be. You gave me centre stage and made me feel anything was achievable.

"My regret is, natural leader that you are, you seem quite content with your role as servant, and totally at ease in this role."

"Young Master, service is a good and noble state. It has its own dignity and integrity. It is, as you have said, part of my contribution. I am content."

"But if only I could give you your freedom. Surely, after all these centuries you've fulfilled your obligations of service."

"Young Master, it is not for me to say. When your coin touched the sword of my former master, I, by the Law of Contiguity, became bound to you for ever."

"If I may for a moment interject," said the High Master. "There is a way in which what you desire, young man, can be done, and it lies within your gift if only you will seek it out."

"In my gift? How? Tell me!"

"What is the one outstanding thing that you have still not resolved?"

The Young Magician was puzzled. He could think of nothing. His mind raced back to the beginning of his journey. The meaning of the dream was now clear, so what else could it be? He racked his brains. He suddenly became aware of the notebook he was holding. The parcel! The High Master had given him a parcel. The notebook and pencil, the polychromatic sunglasses, the map and compass, even the apple, all were clear.

The Young Magician shoved his hand deep into his right pocket, and together with several small coins he pulled out something round and brittle.

"Exactly," said the High Master, "the plastic token." She left a pause to let her words sink in before continuing.

"In ancient days, salt was the currency that was internationally traded instead of money. People were paid in salt, and a master could liberate his slave by giving him a symbolic parcel of salt to represent his freedom."

"But what has that to do with this piece of plastic?"

"Good. So while you're thinking about that perhaps you'd like to share the list of leadership attributes you've made, and where I can find them in your manuscript."

The Young Magician took a couple of pages from his loose-leaf file and handed them over to the High Master.

The High Master began to read. And what she read was exactly the same information as you can find in the Introduction to this book, between pages xix and xxii, under the heading: "The Stories by Theme".

Section 7
Unravelling the Threads

"I still haven't got it," said the Young Magician after the High Master had finished reading. "I still can't work out the relevance of this plastic token to the task of giving Al Sayyid his freedom."

"Spell out the letters. Write them here on Al Sayyid's panel."

P L A S T I C T O K E N

"Here's a hint. Write them in a circle."

The Young Magician carefully drew the letters in the rich pile.

<pre>
            P   L
        N   A
      E   S
    K
      O   T
        T   I
            C
</pre>

"An anagram?"

"Indeed."

PINE LOST TACK
TIN STOLE PACK
TACK STOLE PIN
STATE PIN LOCK
PLATE IN STOCK
KITS NICE PLOT
ANT STICK POLE
ANT STOCKPILE
STICK ON PLATE

STICK TO PLANE

The Young Magician looked hopeful at this vague reference to flying.

The High Master shook her head; Al Sayyid sighed.

"I gave you a clue earlier. Ancient traditions."

"Ah, yes. The Salt."

SALT ON PICKET

"Some kind of a strike or demonstration?" he said hopefully.

Another shake of the head.

NOTE SALTPICK

"A gruesome attack? À la Vladimir Ilych?"

Another shake.

"Aha. Could it be ...?"

SALT IN POCKET

A smile.

"It's a symbol, right? A metaphor?" He took the token in his right hand and gently inserted it into Al Sayyid's pocket, the one at the mouth of the chalice.

There was silence.

And then Al Sayyid quietly said, "Young man, from the warp and weft of my weave, I thank you. Everything has a pattern and everything has a design. Remember that always as I shall remember you. And you, High Master, I thank you too."

A shiver passed through his length and breadth, and then effortlessly Al Sayyid rose into the air, hovered a moment or two above their heads, and then set off at speed towards the East.

The two of them watched until he was just a speck that vanished into the dusk.

Appendices

Appendix A

A Short Introduction to Spiral Dynamics

Overview

Spiral Dynamics (SD) is a model that makes sense of how people think, how they are motivated, what kind of leaders they prefer, how they learn, how they change and how development occurs in individuals, groups, organisations, nation states and the world generally.

It is a model that is increasingly being applied in a wide range of contexts, including education, business, politics, governance, social reform, health, coaching and relationships. It offers incisive insights into why people behave and think as they do.

Spiral Dynamics is based on the work of Clare W. Graves, emeritus professor of psychology at Union College, Schenectady, in New York State. His research programme, which began in the early 1950s and continued for over thirty years, was aimed at making sense of the myriad psychological theories of the time and understanding human nature.

After Graves's death in 1986, the work was developed further by others, including Don Edward Beck and Christopher C. Cowan, whose book, *Spiral Dynamics: Mastering Values, Leadership, and Change*, published in 1996, is the seminal work. What follows is my much-simplified interpretation of the concepts presented in the book, and from those seminars of theirs which I have attended. For those readers who desire to know more, a thorough reading of the book and attendance at a certified seminar is thoroughly recommended. For further details, refer to the Bibliography.

What is Spiral Dynamics (SD)?

SD is an open-ended model of adult (i.e. 18+) human biopsy-chosocial systems development, which applies as much to entire cultures as to individuals. It proposes an interdependent nested hierarchy of eight stages of human development – with more to come as the world we inhabit increases in complexity.

A key underpinning theory is that all humans have the latent capacity to unlock new potential in the brain, but this happens only as the conditions in which we live become more complex.[1] The stages are coded in colours to aid memorability. Although these colours are divided into warm and cool to denote expressive and sacrificial systems, the colours themselves have no inherent significance. The colours were the idea of Chris Cowan to simplify and make more accessible the alphabetical codings that Clare Graves had used.

Imagine a lighthouse with an internal spiral staircase. At each level there is a landing, and a room where you can rest as long as you like before deciding to continue your journey. To reach the upper levels, you have to visit each of the landings: you cannot miss a landing, for some knowledge of each stage is essential to progress to greater levels of complexity, but you need not choose to stay at a stage any longer than is necessary to master its requirements.

On the other hand you may find that the conditions provided at a certain level feel very comfortable. You may take up residence here; you may not even notice that there are higher floors; or you may just feel a sense of inertia. And if the conditions in which you live take a turn for the worse – for example, loss of income, civil war etc. – you may even go back down the staircase. In other words, it can be the conditions in which you live that determine your valuing and thinking systems as much as your own inner compass and sense of choice.

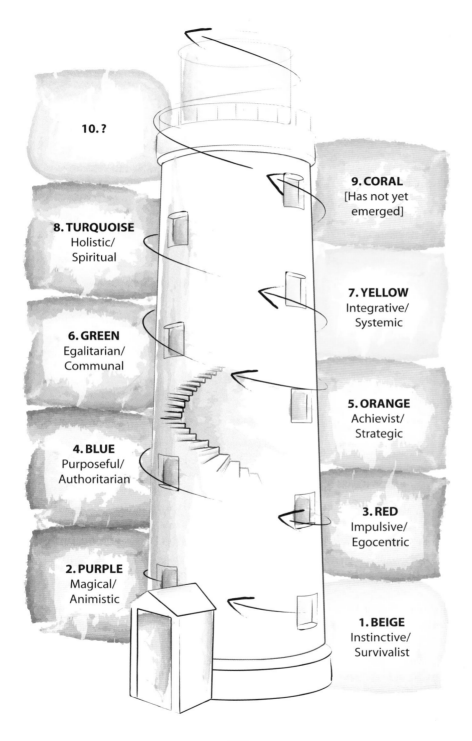

309

COMMUNAL SYSTEMS: WE	INDIVIDUAL SYSTEMS: ME
(cool colours)	(warm colours)
Serve others	Assert self
Externally referenced	Internally referenced
Come to peace within through order:	Change the external world through:
Sacrifice for the tribe (PURPLE)	Power (RED)
Sacrifice for the "truth" (BLUE)	Reason and knowledge (ORANGE)
Sacrifice to reach consensus (GREEN)	Systemic understanding (YELLOW)
Sacrifice to save the planet (TURQUOISE)	

The relationship between valuing the community and valuing oneself, and between external and internal reference, has also been noted by many other social scientists including Maslow, Loevinger and Jung. But the idea of *oscillation* between the two systems, first one then the other, and back again is a distinct contribution of Clare Graves.

Graves on Graves

"The psychology of the mature human being is an unfolding, emergent, oscillating, spiralling process marked by progressive subordination of older, lower-order behaviour systems to newer, higher-order systems as man's existential problems change."

Basic characteristics of the eight systems

"We do not see the world the way it is, we see the world the way we think it is."[2]

As the complexity of the conditions in which we live increases, we have to develop the complexity of our thinking and behavioural strategies to cope. The thinking and valuing system each of us adopts to deal with the conditions absolutely influences the way we perceive reality. Each of the eight systems experiences reality differently, is motivated differently and responds to stimuli differently.

It's not possible, however, to recognise the operating system in a person or group simply by observing their behaviour – *what* they do. You need to discover the underlying valuing patterns by asking *why* a person is doing or saying certain things **and** pay attention to what they are doing. Patterns of behaviour observed over time are one of the most reliable forms of feedback. Observe what the feet do just as much as what the mouth says.

BEIGE:
Emerges mainly when survival is threatened. For example, deep grief, serious illness, intensive-care units.
Leadership role: Caretaker

PURPLE:
Repetition, routines and rituals help people centred here feel safe and secure in a mysterious, unknowable world.
Leadership role: Caring Parent

RED:
People centred here see the world as a jungle. They play the role of warrior or aggressor to survive.
Leadership role: Big Boss who can give tough love and police the boundaries

BLUE:
People centred here believe there is only "one right way" and with this belief seek order, meaning and purpose in life.
Leadership role: Rightful Authority

ORANGE:
People centred here seek influence, possibilities, status and hi-tech tools and toys to play and work with. They like to be winners and will negotiate WIN–WIN situations.
Leadership role: Snappy, well-briefed colleague who demands the best

GREEN:
People centred here seek mutually agreed ways of working together with management and colleagues. Their concerns are to build a better world for all and share common resources with those who have less.
Leadership role: Sensitive Facilitator

YELLOW:
People centred here seek ways to understand the complexity of integrated living systems of which they are a part. Their key drivers are knowledge and competence. They often prefer working alone. Leaders need to get out of their way and be available as a resource.
Leadership role: Competent Partner/Consultant

TURQUOISE:
Very few people are centred here. The system is only just beginning to emerge.
Leadership role: Spiritual Counsellor

Complex Characteristics of the Eight Systems: Entering, Peak, Exiting

It is more accurate to consider 21 systems rather than eight, since systems are not jumped in nice clean breaks. Each wave has its Exiting period as it begins to prepare to leave one system, and an Entering period as it starts to engage with the next system. So a person or organisation just exiting BLUE and tentatively flirting with ORANGE in SD language is described as BLUE/orange. Once they are more established in the new system with only a few manifestations of the previous one they may be described as ORANGE/blue. Once a person is immersed in the new system, it is described as Peak stage.

The theory of change

You cannot step into the same river twice – Heraclitus, 500 BC

Change is present and inevitable, just faster than 2,500 years ago. So how does it occur? SD is based on the premise that there is a never-ending dance in operation between the life conditions in which we live and the coping strategies that individuals, groups, institutions and cultures develop to survive effectively within their particular conditions.

Life conditions consist of four key factors:

- *geographical location:* the physical conditions, natural or man-made, in which we live (e.g. urban jungle or Saharan cave dwelling);
- *historical epoch:* our culture's stage of emergence (e.g. twenty-first-century Paris or sixteenth-century Kabul);
- *human issues:* our requirements for existence and survival (how far do you need to walk from home to get fresh, clean drinking water?); and
- *societal circumstances:* our placement within hierarchies of power, status and influence (whether you were born, say, poor, black, female, unattractive, for in many societies these factors absolutely unfairly militate against people).

Consider this diagram:

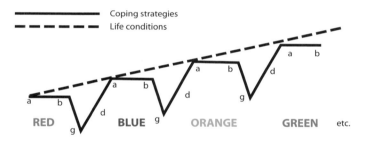

When our coping strategies are in step with our life conditions at Point a, everything seems fine with our world, and we think it will always be so. But, as life conditions become increasingly complex, a gap emerges (b). Sensible people, organisations and societies plan for this and can make a smooth transition to the more complex thinking of a new Point (a) at the next stage of the Spiral – before the gap becomes too great for the current Coping Strategies to deal with.

But those without such foresight, or who are just taken by surprise at the speed of change, get caught in a trap (g), a time of huge frustration as they desperately search for ways to catch up. This releases a huge surge of energy and creativity (d), which is necessary for "break-out". Of course, it doesn't always work. This is when individuals, organisations or whole nation states can fail to develop to the next stage of emergence. They disintegrate, get stuck, or even regress to former levels of existence.

But, if they do make it, then the cycle starts again. Everything seems fine, until ... the next cycle.

SD and conflict

Many of the problems that exist within a family, a team, a school, a boardroom, an organisation and the world are caused by a clash in valuing systems. Clashes can occur both *between* thinking and valuing systems and *within* the same system.

How do your colleagues respond to different styles of management or leadership? How do they respond to different educational methodologies? How willing are they – or are you – to try new ideas or see different perspectives? Is your style appropriate for those who look to you as a leader? What does a colleague, or an employee, or a student, or a child need from you, the leader or manager or teacher or parent? How do people respond to each other? What valuing and thinking systems do they have in common that brings them together? What valuing and thinking systems are they running that cause mistrust and friction between themselves and others?

And how do you, the leader, respond to people in different valuing and thinking systems? The stage in the Spiral where you are centred is a filter. Do you see and experience the world from a RED, BLUE, ORANGE or other perspective? People naturally tend to see their own level as the one that makes most sense. Yet BLUE thinking, under the right conditions, can accept that others can make different choices based on principle. ORANGE is accepting of pluralism, and is willing and able to recognise and make use of differences in types of thinking.

SD and systemic thinking: the big picture

Graves hypothesised that the shift to YELLOW would herald a huge development in human thinking. YELLOW processing is characterised by systemic thinking and seeks to facilitate the *interdependence* of the whole Spiral. It promotes the idea that all stages are necessary and all have a part to play in human emergence. You might think that from a YELLOW big picture perspective it would become possible to lead others more effectively, and in ways appropriate to their valuing systems. This may be the case, yet the fascinating paradox is that individuals centred in YELLOW often prefer not to seek out leadership roles. They are not averse, however, to influencing from behind the scenes as consultants, advisers or prophets.

SD and appropriate leadership styles

Thus, leading from a YELLOW perspective is by no means necessary. The vast majority of people in the world today are centred in RED, BLUE and ORANGE. If you have teams or students centred in RED, then RED leadership or management is perfectly appropriate. But if you want your teams to develop from, say, ORANGE to GREEN you will need a different kind leadership, perhaps half a step ahead of the team.

Spiral Dynamics proposes three types of leader:

* stage wizards
* change wizards, and
* spiral wizards.

The stage wizard

This type of leader is centred in the same thinking and valuing system as the people in her team. If they are centred in BLUE, she will also be centred in BLUE. She knows how to motivate and influence them; she knows how they respond best; and she knows what they need and how they think. She is a guide who knows the terrain, the shortcuts and the journey's destination. However, she may struggle with team members and colleagues who are not centred in her system.

The change wizard

This type of leader is already making the transition to the next stage. If the team are centred in BLUE, he will be in the BLUE/ORANGE transitional stage. He knows how to coach his people to make the necessary changes in their mindset to achieve deeper levels of challenge, questioning and complexity. He will be no more than half a step ahead of them, so he can be sympathetic to, and supportive of, their struggle.

The spiral wizard

This type of leader is likely to be able to access YELLOW thinking or above. But she may not be a leader in any traditional sense. She can be found at any level within an organisation. She looks for patterns and relationships, scans for future trends, and seeks to connect details to the bigger picture. She can adapt easily to periods of stability or transformation, order or chaos. Understanding the thinking behind different systems, she can be an effective mediator. She may assist *horizontal* development within a system to keep it active and healthy. She may work to keep the Spiral open *vertically* so that new valuing and thinking systems may emerge. Or she may encourage oblique development so that existing patterns can adapt to changing Life Conditions.

Spiral wizards have the skills to *'integrate, align, and synthesise'* all elements of an organisation into a co-operative effort. They can detect the blockages in the system, and know where to tap in order to release them. They value competency above seniority, and knowledge above status. They can be seen as gurus, or be completely misunderstood and ignored as irrelevant star gazers.

Leadership issues

As complexity in thinking increases, the more developed systems begin to recognise that all the systems are important in the development of a healthy habitat, and that all systems have a part to play. It is useful to recognise that as each of us progresses along the

Spiral each of the previous systems from BEIGE onwards remain present within ourselves. So more complex systems are able to access RED thinking and behaviours when working with RED, ORANGE thinking and behaviours when working with ORANGE, and so on. The greater the complexity of thinking, the more skilful and flexible this is likely to be.

YELLOW recognises that progress through the Spiral is essential to a person's, group's or organisation's development. So YELLOW works very hard to keep the Spiral healthy, open and flowing.

This doesn't, of course, necessarily mean that a leader has to be centred in the most complex types of thinking to run a large organisation. There is no reason why a dynamic, creative entrepreneur centred in healthy, open RED, for example, shouldn't employ ORANGE-, GREEN- or YELLOW-centred thinkers to manage aspects of his business. Spiral Dynamics doesn't measure intelligence; you can find intelligence or lack of it at all levels. Spiral Dynamics measures *types of thinking and valuing in people*, and that's what is particularly useful if you want to lead, influence and motivate people, and manage change programmes effectively.

Complexity in people

Each one of us has potential at all levels of the Spiral. It takes complexity in the life conditions to trigger the necessary chemical and neurological changes in the brain to shift the valuing and thinking systems. Keep in mind, too, that *each stage includes and transcends previous stages*. So it might be useful to use the analogy of the layers of an onion when thinking about complexity in individuals.

Take a senior manager who may be centred in GREEN. With her family and team she builds relationships based on consensus and harmony. But she is also aiming for an important promotion, and is competitively striving to ensure she achieves it (ORANGE). She goes to confession at church twice a week (BLUE), and aggressively plays every game of tennis at her club to win (RED). She never walks under ladders because of the superstitious beliefs she has carried from childhood (PURPLE).

At this point, Al Sayyid, the flying carpet, might say, "Possibly." This could be far too simple an analysis. It will be necessary to ask her why she does as she does in order to ascertain the underlying reasons and valuing systems. We may need to discover the external conditions in which she is operating, and what her overall motives are for each aspect of her behaviour. Is her not walking under ladders really superstitious? Or is it merely an old habit? Or just plain common sense?

Nevertheless, it is quite possible for most leaders to access various styles and methodologies of leadership. The key factor is to be sensitive to *where* those you manage are centred on the Spiral, *why* you are choosing that particular style and *what* you want to achieve through it. Or to use a Spiral question, "How should who manage whom to do what, and why?"

Estimating potential for change: open, arrested or closed

As well as the eight different valuing and thinking systems, and the five states of change between them – alpha, beta, gamma, delta and new alpha (see page 313) – the systems can also operate in three different ways: Open, Arrested and Closed.

These descriptions "do not refer to a type of person, but to a condition of a value system within the repertoire of an individual or group mindset".[3]

People are willing to change under certain conditions.

OPEN – refers to thinking or behaviour which actively attempts to remove barriers or change existing conditions that hamper self-expression. 'Open' activity will work hard to change the situation 'to fit self as self is' rather than attempting to become something else. 'Open' is always 'in respect to' an issue: thus an individual or organisation can be 'open' to one topic, and 'closed' to another.

ARRESTED – refers to thinking or behaviour that is accepting of a perceived necessity to live within constraints. 'Arrested' thinking operates to do the best one can given the circumstances, and adjusts to fit the existing conditions. "There's nothing we can do about it – Que sera, sera." 'Arrested' thinking can manifest stress and neuroses when feeling trapped and unsupported.

CLOSED – refers to thinking or behaviour that is inclined to resist change and have a low tolerance for anything perceived as a barrier to its current way of operating. 'Closed' thinking frequently demonstrates a denial of what is, and attempts to return to past ways of being and doing. 'Closed' behaviour often exhibits panic or inappropriacy especially when challenged to deliver above its current level of coping skills. It can be aggressive or even violent when pushed to the edge.

Take a look at a busy street in a bustling city or even a small rural village. Among the cross section of people there your eyes may rest upon 'Closed RED Gamma' [the mugger sourcing his cocaine habit]; 'Arrested BLUE Alpha' [the public sector worker doing the minimum possible to get by as stipulated in the contract of work]; or 'Open ORANGE Delta' [the thrusting young businessman setting up a dynamic commercial venture].

You will have to deal with a wide range of people in the course of your everyday life whether professionally or personally. The days of one-size-fits-all thinking are gone. Leading and managing people effectively requires the factoring in of Value Systems, Change States, and O-A-C status. It's more complicated but it makes no sense to pretend things are simpler than they really are. Quick fixes are generally short fixes.

Spiral leadership

Spiral leadership puts emphasis on building and maintaining positive relationships between people. This can be achieved in three ways:

- POA: *p*oliteness, *o*penness, *a*utocracy;
- honour and recognise each of the valuing and thinking systems at a personal and organisational level; and
- adapt to different people and different situations with a variety of appropriate styles.

Politeness is:

- civil rather than rude;
- considerate rather than cynical;
- sensitive rather than judgemental; and
- empathetic rather than critical.

Politeness respects cultural differences and people's right to be who they are. Politeness meets the needs and values of all levels of the Spiral.

Openness is:

- authentic rather than withholding;
- transparent rather than closed;
- available rather than aloof;
- sharing rather than self-protective; and
- open rather than biased.

Openness fosters a climate of communication and honesty. Critics are listened to, and psychological games are rare. Openness fosters the participation of all levels on the Spiral.

Warning: Trust is essential for openness to work well. If trust is weak, openness is high-risk behaviour.

Autocracy means:

Taking charge, accepting responsibility, being willing to carry the can. While GREEN, YELLOW and TURQUOISE systems tend to be self-managing and require participative management, the need for accountability does not disappear. PURPLE through to BLUE, and even some ORANGE, demand someone to be in charge.

Autocracy by itself is not an option but part of a package: POA. Politeness and openness without autocracy can seem flaky and fuzzy.

POA is key to the establishment of an ideal working habitat in which all can contribute and all can thrive.

Horizontal and Vertical Development

The concepts of horizontal and vertical development suggest that change is possible within systems as well as across and between systems. Horizontal change is to do with improvements to the system in which a person, team, or organisation is currently operating. It might be a matter of developing new skills, or upgrading software, or improving communication hardware. It is essentially a question of making the best of what can be done within the existing external conditions. This is sometimes referred to as 1st Order change: change within the current mindset.

Vertical change is a fundamental shift from one way of thinking to another. This occurs when greater complexity in external conditions requires a shift of valuing and thinking to create more effective coping strategies. Completely new and different solutions are found to deal with existing problems and barriers. A surge of creativity blows away old thinking and ushers in the dawn of revolutionary new approaches. This is sometimes referred to as 2nd Order change.

Greater complexity in thinking and behaviour brought about by vertical shift should not be considered 'better' than previous forms of coping. It is simply more appropriate to the changed external conditions. Shifting Value Systems is only useful when circumstances require it. Nor do these changes happen overnight. Often they take considerable time to move from one Peak stage through Exiting and Entering stages to the next Peak stage.

Vertical change can also revert to *previous* systems if sudden catastrophic changes occur in the external conditions: civil war, loss of employment, serious illness and so on.

Because the sophistication of coping strategies depends upon their appropriateness to existing external conditions it is not useful to think that greater complexity is inherently better than less complexity. It can therefore be useful to thing of the Spiral as a metaphor for the existence and emergence of naturally designed systems. Nature gives us many examples of nested hierarchies *that are essential to the life of the planet*. One such is the progress from atom to molecule to cell to organism to ecosystems to biosphere to universe. This example shows the *difference between levels* in terms of their relative complexity, and the *interdependence* of all levels. While organisms (such as ourselves) are more complex than cells, if all cells were to be destroyed everything more complex would be destroyed also.

In the same way, the health of the planet depends on respect for the interdependence of all levels of the Spiral. To suggest that there are no levels, that there is no complexity and there is no vertical development is to ignore empirical evidence. But to argue that more complex is 'better' is to equally distort the facts. It would be like saying the elevator stop on the sixth floor of a multi-storey building is more important than the elevator stop on the fifth, or any other, floor.

Verticality allows us to recognise that human beings are meaning-making organisations capable of developing and adapting to ever newer and more complex ways of thinking and valuing as our circumstances change. Verticality allows us to understand that we need to apply different strategies and modes of communication and motivation for people situated at different levels of development. Teachers need to use several methodologies, not just one, according to the needs of their different pupils. Managers need to cultivate different managerial and leadership styles to influence and motivate different teams. Verticality suggests that anything resembling a one-size-fits-all strategy should be consigned for good to the dustbin of history.

This is not to deny that "all human beings are born free and equal in dignity and rights" but that – as Lawrence Kohlberg and others have argued – "every human being has equal rights but everything they say and do is not of equal value".[4]

Key elements of Spiral Dynamics

* Eight stages of development have emerged so far.
* The stages develop from less to more complex as external conditions become more complex and demanding
* Each stage teaches the codes necessary to proceed to the next stage

- Each stage appears to include and transcend previous stages.
- Complexity is appropriate only when useful.
- Each stage is necessary to the healthy development of the next.
- Colours do not define types of people, intelligence or temperament, but are a code of *different types of thinking* in people.
- SD is not a tool to pigeonhole or judge people, but a set of guidelines of possible potential in people not yet being realised.
- Change in people occurs when their coping strategies are no longer sufficient to deal with the complexity of their environment provided they have the bio-psychosocial capacity to deal with it
- Complexity can release hidden potential in people's brains – they develop along the Spiral.
- Complexity can overwhelm people – they become stuck or move down the Spiral.

Health warning

Most people have a perfectly natural tendency to overestimate their placement on the Spiral. It is worth reiterating that the best place to be is the place that is most compatible with your current life conditions. It is also worth saying that healthy expressions of each system depend on having healthy expressions of previous systems present within the individual, team or organisation. It is always possible to work on improving the qualities of your PURPLE, RED, BLUE (etc.) expressiveness. In fact, the more confident you are of dealing with issues of previous systems, the more successful you are likely to be in navigating your progress through the Spiral.

Instruments exist for testing your valuing and thinking "stacks". Details of these, and courses on Spiral Dynamics, can be found in the Bibliography. It is advisable to have these interpreted by a qualified SD practitioner.

Notes
[1] E. Harth (1991), *Beyond Evolution and Culture* (Penguin).
[2] D. Lynch and P. Kordis (1989), *Strategy of the Dolphin* (Arrow).
[3] National Values Center: Values Test User Guidelines, p. 33.

[4] L. Kohlberg (1981), *The Philosophy of Moral Development: Moral Stages and Idea of Justice: 1* (HarperCollins).

An earlier and somewhat different version of this appendix, focusing on teaching and the management of education appeared in a series of four articles originally published in *English Teaching Professional* magazine, www.etprofessional.com

Copies of these articles are available from the author at NowenOne@aol.com or info@nickowen.net

Appendix B

Ken Wilber's 4 Quadrant 'A Theory of Everything' Model

Ken Wilber describes his four quadrant model in several ways, alluding also to its origins in classical and romantic thought. These are some of the ways:

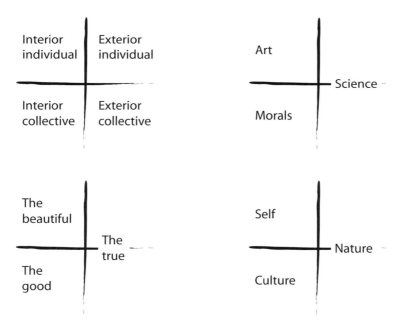

In contemporary terms, these concepts could be translated as:

Mind-consciousness Waves of development Personal awareness	Brain–body Hard sciences Behaviourism
Culture Shared values Shared perceptions Worldview Ethics and morality	Architecture Geopolitical structures Technoeconomic modes Information transfer Social systems and structures

All Quadrants/All Lines (AQAL)

Stages of development within the four quadrants

In his work, Ken Wilber has noted that the waves of Spiral development operate in each of the four quadrants: personal [I], team [WE], professional [IT], and infrastructural [ITS].

- The Upper Left quadrant shows relative stages of personal development and complexity.
- The Lower Left quadrant shows relative stages of cultural development and complexity, whether in a nation, an organisation, a division, a team or a family.
- The Upper Right quadrant shows relative stages of development in an individual's behaviour and skills, and physical, social and intellectual capacities.

- The Lower Right quadrant shows the relative stages of development in the infrastructure. For example, how sophisticated are the computers and other communication devices available within an organisation? What is the style of leadership: feudal, authoritarian, strategic, consensual or integral?

Integral leadership

The Four Quadrant model is a useful tool for the leader/influencer who needs to consider the full range of relationships between the habitat and the 'inhabitants'.

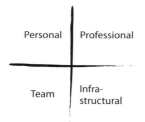

The integral leader recognises, whether consciously or intuitively, that an integral relationship is required *internally* between the personal, team, professional and infrastructural quadrants, and *externally* with the environment and any other relevant systems that operate upon it. The integral leader understands that systemically everything connects to everything else in some way, and that all decisions and actions that are taken will have consequences that need to be considered.

The integral leader strives also to be aware of the different preferences in thinking and valuing systems from BEIGE through YELLOW and beyond. The integral leader recognises how the systems relate to each other *within* each box and *between* the boxes. Sensitive to the relationships and dynamics between these systems, the integral leader will consider how best to communicate with people, influence them and get them motivated *naturally*. The integral leader will, for example, consider how to fit jobs to particular people so that every person will engage fully with what they are doing, rather than fit a person to a particular job. These ideas were first articulated by Beck and Cowan in their book *Spiral Dynamics* in 1996.

Integral leadership is not so much "do unto others as you would have them do unto you" as "do unto others as they would have you do unto them!"[1]

Notes
[1] Laura Frey Horn, student of Professor Clare Graves.

Appendix C

Some Practical Benefits of Spiral Dynamics

1. As a way of understanding and appreciating one's own personal development: charting the shifts and transitions that have occurred in one's life and recognising the changing conditions and critical factors that triggered them. Developing an autobiographical understanding.

2. Gaining greater insights into, and understanding of, other people and the underlying reasons for their behaviours, needs and motivations.

3. As a tool for predicting how to change one's own strategies and behaviours in order to meet and manage others in *their* reality.

4. As a means of analysing and interpreting the arts. For example, exploring the conflicts and contradictions between characters, cultures, organisations etc. in literature, drama, film and so forth.

5. As a way of understanding dynamics within relationships, teams and organisations. Recognising the deeper causes of positive or negative energy that may exist between entities.

6. As a tool for exploring issues and the deeper causes of problems that exist within organisations. A means of getting to the heart of the deeper factors that create the surface symptoms.

7. As a big-picture-framing device that enables a change agent to select from a variety of models and tools the ones that might best serve a particular individual, group or community.

8. As a tool for working with vertical – as well as horizontal – development in individuals, teams, groups, organisations, cultures and geopolitical entities.

9. As a means of recognising the interdependence and interrelationship between our inner and outer realities, and between the individual and the collective; a means of integral thinking.

10. As a reminder that what works for me may well not work for others; different methodologies, styles, strategies and approaches may be required.

11. A way to usefully critique and recognise the types of thinking in other people; to know "where they are coming from".

12. A means of analysing cultures and societies and understanding the underlying causes of social and political conflict and the reasons for social and economic breakdown, and as a framework to interpret history.

13. An instrument to predict the likely consequences of change programmes, and of organisational, cultural and political interventions.

14. A metaphor that is simple to understand but that reveals the underlying complexity of the world we inhabit; a model that contraindicates the desire of modern management for a quick fix, and that teaches the necessity of patient, thoughtful, integral analysis of the issues at hand.

(With thanks to the Spiral Dynamics Integral Yahoo! Group, especially Bruce Gibb and Maria Jeukens.)

Bibliography

Collections of stories

Canfield, J., and Hansen, M. V., 2000, *Chicken Soup for the Soul*, Vermillion, London.

Forstater, M., 2001, *The Spiritual Teachings of the Tao*, Coronet, London.

Gbadamosi, B., and Beier, U., 1968, *Not Even God Is Ripe Enough*, Heinemann AWS, Oxford.

Morgan, J., and Rinvolucri, M., 1983, *Once Upon a Time*, Cambridge University Press, Cambridge.

Okot p'Bitek, 1978, *Hare and Hornbill*, Heinemann AWS, Oxford.

Peseschkian, N., 1982, *Oriental Stories as Tools for Psychotherapy*, Sterling Press, London.

Pinkola Estes, C., 1993, *Women Who Run with the Wolves*, Rider, London.

Rosen, S. (ed.), 1982, *My Voice Will Go With You: The Teaching Tales of Milton H. Erickson*, Norton, New York.

Shah, I., 1968, *The Way of the Sufi*, Penguin Arkana, London.

Shah, I., 1971, *Thinkers of the East*, Octagon Press, London.

Simmons, A., 2002, *The Story Factor*, Perseus Publishing, Cambridge, MA.

Zander, R., and Zander, B., 2002, *The Art of Possibility*, Penguin Putnam, New York.

Articles containing stories

Chan Kim, W., and Mauborgne, R., 1992, Parables of Leadership, *Harvard Business Review*, July–August.

Owen, N., Transforming You Students' Thinking with Stories, *Karen's Linguistic Issues,* www3.telus.net/linguisticissues/Transformingthinking.html, June 2002.

Source books for stories

Berlin, I., 1939, *The Hedgehog and the Fox*, Elephant Paperbacks, Chicago.

Bonder, N., 1999, *Yiddishe Kop*, Shambhala, Boston, MA.

Coelho, P., 1997, *The Pilgrimage*, Thorsons, London.

Coelho, P., 1998, *The Alchemist*, Thorsons, London.

Remen, R., 1996, *Kitchen Table Wisdom*, Pan, London.

Revell, J., and Norman, S., 1997, *In Your Hands*, Saffire Press, London.

Revell, J., and Norman, S., 1999, *Handing Over,* Saffire Press, London.

Wright, A., 1995, *Storytelling for Children*, Oxford University Press, Oxford.

Books on applications of metaphor

Berman, M., and Brown, D., 2000, *The Power of Metaphor*, Crown House Publishing, Carmarthen, Wales.

Gordon, D., 1978, *Therapeutic Metaphors*, Meta Publications, Capitola, CA.

Lakoff, G., and Johnson, M., 1980, *Metaphors We Live By*, University of Chicago Press, Chicago, IL.

Lawley, J., and Tompkins, P., 2000, *Metaphors in Mind*, Developing Company Press, London.

Useful background reading on leading, influencing and motivating

Adizes, I., 1988, *Corporate Life Cycles: The Theory of How and Why Corporations Grow and Die and What to Do About It*, Prentice Hall Direct, Upper Saddle River, NJ.

Charvet, S. R., 1995, *Words That Change Minds*, Kendall Hunt, Dubuque, IA.

Collins, J., 2001, *Good to Great*, Random House, London.

Covey, S., 1989, *Seven Habits of Highly Effective People*, Simon & Schuster, London.

Deering, A., Dilts, R., and Russell, J., 2002, *Alpha Leadership*, John Wiley & Sons, Chichester.

Johnson, S., 1998, *Who Moved My Cheese?*, Vermillion, London.

Kotter, J., 1996, *Leading Change*, Harvard Business School Press, Cambridge, MA.

Kouzes, J., and Posner, B., 2002, *The Leadership Challenge*, Jossey Bass Wiley, Indianapolis, IN.

Laborde, G., 1998, *Influencing with Integrity*, Crown House Publishing, Carmarthen, Wales.

Lynch, D., and Kordis, P., 1989, *Strategy of the Dolphin*, Arrow, London.

O'Connor, J., 1998, *Leading With NLP*, Thorsons, London.

O'Connor, J., 2001, *NLP Workbook*, Thorsons, London.

Owen, H., 1997, *Open Space Technology*, Berrett-Koehler, San Francisco, CA.

Owen, N., 2001, *The Magic of Metaphor*, Crown House Publishing, Carmarthen, Wales.

Pearson, C., 1991, *Awakening the Heroes Within*, Harper, San Francisco, CA.

Riso, D., and Hudson, R., 1999, *The Wisdom of the Enneagram*, Bantam, New York.

Senge, P., 1990, *The Fifth Discipline*, Random House, London.

Shlain, L., 2000, *The Alphabet versus the Goddess*, Penguin, London.

Sun Tzu, 1963, *The Art of War*, Oxford University Press, Oxford.

Tolle, E., 1999, *The Power of Now*, Hodder & Stoughton, London.

Torbert, W., 1991, *The Power Balance: Transforming Self, Society, and Scientific Inquiry*, Sage Publications, Thousand Oaks, CA.

Torbert, W., 2004, *Action Inquiry*, Berrett-Koehler, San Francisco, CA.

Books and articles on valuing and thinking systems, Spiral Dynamics, and integral thinking

Beck, D., and Cowan, C., 1996, *Spiral Dynamics: Mastering Values, Leadership and Change*, Blackwell, Oxford.

James, T., and Woodsmall, W., 1988, *Time Line Therapy & The Basis of Personality*, Meta Publications, Capitola, CA.

Lynch, D., 2003, *The Mother of All Minds*, Brain Technologies Press, Plano, TX.

Martin, C., 2001, *The Life Coaching Handbook*, Crown House Publishing, Carmarthen, Wales.

Owen, N., 2003/4, Spiral Dynamics: Applications in Education, *English Teaching Professional* magazine, London, Vols 27–30.

Pirsig, R., 1989, *Zen and the Art of Motorcycle Maintenance: An Inquiry into Values*, Vintage, London.

Pirsig, R. Lila, 1992, *An Inquiry into Morals*, Corgi, London.

Wilber, K., 2001, *A Theory of Everything*, Gateway, Boston, MA.

Wilber, K., 2000, *Integral Psychology*, Shambhala, Boston, MA.

Websites for stories and storytelling

Australian Storytelling Guild, http://www.home.aone.net.au/stories/index4.html

Finley, Guy, http://www.guyfinley.com

Lawley, James & Tompkins, Penny, http://www.cleanlanguage.co.uk

Metaphor, The, http://www.compapp.dcu.ie/storyv/metaphor.html

Suler, John, http://www.rider.edu/~suler/zenstory/zenstory.html

US National Storytelling Association,
http://www.enigmagraphics.com/stories/storytelling

More useful websites

http://www.clarewgraves.com
http://www.etprofessional.com
http://www.integralinstitute.org
http://www.integralnaked.org
http://www.integraluniversity.org
http://www.nordicintegral.com
http://www.spiraldynamics.net
http://www.spiraldynamics.org

The Magic of Metaphor
77 Stories for Teachers, Trainers & Thinkers
Nick Owen

Foreword by *Judith DeLozier*

the Magic of Metaphor

77 Stories for Teachers, Trainers & Thinkers

Nick Owen

Already on its fourth reprint this volume presents a collection of powerful stories designed to engage, inspire and transform the listener as well as the reader.

Promoting positive feelings, confidence, direction, and vision, *The Magic of Metaphor* supplies a wealth of advice and information on the art of creating metaphor and storytelling.

"A treasure trove of wisdom and fun! Stories for leaders to use on every occasion to enhance their effectiveness."
Richard D. Field OBE, Industrialist, Leadership Coach and Student

"This book gives the communicator a refreshing and creative way of cutting through the language barrier of Information Technology and delivering clear messages to often diverse audiences."
Alison Hood, Managing Consultant and Operations Director for the Wholesale Investment Banking Practice

"The book appeals on diverse levels with insights and enlightening illustrations that will illuminate teaching and learning. Drawn from ancient oriental traditions, contemporary sources and the author's own repertoire - the experience is challenging, life-affirming and enriching."
Mick Reid, Voluntary Service Overseas, London

Paperback 234mm x 154mm 256 pages
ISBN: 1899836705 £16.99 $27.95